Critical Incidents in Clinical Supervision

Addictions, Community, and School Counseling

Edited by

Lawrence E. Tyson
John R. Culbreth
Judith A. Harrington

AMERICAN COUNSELING ASSOCIATION
5999 Stevenson Avenue
Alexandria, VA 22304
www.counseling.org

Critical Incidents
in Clinical Supervision
Addictions, Community, and
School Counseling

10   9   8   7   6   5   4   3   2   1

American Counseling Association
5999 Stevenson Avenue • Alexandria, VA 22304

Director of Publications • Carolyn C. Baker

Production Manager • Bonny E. Gaston

Copy Editor • Christine Calorusso

Editorial Assistant • Catherine A. Brumley

Cover and text design by Bonny E. Gaston.

Library of Congress Cataloging-in-Publication Data
Critical incidents in clinical supervision: addictions, community, and school counseling/edited by Lawrence E. Tyson, John R. Culbreth, and Judith A. Harrington.
   p. ; cm.
     Includes bibliographical references.
     ISBN 978-1-55620-260-5 (alk. paper)
1. Mental health counselors—Supervision of. 2. Drug abuse counselors—Supervision of. 3. Student counselors—Supervision of. 4. Critical incident technique. I. Tyson, Lawrence E. II. Culbreth, John R. III. Harrington, Judith A. IV. American Counseling Association.
[DNLM: 1. Ethics, Professional. 2. Psychology, Clinical. 3. Counseling—ethics. 4. Interprofessional Relations—ethics. 5. Professional Misconduct. 6. Professional Role—psychology. WM 21 C9335 2007]

RC466.C75 2007
362.2'04256—dc22   2007025835

Contents

Part I: Addictions Counseling

Part II: Community Counseling

Part III: School Counseling

Acknowledgments

This book would not exist were it not for the 92 contributors who were willing to share their foibles and their narratives, their standards and their reasoning, and their patience and diligence. We have found it very exciting to see so much interest from so many across the country, representing many levels of experience and perspectives in the field, and many cultures and professional specializations. Thank you, each of you, for your commitment and contribution.

Additionally, we are grateful to the American Counseling Association for endorsing and providing for this publication. It is edifying to know that this project, unique to the field of clinical supervision, is buoyed by not only the many Association for Counselor Education and Supervision–affiliated authors and contributors but also our parent organization, the American Counseling Association. Carolyn Baker has been a forward scout for us, and we are most appreciative of her adroit leadership and editorial assistance throughout the process.

We would like to acknowledge and honor the many self-evident risk takers and those who are more invisible through their tales and stories that might have been "anonymized" in this book. Sometimes the best learning can be done from our mistakes, and it is a wise person who can risk sharing such mistakes with a readership of one's own colleagues. And perhaps it is even more courageous to risk sharing when one has been on the receiving end of a colleague's mistake. We thank you, including those of you who may not even know that you are the subject of a critical incident account such as one of the 33 in this text.

Similarly, thank you to the supervisors, supervisees, and clients, who are at the heart of all we do. Perhaps in the long run we are all one and the same— overseers, learners, and consumers. Special thanks go to our inspiration for this book, namely our previous and current supervisors and consultants, and past and present supervisees, all of whom have taught us so much and continue to leave much for us to draw on in the well.

And finally, we are most thankful to our families who, alongside our contributing authors, made room for this project, even when doing so cost valuable time personally.

—*Judith A. Harrington*

Special Thanks

I have a passion for training school counselors. This passion was instilled in me from very specific mentors and colleagues. I am indebted to the following for their personal and professional involvement: Dr. Jeff Siskind, who was my first true school counseling colleague; Drs. Ted Remley, Dwight Hare, Anne Bailey, Warren Housley, and Joe Ray Underwood, who taught me how to think while at Mississippi State University; and Drs. Michael Brooks, Barry Stephens, and David Macrina and Ms. Patti Sheets, who were and are always supportive of projects such as this.

—*Lawrence E. Tyson*

I would like to acknowledge all of the family, friends, and colleagues who have helped me get to this point in my career where I can actually write an acknowledgements page in a book. Pretty cool! I would like to dedicate this book to Barbara and Alex. Your love, support, and friendship have been an inspiration to me and a critical part of my life, both now and always. Thank you for all that you are and all you have been over these past years.

—*John R. Culbreth*

Supervision has become a passion of mine, both as a younger counselor receiving supervision and now as a provider of supervision and supervision training. My supervisors and consultants have had the most to do with my anchoring within the field, second only in inspiration to my clients. My incalculable appreciation goes to the many shining supervisees who have taught me so much in addition to my own supervisors and consultants: Elbert LaLande, Charles Alexander, Sam Gladding, Jamie Satcher, Robert Friedl (Chief of Psychiatry at University of Alabama at Birmingham), the late Larry DePalma (psychiatrist and priest), Harriet Schaffer, Jeannie Ingram, Quinn Pearson, Mary Stinson, Kathleen Friery, and my group of peer consultants that has been meeting for 19 years: Marian Bell, Donica Creasy, Glenda Elliott, Vicky Farley, Grace Reed, Beebe Roberts, and Caroline West. Behind the scenery of this deeply gratifying work is my collaborator, mentor, and husband, Dr. Steven Webb, and our young son, William Kelson Webb, whose arrival came only weeks after this book was approved.

—*Judith A. Harrington*

Preface

Critical Incidents in Clinical Supervision is a practical text for counselor educators, clinical supervisors, clinical directors, counselors and supervisees in the field, and counselor education students, as well as those who have a general interest in the counseling profession. Each chapter contains a description of a critical incident, followed by two responses. The incidents are based on common experiences specific to the clinical supervision setting and challenge the reader to think about the factors present in the described incident and how those factors may be addressed.

The responses allow the reader to view two approaches in deciding on appropriate professional behaviors that the counseling supervisor may follow to meet the challenges presented in the described incident. Opportunities for further learning exist for group discussion or individual analysis of the incident and responses to provide insight into what might be considered as best practice in clinical supervision.

The topics for the clinical supervision incidents were generated by the editors on the basis of their experience and knowledge in supervision in the areas of community, addictions, and school counseling. Topics were placed in one of five categories representing a broad range of group-work issues: (1) legal and ethical, (2) professional development, (3) methodology and techniques, (4) contractual, and (5) working alliance. The basic plan was to provide supervision incidents that might occur across a variety of work contexts (i.e., schools, community agencies, and addictions). Furthermore, given the number of differences among contributing writers, a variety of presenting problems in supervision are depicted.

The editors each had responsibility for one of the three settings. Once an incident was received, it was edited and sent out to the two respondents, who independently wrote their responses and sent them back to the appropriate editor. The editors communicated with each other via e-mail and telephone to maintain a consistent editing approach and format for the book.

A broad approach was used in soliciting writers to contribute to this book. The editors developed a list of professionals in the supervision field perceived to be well-known authors, skilled practitioners, or knowledgeable educators. An invitation was developed and sent to those professionals, asking them to contribute to *Critical Incidents in Clinical Supervision* by writing an incident or a response in connection with the topics that had been generated. The invitation included an example of a chapter (i.e., an incident and two responses) to explain the expected format. Each contributor could write one or two incidents and one or two responses, with a limit of two contributions in total. A contributor could not write both an incident and a response on the same topic. In addition, a general call for contributions was placed on the Counselor Education and Supervision Network Listserv (CESNET) and the International Counselors Network (ICN) to provide for a wider range of contributions.

Contributors were asked to consider the ethical, legal, and clinical implications, as well as training standards that might apply to their incident or response. The law, ethics, and training standards guide the work of professional counselors in striving to serve the best interest of their clients, whether it is in a group or an individual supervisory setting. Some of the citations made by the contributors included the *Code of Ethics* of the American Counseling Association (2005) and the American School Counselor Association's *Ethical Standards for School Counselors* (1998).

The novice, as well as the experienced supervisor, will benefit from *Critical Incidents in Clinical Supervision*. The editors consider this book to be a valuable resource for clinical supervisors and clinical directors in schools, community agencies and mental health centers, treatment centers and clinics, hospitals, and private practices; supervisees ranging from the practicum student to the licensure-seeking supervisee and beyond; supervisors-in-training; supervisors of supervisors; site supervisors for approved training experiences; counselors-in-training; peer consultants; and mentors and protégés.

As a text, supplementary text, or reference for advanced or beginning courses in supervision, ethical and legal issues, professional issues, practicum, internship, and other counseling courses, the counselor- or supervisor-in-training will benefit from working on some of the "real" issues he or she will face in supervisory situations. On reading the incident, the student and experienced professional alike may analyze the factors presented and reflect on what they may have done the same or differently if faced with a similar situation. In addition, it is suggested the reader focus on the two responses and reflect on points of agreement and disagreement in deciding on an appropriate course of action. Consideration of the ethical codes, the law, and standards of practice and care should be applied as well. It is recognized that there can be more than one appropriate course of action applied to a specific incident. In this way, responses to incidents are provided not as ideal responses but as viewpoints that can be discussed and debated.

The editors hope that readers will embrace *Critical Incidents in Clinical Supervision* as a practical text that provides the means to examine critical incidents that occur in the supervisory setting. Readers are encouraged to be actively involved in determining appropriate courses of action, based on their reflections in reading the two responses to each incident as well as their own training, education, and level of supervisory skill development.

—*Lawrence E. Tyson*
John R. Culbreth
Judith A. Harrington

About the Editors

Lawrence E. Tyson, PhD, NCSC, is an associate professor in the Counselor Education Program, within the Department of Human Studies, in the School of Education at the University of Alabama at Birmingham (UAB). He is a coeditor of *Critical Incidents in School Counseling* and *Critical Incidents in Group Counseling*. For the past nine years, he has served as the advisor for the school counseling concentration within the Counselor Education Program at UAB. Additionally, he oversees the placement of UAB practicum and intern school counseling students in area schools, as well as UAB school counseling students who are involved in clinical placements outside of Alabama. He holds a master's degree from Rollins College and a doctorate in philosophy from Mississippi State University. He is a National Certified Counselor and a National Certified School Counselor.

John R. Culbreth, PhD, NCC, ACS, MAC, NCLPC, NCLCAS, NCLSC, is an associate professor in the Department of Counseling at The University of North Carolina at Charlotte. Before coming to UNC Charlotte, Jack was on the faculty at The Pennsylvania State University and the University of Virginia. Jack conducts research in the areas of clinical supervision in the chemical dependency counseling field, supervisor developmental processes, school counselor supervision, and the professional development of counselors in the United States and in different parts of the world. Prior to becoming a professor, Jack worked in a variety of treatment settings as a mental health counselor, a chemical dependency treatment counselor, and a substance abuse prevention counselor at the middle and high school levels. He currently has a counseling and supervision private practice.

Jack is a National Certified Counselor, Approved Clinical Supervisor, and Master Addictions Counselor and is recognized by the state of North Carolina as a Licensed Professional Counselor, a Licensed Chemical Addiction Specialist, and a Licensed K–12 School Counselor. Jack is currently the chair of the CACREP Board of Directors and is an active member in the American Counseling Association, the Association for Counselor Education and Supervision, and the International Association of Addictions and Offender Counseling. He serves on the editorial review boards of two journals, the *Journal of Addictions & Offender Counseling* and *The Clinical Supervisor,* and is an ad hoc reviewer for the *Journal of Counseling & Development* and *Counselor Education and Supervision.*

Judith A. Harrington has been a mental health professional since 1979, having served most of her career since 1988 in full-time private practice and community counseling in Birmingham, Alabama. She has served as a clinical director of two public counseling agencies and specializes in providing clinical supervision of licensure-seeking counselors in her state of Alabama. In addition to mentoring licensees, since 1994 she has also trained several hundred counselors wishing to comply with her state's Board of Examiners in Counseling supervisor regulations. She has provided extensive service to the profession, having served in a variety of elected and appointed positions in state and regional associations, including president of the Alabama Association of Counselor Education and Supervision and the Alabama Mental Health Counselors Association, coeditor of the Southern Association of Counselor Education Newsletter, SACES Long Range Planning Committee chairperson, and SACES Supervision Interest Network cochairperson. She has maintained an active adjunct teaching role since 1993 in her area, having taught master's and EdS courses in clinical supervision and *DSM-IV-TR* diagnosis and treatment, among others.

She holds credentials as a Licensed Professional Counselor, a Licensed Marriage and Family Therapist, a Certified Clinical Mental Health Counselor, a Certified Clinical Supervisor, and a Certified Alcohol and Drug Abuse Professional. Among several honors, she was selected by the Alabama Counseling Association as Outstanding Practitioner of the Year in its inaugural year of 2006 and earned her state's highest honor as the Wilbur Tincher Humanitarian and Caring Person of the Year in 2002. Recently, she was honored as the Mental Health Counselor of the Year by the American Mental Health Counselors Association.

Contributors

Lyndon Abrams, PhD, NCC, The University of North Carolina at Charlotte
Paul Baird, PhD, LPC, NCC, University of North Alabama
Marjorie Baker, MS, LPC-S, Family Sunshine Center, Montgomery, AL
Phillip W. Barbee, PhD, University of Texas at El Paso
Paul Barnes, PhD, NCC, NCSC, University of Nebraska at Omaha
Christine Suniti Bhat, PhD, Ohio University
Wendy Charkow Bordeau, PhD, NCC, LPC, Georgian Court University, NJ
Judy Bowers, EdD, Tucson Unified School District, AZ
Michael Brooks, PhD, LPC, LMHC, NCC, University of Alabama at Birmingham
Lori L. Brown, PhD, LPC, NCC, NCSC, ACS, The University of North Carolina
   at Greensboro
Nancy G. Calley, PhD, LPC, University of Detroit Mercy and Spectrum Human
   Services, Inc. & Affiliated Companies
Catherine Clark, EdD, Appalachian State University, NC
Diane M. Clark, PhD, NCC, LPC, Austin Peay State University, TN
Kenneth M. Coll, PhD, NCC, MAC, LPC, Boise State University, ID
Katrina Cook, MA, LPC, LMFT, University of Texas at San Antonio
Joseph B. Cooper, PhD, NCC, LPC, Marymount University, VA
Hugh C. Crethar, PhD, University of Arizona
John R. Culbreth, PhD, NCC, ACS, MAC, NCLPC, NCLCAS, NCLSC, The
   University of North Carolina at Charlotte
Carol A. Dahir, EdD, New York Institute of Technology
Heidi S. Deschamps, PhD, University of New Mexico
Ginger L. Dickson, PhD, NCC, University of Texas at El Paso
Kevin Doyle, EdD, LPC, LSATP, University of Virginia
Cher N. Edwards, PhD, Seattle Pacific University
Scott Edwards, PhD, LMFT, Seattle Pacific University
Lori Ellison, PhD, LPC, LMFT, Texas A&M University (Commerce)
Karen Eriksen, PhD, NCC, Florida Atlantic University
R. Reneè Evans, PhD, LPC, NCLSC, Appalachian State University, NC
Linda H. Foster, PhD, NCC, NCSC, LPC, University of Alabama at Birmingham
Perry C. Francis, EdD, LPC, NCC, Eastern Michigan University
Jill A. Geltner, PhD, NCSC, Queen of Peace Catholic Academy, FL
Harriet L. Glosoff, PhD, LPC, NCC, ACS, University of Virginia
Gary Goodnough, PhD, LCMHC, Plymouth State University, NH

Darcy Haag Granello, PhD, LPCC-S, Ohio State University

Charles F. Gressard, PhD, NCC, MAC, LPC, LSATP, College of William and Mary, VA

Marc A. Grimmett, PhD, HSP-P, North Carolina State University

W. Bryce Hagedorn, PhD, NCC, MAC, LMHC, University of Central Florida

Judith A. Harrington, PhD, LPC, LMFT, private practice, Birmingham, AL

Trish Hatch, PhD, San Diego State University

Rose Marie Hoffman, PhD, California State University, Long Beach

Joseph P. Jordan, PhD, NCC, MAC, LPC, LCAS, CCS, private practice, Greensboro, NC

Gerald A. Juhnke, EdD, NCC, MAC, LPC, CCAS, University of Texas at San Antonio

Virginia A. Kelly, PhD, NCC, LPC, Fairfield University, CT

Simone Lambert, PhD, NCC, LPC, Virginia Polytechnic Institute and State University

Pamela S. Lassiter, PhD, NCC, LPC, LCAS, CCS, LMFT, The University of North Carolina at Charlotte

Robin Wilbourn Lee, PhD, LPC, NCC, Middle Tennessee State University

Todd F. Lewis, PhD, NCC, LPC, The University of North Carolina at Greensboro

Jeremy M. Linton, PhD, NCC, LMHC, Indiana University South Bend

Stephanie L. Lusk, PhD, CRC, North Carolina A&T State University

Virginia Magnus, PhD, LPC, CSC, University of Tennessee at Chattanooga

Krista Malott, PhD, NCC, Villanova University, PA

Michele P. Mannion, PhD, LCPC, Capella University

Geri Miller, PhD, LPC, LCAS, CCS, Appalachian State University, NC

Oliver J. Morgan, PhD, NCC, LMFT, ACS, University of Scranton, PA

Allan A. Morotti, PhD, NCC, LPC, University of Alaska Fairbanks

Sullivan Moseley, PhD, NCC, LPC, private practice, Charlotte, NC

Louise Napolitano, PhD, LPC, private practice, Charlotte, NC

Patricia J. Neufeld, PhD, LCPC, NCC, Emporia State University, KS

Quinn M. Pearson, PhD, LPC, University of North Alabama

Rachelle Pérusse, PhD, NCC, NCSC, University of Connecticut

Jean Sunde Peterson, PhD, NCC, LMHC, Purdue University, IN

Emily Phillips, PhD, NCC, State University of New York at Oneonta

Rhiannon Horne Price, MA, University of Tennessee

Theodore P. Remley Jr., JD, PhD, LPC, NCC, Old Dominion University, VA

Solange Ribeiro, MS, LPC-S, private practice, Birmingham, AL

Walter B. Roberts Jr., EdD, LPC, LSC, NCC, NCSC, ACS, Minnesota State University

P. Clay Rowell, PhD, NCC, The University of North Carolina at Greensboro

James R. Ruby, PhD, LCPC, NCC, Northeastern Illinois University

Jill Russett, MSW, CSAC, College of William and Mary, VA

Carmen Salazar, PhD, NCC, Texas A&M University–Commerce

Kathleen M. Salyers, PhD, LPC, LICDC, University of Toledo

Cheri Smith, PhD, LPC, NCC, Southern Connecticut State University

LeAnne Steen, PhD, LPC, RPT-S, Loyola University New Orleans

Matthew J. Stefanelli, MS, CAC, CRC, Marworth Treatment Center

Carolyn B. Stone, EdD, University of North Florida
Jeannine R. Studer, EdD, University of Tennessee
Toni Roth Sullivan, EdD, LCPC, ACS, private practice, Easton, MD
Michael J. Taleff, PhD, MAC, CSAC, University of Hawaii at Manoa
Lisa Tang, PhD, NCC, State University of New York at Oneonta
Warren Throckmorton, PhD, Grove City College, PA
Heather C. Trepal, PhD, LPC, University of Texas at San Antonio
Barbara C. Trolley, PhD, CRC, St. Bonaventure University, NY
Lawrence E. Tyson, PhD, NCSC, University of Alabama at Birmingham
Robert Urofsky, PhD, Clemson University, SC
Laura J. Veach, PhD, LPC, LCAS, CCS, Wake Forest University, NC
Riley Venable, PhD, NCC, RN, LPC, LPCS, Texas Southern University
Consuelo Viteri, MS, LPC, Oasis Women's Counseling Center, Birmingham, AL
Laurae K. Wartinger, PhD, NCC, The Sage Colleges, NY
Tyra Turner Whittaker, RhD, CRC, LPC, North Carolina A&T State University
David Whittinghill, PhD, NCC, MAC, LMHC, University of North Florida
Laurie L. Williamson, EdD, LPC, ACS, Appalachian State University, NC
Nona Wilson, PhD, St. Cloud State University, MN
Geof Yager, PhD, PCC, NCC, ACS, University of Cincinnati and Holistic Counseling Care of Cincinnati

Part I

Addictions Counseling

Chapter 1

You're Not One of Us: The Age-Old Question of Counselor Recovery Status

Kevin Doyle

Topics

- Recovery issues among supervisees
- Supervisor validity
- Personal recovery as a credential

Background

Cecil is a White 45-year-old professional counselor who has practiced his entire career in the addiction treatment field. He attributes his interest in this area to an internship at a treatment center that he completed while in graduate school and not to any personal issues of his own. He is not a recovering alcoholic or addict, unlike many of the staff at his workplace.

For the past several years, Cecil has conducted a supervision group for several of his coworkers who are seeking licensure as professional counselors in his state. The group meets weekly for 90 minutes. Group members bring difficult cases, ethical scenarios, and other topics for peer review and discussion, under Cecil's supervision. He is responsible for completing regular paperwork for submission to the state board, which will be considered part of each member's application as he or she works to become eligible to take the licensure exam.

Carol is a 33-year-old African American woman and a recovering heroin addict who has worked at the agency for 10 years. She began working 2 years after entering recovery, at which time she had completed only a few college courses. Over the subsequent 10 years, she has returned to school and earned both her bachelor's and master's degrees. She now works as a counselor in the women's program at the agency. She has been attending Cecil's supervision group for several months.

Roberto is a 55-year-old Hispanic man who came to the United States from El Salvador 12 years ago. Roberto is also in recovery, having seen his drinking increase dramatically after his move to this country, leading to his successful treatment several years after his arrival here. He also recently received his master's degree from a local university and is making progress toward state licensure. He is a counselor in the agency's adult program, reporting directly to Cecil. He is relatively new to the supervision group, having attended for approximately 2 months.

Ellen is a White, 49-year-old mother of four who reentered the workforce after her three kids were in school. She attributes her interest in the addiction treatment field to her childhood experiences of being raised in a home with an alcoholic father who eventually received treatment and entered recovery during her early adulthood. She has participated in Al-Anon occasionally over the years. She also holds a master's degree in counseling, has been participating in the supervision group for the past year, and works as a counselor in the agency's adolescent treatment program.

Incident

One day the following exchange occurred at the beginning of the supervision group:

Cecil: Welcome everyone. [Group members respond accordingly.] I hope everyone is having a good week so far. Is there anything anyone would like to start with today?

Roberto: Yes, I have a topic that has been on my mind recently that I would like to share.

Cecil: Thanks, Roberto, please go ahead.

Roberto: Well, I have been doing some reading and talking with my sponsor a bit and am curious about your [gesturing toward Cecil] opinion about whether people who are not in recovery can be effective as counselors. I have read the history of Alcoholics Anonymous and seen for myself how the value of one alcoholic or addict helping another is without parallel. I am just not sure that effective drug counselors can be taught in classes or from books. I know that my personal experiences are what help me in working with our clients, and I know that you are not in recovery, Cecil, so I was wondering what your position was on this.

Cecil: Before I comment, I would like to hear what other members of the group think.

Ellen: Well, I totally disagree. I am also not in recovery, but I grew up in an alcoholic home and I think I have quite a good understanding of this disease from that perspective. So, I think you don't have to be in recovery to be effective.

Carol: OK, but there are some things that you just can't understand unless you've been there. Empathy—which we all learned about in school—is a great thing, but I know what it's like when the women I work with talk about their "heroin jones." I know what it's like to steal money from family members to buy drugs. I am able to draw on these experiences when I work with these women. I think a more interesting discussion would be to talk about how much to self-disclose.

Cecil: Well, let's come back to the self-disclosure issue. I have a couple of thoughts about the recovery versus nonrecovery thing. First, I guess I am wondering if the group is somehow doubting my competence as your supervisor because of my status of not being in recovery. I guess I am feeling a bit unappreciated or maybe disrespected right now. Second, I do think that it is possible to be effective as a counselor even though I have not had personal experience as an alcoholic or addict. After all, you don't have to have had a brain surgery to be a good brain surgeon, right? I know that my clients don't know if I am in recovery or not.

Carol: Yes, they do—they can tell!

Cecil: Well, I don't tell them, so they would just be guessing. What I am trying to say is that my clients are able to benefit from what I have learned in school. I haven't attended AA or NA meetings like they do, but I still am able to share with them what they need to do to recover. Now, let's move on to the self-disclosure issue that Carol raised.

Discussion

Cecil has been handed the ongoing question in the addiction field regarding counselor, or in this case supervisor, recovery status. Personal experience with recovery continues to be a sticking point for many counselors, even though many research studies have indicated that it should not be a criteria for effective alcohol or drug addiction counseling (Aiken, LoSciuto, Ausetts, & Brown, 1984; Brown & Thompson, 1976; McLellan, Woody, Luborsky, & Goehl, 1988). However, the issue is very important as it relates to the perception of Cecil in the eyes of his counselors. It may indicate some level of anxiety about Cecil's ability to understand the counselors' perspective and to appreciate what recovering counselors bring to their work. How supervisors manage this conversation and how they manage interactions related to personal recovery can affect the supervisory relationship.

Questions

1. Discuss how Cecil handled the issue of personal recovery as it was raised in the group. Did you feel he was effective in his response? Why or why not? What could he have done differently?
2. How should supervisors respond in the group setting when their competence or qualifications are challenged by a group member or members? Did Cecil respond effectively?
3. Consider your feelings about personal recovery for the counselor and how it might arise in the supervisory setting. Should you re-

veal your status to those you supervise? To your clients? Are there any potential ethical problems that could result?

4. Could the dialogue above cause any lingering problems in the group? What, if anything, would you recommend Cecil do additionally to address some of the issues that were raised in the session?

References

Aiken, L. S., LoSciuto, L. A., Ausetts, M. A., & Brown, B. S. (1984). Paraprofessional versus professional drug counselors: The progress of clients in treatment. *International Journal of the Addictions, 19,* 383–401.

Brown, B. S., & Thompson, R. F. (1976). The effectiveness of formerly addicted and nonaddicted counselors on client functioning. *Drug Forum, 5,* 123–129.

McLellan, A. T., Woody, G. E., Luborsky, L., & Goehl, L. (1988). Is the counselor an "active ingredient" in substance abuse rehabilitation? An examination of treatment success among four counselors. *Journal of Nervous and Mental Disease, 176,* 423–430.

Response

Jeremy M. Linton

This critical incident highlights several issues that can arise in the supervision of substance abuse counselors. These include perceived challenges to supervisor competence, differences in supervisor and supervisee backgrounds, and conflict in group supervision. Cecil's initial actions in addressing this incident were both effective and appropriate to the situation. He started off well by addressing head on Roberto's question regarding counselor recovery status. Supervisees need to feel comfortable expressing concerns, and by attending to Roberto's question, Cecil likely assisted in this process (Bernard & Goodyear, 1998). Cecil also demonstrated effective group management skills by asking other group members for their input and keeping the group on topic. When this is done well, it serves to keep all group members actively involved in their professional development.

Unfortunately, Cecil's defensive manner undermined any positive effects that occurred because of the actions specified above. By assuming almost immediately that the group was being disrespectful to him and doubting his competence, Cecil helped to create a conflictual atmosphere in the group, thereby making productive discussion unlikely. Furthermore, his example about brain surgery was perfunctory and has little relevance to substance abuse counseling. This may have served to belittle the issue in the eyes of the group. More germane illustrations could involve depression or suicide. Perhaps Cecil let some of his personal feelings affect his response to the incident. Cecil has likely been asked on numerous occasions to defend the stance that nonrecovering counselors can be effective in addictions treatment. Cecil may have had some difficulty separating any resulting frustration about this topic from his supervisory role.

Supervision contracts can be used as a preventative measure for incidents such as this one (Lockett, 2001). These contracts can be used to set supervision goals, rules, roles, and norms and to specify the focus of supervision (e.g., improve professional skills, understand personal issues related to service delivery). In this incident, Cecil could have referred to these contracts to frame the discussion of Roberto's question and to steer the conversation away from personal debates and toward professional development.

When supervisors believe that their competence is being challenged, they should refrain from inferring meaning about the challenge. Because it is possible that a supervisee's question or comment has been incorrectly interpreted as a challenge, the supervisor should first engage in some fact finding about the supervisee's motives. This would involve questioning the supervisee about the issue being raised and what he or she hopes to gain from the discussion. The group should also be engaged in this questioning. Following this, the supervisor can make a more informed judgment about whether his or her competence is being challenged and proceed accordingly.

Self-disclosure regarding recovery status, as highlighted by this incident, is never a dichotomous issue, and several factors must be considered before such a disclosure is made. In the addictions treatment field, counselors and supervisors are apt to feel great pressure to disclose their personal drug and alcohol use history (i.e., recovery status). As with all self-disclosure, this should be a personal choice on the part of the professional involved. If a disclosure is made, the professional must make certain that the purpose of the disclosure is for the benefit of the client or supervisee (e.g., telling his or her personal story to strengthen the client's resolve in recovery) and not for personal gain. Otherwise, a potential ethical violation has occurred.

Specific to supervision, the debate regarding counselor recovery status, and self-disclosure of such, is likely to occur when the supervisor and supervisee are of differing recovery backgrounds (Culbreth & Borders, 1999). Guidelines set forth by the Association for Counselor Education and Supervision (ACES, 1993) say little about supervisor self-disclosure with supervisees. ACES guidelines do, however, specify that supervisors should inform their supervisees of their theoretical approaches to both counseling and supervision. The substance abuse treatment field is unique from other specializations because certain models of treatment are rooted in the counselor's own experiences with addiction. For some counselors and supervisors, then, disclosure about theoretical orientation may entail revealing one's personal recovery status. However, when the focus remains on assisting the supervisee to improve services offered to clients, disclosure of recovery status need not be imperative if the supervisor does not deem it so.

In the substance abuse treatment field, clients and treatment professionals alike often believe that they are entitled to know the recovery status of their counselors or coworkers. In reality, counselor and supervisor recovery status is not at all relevant to the counseling or supervisory process unless it is a part of the provider's personal model of service delivery. If the client or supervisee continues to inquire about counselor or supervisor recovery status, even after the counselor or supervisor has declined to share that information, then perhaps this persistence should be addressed as a counseling or supervision issue.

It is likely that the conflict created by this critical incident will cause some lingering effects for future group meetings, and it is imperative that these effects be addressed (Enyedy et al., 2003; Linton, 2003). In these instances, the supervisor should begin to address the conflict by taking ownership and accountability for his or her actions. Group members should also be involved in the reparative process and encouraged to develop plans to fix any resulting damage. Finally, to minimize such conflicts in the future, the supervisor should gain a more thorough understanding of group supervision and the processes inherent within through training and a review of the literature. To practice group supervision without this understanding may be an ethical violation at best and detrimental to client welfare at worst (Borders, 1989).

References

Association for Counselor Education and Supervision. (1993). Ethical guidelines for counseling supervisors. *ACES Spectrum, 53*(4), 5-8.

Bernard, J. M., & Goodyear, R. K. (1998). *Fundamentals of clinical supervision* (2nd ed.). Boston: Allyn & Bacon.

Borders, L. D. (1989). A pragmatic agenda for developmental supervision research. *Counselor Education and Supervision, 29*, 16-24.

Culbreth, J. R., & Borders, L. D. (1999). Perceptions of the supervisory relationship: Recovering and non-recovering substance abuse counselors. *Journal of Counseling & Development, 77*, 330-338.

Enyedy, K., Arcinue, F., Puri, N., Carter, J., Goodyear, R., & Getzelman, M. (2003). Hindering phenomena in group supervision: Implications for practice. *Professional Psychology: Research and Practice, 43*, 312-317.

Linton, J. (2003). A preliminary qualitative investigation of group processes in group supervision: Perspectives of master's level practicum students. *Journal for Specialists in Group Work, 28*, 215-226.

Lockett, M. (2001). The responsibilities of group supervisors. In S. Wheeler & D. King (Eds.), *Supervising counsellors: Issues of responsibility* (pp. 153-166). London: Sage.

Response

Oliver J. Morgan and Matthew J. Stefanelli

Cecil's initial response to the questions of recovery status, self-disclosure, and clinical effectiveness was a good one. He tried to engage a group process of reflection and discussion. Quickly, however, his own discomfort with the issues pushed him to short-circuit the discussion, overly personalize the issues, and lay the groundwork for frustration and dissatisfaction within the group. A better prepared and more self-assured supervisor would have allowed the group to surface its questions and perhaps wondered aloud about the timing and underlying thinking that were the catalysts for these questions. This may have revealed other issues that were relevant to the supervision process.

The timing and initiation of this entire conversation could (and should) have occurred differently. In the world of chemical dependency, this set of issues truly is an age-old question. Why, then, wouldn't Cecil have introduced the topic as part of the group's initial contracting for supervision?

Current best practices for supervisors now call for an initial process of informed consent and discussion of goals, credentials, expectations, and relevant questions within the beginning supervisory relationship (Bradley & Ladany, 2001; Todd & Storm, 2002). We believe that recovery status and its relationship to clinical effectiveness, although an issue in the clinical relationship that needs delicate handling to serve therapeutic purposes, is also a critical issue in the supervisory relationship that needs to be dealt with forthrightly. These issues can be seen as central to the supervisor's credentials and critical to the group members' informed consent to embarking on this supervisory relationship. How the supervisor thinks about these issues, and what she or he brings to the table in terms of recovery knowledge either as an "insider" or as an "empathic observer," is as important to the process of supervision here as his or her clinical and supervisory training, competence, and use of models of supervision. Supervisees have a right to this information up front.

Issues such as the counselor's recovery status are unremarkable in chemical dependency settings. Any clinician or supervisor working in such settings should be prepared for them, understanding that at the core of the addicts' problems and treatment is trust. Who can they trust? To whom can they confide what is really going on? How can someone who doesn't experientially understand their world, their language, and their culture really be of any help to them? Rather than seeing these questions as some kind of personal challenge, as resistance, or as "addictive exceptionalism" (i.e., trying to have it all my way), a good clinician or supervisor understands them as a yearning for someone to trust. Cecil failed this test with his supervisees.

In addition, Cecil's disclosure of nonattendance at Alcoholics Anonymous or Narcotics Anonymous meetings confirms for us a certain naïveté (at best) or unwillingness or resistance to learn (at worst) in relation to addictive and recovery cultures (see White, 1996). We believe some ongoing learning about addictive and recovery language, mores, thinking, beliefs, feelings, and experiences is essential to concretely and ethically build an empathic bond with this population.

What many recovering persons say is obviously true, we think: They need somebody in their lives who knows recovery as an insider. This inside perspective has traditionally been the role of the recovery sponsor and 12-step group. Notwithstanding a long tradition of recovering counselors, however, this inside angle is not a qualification for an ethical or effective therapist. Counselors and therapists have a different role to play, as a number of nonrecovering therapists and clergy (e.g., Dr. Harry Tiebout or Rabbi Abraham Twerski) have throughout the history of the recovery movement.

We believe that effective therapists working within the chemical dependency field should have some level of personal experience with the 12-step recovery program. Witnessing 12-step meetings gives the nonrecovering counselor a firsthand look at what we ask our clients to do. Having personal experience with 12-step programs also allows nonrecovering counselors to understand that they are a "formula for mature, responsible living" beyond abstinence from mood-altering substances (Twerski, 2005, p. 22). Attendance at 12-step meetings can be an avenue for personal and spiritual enlightenment for any open person.

It seems to us that Cecil now needs to readdress the group in terms of supervision contracting. The points raised here could be the basis for this meeting. However, the group also needs to make an informed decision about the kind of supervision goals they have together. The issue here is context.

Cecil is providing supervision for licensure in professional counseling. He has a number of roles in this regard, including enhancing the professional functioning of his group members and monitoring client care as well as evaluation and gatekeeping (see, e.g., Bernard & Goodyear, 1998). These central supervisory tasks have little to do with his or the group members' recovery status. Both Cecil and the group need to attend to these tasks for there to be any chance of regaining the group's trust and reestablishing a working supervisory group that is focused on a common goal.

References

Bernard, J. M., & Goodyear, R. K. (1998). *Fundamentals of clinical supervision* (2nd ed.). Boston: Allyn & Bacon.

Bradley, L., & Ladany, N. (2001). *Counselor supervision: Principles, process, and practice*. Philadelphia: Brunner-Routledge.

Todd, T. C., & Storm, C. L. (2002). *The complete systemic supervisor: Context, philosophy, and pragmatics.* New York: Authors Choice Press.

Twerski, A. J. (2005). *From pulpit ... To couch.* Pittsburgh: Mirkov Publications.

White, W. L. (1996). *Pathways from the culture of addiction to the culture of recovery: A travel guide for addiction professionals* (2nd ed.). Center City, MN: Hazelden.

Chapter 2

Is This Love That I'm Feeling? Intimacy and Attraction in Supervision

W. Bryce Hagedorn

Topics

- Parallel process issues in supervision
- Sexual attraction in the supervisory relationship
- Unique characteristics of process addictions

Background

Dr. Vasquez is a 42-year-old Hispanic woman who has worked as an assistant professor in a Council for Accreditation of Counseling and Related Educational Programs–accredited counselor education program at State University for 4 years. Prior to attaining her doctoral degree, Dr. Vasquez worked primarily in substance abuse treatment facilities for a total of 8 years. Her research background is in addictions counseling, couples and family therapy, and gender identity development. As a part of her teaching responsibilities, she supervises 10 mental health counseling internship students enrolled in the master's program. In addition to facilitating the group supervision element of these students on a weekly basis, she also meets with each student on a bimonthly basis.

Incident

Nicolas, one of the master's students supervised by Dr. Vasquez, is a 35-year-old Caucasian man who is in his last semester of his master's degree. Nicolas has chosen a community mental health clinic as his internship site. He works with a variety of clients presenting with concerns ranging from substance abuse disorders, psychiatric disorders, and dual diagnoses. This setting offers individual and group counseling, medication consultations, and intensive outpatient programs.

Unbeknownst to Dr. Vasquez, Nicolas is attracted to her. On a cognitive level, Nicholas is aware of his attraction and begrudgingly admits that there can be no relationship between the two of them. On an emotional level, however, Nicolas often finds himself fantasizing over how such a relationship might evolve if it were ever to come to fruition.

In the 7th week of Nicolas' second semester of internship, he was assigned Rosie as a client. Rosie, a 29-year-old biracial woman (father is African American, mother is Hispanic) who has one child by a prior marriage, sought counseling for reoccurring substance dependence to cocaine and alcohol. She currently works as a chef at a local restaurant, and although her addictive use of substances has not impeded her performance thus far, she is concerned with her escalating use. She has been drinking after work on a daily basis for the past 2 years and uses cocaine "whenever I can get my hands on some." Both her alcohol and cocaine use have increased to the point where she is concerned about her ability to maintain her job, care for her daughter, and maintain her self-respect. She reports feelings of low self-esteem and depression and states that she has "never been able to maintain a long-term relationship with a good man." This is Rosie's second time seeking counseling—the first time she admitted herself to inpatient detox (from alcohol) 4 years ago. Although she has attended AA, her attendance has decreased progressively to a point where she attends "once every couple of months." Rosie was able to maintain her sobriety for 8 months following discharge until she met a man at work "who drank more than I did" and didn't think that she had a problem. The recent break-up of this relationship led to a week-long binge while Rosie's daughter stayed with her grandparents, an incident that frightened her for reasons that she has thus far kept to herself.

In the sixth counseling session, Rosie began to share more intimate details of her recent drug and alcohol binge episode, most notably that during that time she engaged in multiple sexual encounters including one with a woman. In the session, Nicolas explored details of the binge episode, how Rosie felt about the events, and how it felt for Rosie to discuss the issue with Nicolas. Rosie also shared her concerns about her interest in pornography and an apparent developing addiction to Internet porn. She stated that she felt this behavior was abnormal for a woman and shared that she has been recently looking at pornography that she considers "weird and perverse." Rosie indicated that she felt uncomfortable sharing these details with a man and that she was worried that Nicolas would think that she "was some kind of pervert." Rosie consistently asked for validation from Nicolas in the session and was concerned about his impression of her. Rosie also maintained that whereas she did not believe herself to be gay, it seemed that being with a woman was easier than being with a man. Throughout the session, Nicolas got the impression that Rosie was deliberately sharing explicit details in order to arouse him, and as a result, he struggled to find the right words for Rosie.

In supervision, Nicolas shared with Dr. Vasquez the events of the session with Rosie and his struggle with how to respond appropriately. Dr. Vasquez asked about Rosie's exploration of her sexual identity and discussed the Internet porn issue. Dr. Vasquez suggested that maybe Rosie has an underlying sexual addiction in addition to her polysubstance abuse. As the conversation progressed, Dr. Vasquez turned her attention to how Nicolas felt during the session with Rosie. Nicolas stated that hearing the details of Rosie's encounters had been slightly uncomfortable. He had a difficult time explaining this discomfort to Dr. Vasquez, stating that he did not think that Rosie's issues were "weird," but that talking about it further was slightly embarrassing for him. Dr. Vasquez brought up the gender differences in the discussion, suggesting that Nicolas may feel uncomfortable because Dr. Vasquez was a woman. Nicolas agreed with this idea and stated that he did feel "weird" and uncomfortable talking with Dr. Vasquez about the details of Rosie's conversation.

Questions

1. Is Nicolas's attraction to Dr. Vasquez affecting this supervision interaction? If so, how?
2. What way would you suggest to appropriately address this attraction in the supervisory relationship if it became a more pronounced issue?
3. In reviewing what is happening during the supervision session and comparing it to what happened in the counseling session, discuss how this may or may not be an example of parallel process.
4. Why would Dr. Vasquez suggest an underlying sexual addiction? Does Nicholas have enough information to form a provisional diagnosis?

Response

Diane M. Clark

There are multiple connections taking place in this case study that need to be attended to in supervision. The attraction that Nicolas is feeling toward his supervisor, Dr. Vasquez, is of primary importance in that it is evident during portions of Nicolas's conversation with Dr. Vasquez about his client's sexual behavior. It is somewhat unclear whether Dr. Vasquez has recognized the attraction, but the fact that it exists affects the way that Nicolas responds to Dr. Vasquez's questions. It is not unusual for a supervisee to feel some degree of attraction to his or her supervisor. The close, collegial atmosphere of supervisory relationships can cause both supervisor and supervisee to lose track of the evaluative nature of supervision and cause the parties to view each other as social friends or colleagues (Falvey, 2002). Although collegial in nature, it must be remembered that the relationship between supervisor and supervisee is not one of professional equals.

When the attraction is one of a more intimate, sexual nature, it becomes ethically dangerous. Although Nicolas is cognitively aware that his feelings for his supervisor are inappropriate, on a less conscious level he may be unable to control them. That being the case, he should bring the issue up during the supervisory discussion. It would be useful for Dr. Vasquez to recognize the attraction in order to further discuss the transference and countertransference that is taking place in the relationship. Furthermore, it is important that Nicolas not deny the attraction, as attending to it may be useful in increasing his understanding of his client (Bernard & Goodyear, 1998).

In order to fully understand the parallel process that is occurring during this supervision session, both Dr. Vasquez and Nicolas would need to be aware of the underlying attraction that Nicolas has for his supervisor. This attraction appears to be the basis for Nicolas' transference issues. He has selected a part of the client's problem that he shares (sexual attraction) and is acting out the impasse that occurred between himself and the client regarding her sexual conduct during his supervisory experience.

Specifically, during their session Rosie (the client) has shared with Nicolas intimate details concerning her sexual activities and admits to feeling uncomfortable sharing these details with her male counselor. She looks for consistent validation from Nicolas during the session. Nicolas feels that Rosie is attempting to arouse him and has a difficult time responding to her therapeutic needs. In the same fashion, during supervision Nicolas admits to feeling uncomfortable describing the session to Dr. Vasquez and admits that the gender dynamic adds to his embarrassment. He skirts the issue of his attraction to Dr. Vasquez and focuses on his discomfort as it relates to talking to a woman about sexually charged issues.

Both Nicolas and Dr. Vasquez could take advantage of the parallel process that is taking place in this exchange. Instead of giving Nicolas a reason for his feelings of discomfort by suggesting the difference in their genders, Dr. Vasquez might instead use the skill of immediacy and say, "While you were describing your client's behavior, I noticed that I felt completely comfortable. However, you seem to be a little embarrassed, as did your client when she spoke to you about her sexual activity. What do you make of this?" In this way, Nicolas might make a conscious connection between what happened in the therapeutic process and what is taking place in the supervision experience. On the other hand, he may register his response to the feedback unconsciously, and it may find its way back into the therapeutic relationship by a delayed awareness of what is happening during the counseling session (Morrissey & Tribe, 2001). Either way, the parallel process taking place becomes a therapeutic tool and should not be ignored. Examination of the parallel process may help Nicolas look beyond the client–therapist dyad in examining the interactional field (Morrissey & Tribe, 2001). In other words, it could help him to understand the effect his attraction to Dr. Vasquez has on the supervisory relationship and assist him in bringing the problem to light with his supervisor, thus leading to a meaningful discussion within the supervisory session.

In addition to the parallel process that is taking place during supervision, Dr. Vasquez has suggested that Nicolas look a little more closely at Rosie's exploration of her sexual identity and her Internet porn use. Her suggestion that Rosie may suffer from a sexual addiction may be correct. Her cycle of avoidance followed by excessive sexual activity during a binge episode certainly fits the description of addictive behavior. Her thought process about her recent behavior has become one of judging as opposed to judgment (Schneider, Sealy, Montgomery, & Irons, 2005). Schneider et al. (2005) recently spoke to the ritualization that accompanies sexual addiction and its connection to drug addiction. They posit that Internet porn has become a powerful form of solo polyaddictive behavior by which the user can actually satisfy several addictive behaviors at once without involving other human beings. As with all addictions, it fits into a ritualized cycle, satisfying impulsive desire while shutting out the need for human contact.

Certainly Nicolas has a basis for a preliminary diagnosis of sexual addiction that needs further investigation. Nicolas may reject this diagnosis, however, if he does not acknowledge the transference and countertransference that is going on between himself and his client and during the supervisory session. To accept that Rosie has a sexual addiction without recognizing the parallel process dynamics at play within supervision could lead Nicolas to question his own ability to control sexual urges.

References

Bernard, J. M., & Goodyear, R. K. (1998). *Fundamentals of clinical supervision* (2nd ed.). Boston: Allyn & Bacon.

Falvey, J. E. (2002). *Managing clinical supervision: Ethical practice and clinical risk.* Pacific Grove, CA: Brooks/Cole.

Morrissey, J., & Tribe, R. (2001). Parallel process in supervision. *Counselling Psychology Quarterly, 14*, 103–110.

Schneider, J. P., Sealy, J., Montgomery, J., & Irons, R. R. (2005). Ritualization and reinforcement: Keys to understanding mixed addiction involving sex and drugs. *Sexual Addiction & Compulsivity, 12*, 121–148.

Response

Pamela S. Lassiter

Clinical work within the internship experience can bring up personal and difficult material for students. Because of the nature of our work, supervisors must be prepared not only to assist students in clinical skill-building but also to assist them with learning to manage the complex emotional and intellectual challenges they may personally face in their training (Aponte, 1994). Although there are definite differences between supervision and therapy, it is sometimes necessary to deal with the intern's personal issues within the context of the supervisory relationship, especially when those issues may be interfering with the student's clinical work or professional development (Bradley & Post, 1991). In this situation, the intern's intense personal feelings for the supervisor and his reactions to the client may be interfering with his ability to work effectively with either. At the least, these strong personal reactions offer an opportunity for professional and personal growth, which may be precluded here by the supervisor's ethical responsibility to protect the welfare of the client.

It appears that Nicolas's attraction to his supervisor is affecting his supervision because of the awkwardness he is experiencing in attempting to describe his feelings from the client's session. He does not seem to be able to go beyond a vague description of discomfort and embarrassment. Dr. Vasquez's initial attempt at exploration focused on the gender difference between herself and Nicolas. He is constrained in sharing a full description of his reactions to the client, thus severely limiting the available information for exploration in supervision. The potency of the counselor–client interaction described here could easily result in unethical behavior by the counselor-in-training. If not dealt with directly in supervision, the client's behavior could at the least serve to sabotage any progress in counseling. Nicolas is also not sharing his own personal feelings about Dr. Vasquez, which serves to create the "not yet said" or hidden agenda within the supervisory relationship. There appear to be two possibilities here surrounding the intern's discomfort. Is his discomfort due solely to the fact that his supervisor is female, or is it also due to his attraction to her? Nicolas's inability to openly explore his feelings about the client and about the supervisor is likely having a negative effect on both relationships as well as on his progress as a new counselor.

In this situation, it might be helpful if the attraction issues became more pronounced. Nicolas's newly overt behavior toward Dr. Vasquez would give her something to address more openly. She could explain to Nicolas how important it is to discuss such feelings and that it is safe to do so because the relationship would remain a professional one with clear boundaries. She might do this by saying, "I am glad that you shared your feelings of attraction toward me, and I believe it is important to do so. You are safe doing that here because we will continue to have a purely professional relationship that will not go beyond ethical boundaries. This is a valuable opportunity for you to explore those feelings, especially as they relate to your client work. It is normal to experience attractions in this work. Those attractions can reveal a great deal about us. In order to remain ethical within your practice, it is important to discuss them openly within supervision." Dr. Vasquez could also then explain the usefulness of parallel process, exploring the similarities between their relationship dynamics and the relationship between Nicolas and Rosie. The supervisor in this situation has the opportunity to model appropriate facilitation of an awkward topic and to show how to set appropriate therapeutic boundaries. Dr. Vasquez must first deal with her own responses and feelings about Nicolas's attraction. Her level of maturity, honesty, and genuineness will potentially set the tone for a similar conversation Nicolas may need to have with his client.

Parallel process is a unique concept in clinical supervision that uses the supervision relationship itself as the teaching medium (Borders & Brown, 2005). It is essentially a reflective process by which the dynamics that exist between the client and the counselor are reflected in the relationship between the counselor and the supervisor (Searles, 1955). The dynamics, if made conscious, can lead to powerful insights. Although supervision is clearly not therapy, good supervision challenges supervisees to grow both personally and professionally. The focus of supervision should remain on the supervisee's actions in counseling, but in this case, the dynamics between the supervisor and the intern warrant personal exploration within clearly defined boundaries. There are many opportunities for Nicolas to take what emerges in supervision and explore those issues further in his own personal counseling, and his supervisor should encourage him to invest in an outside therapeutic process. If left unconscious, this unspoken dynamic might sabotage progress. It does seem that there are potentially powerful elements of parallel process at play here.

Rosie describes feeling "weird" discussing the details of her sexual experiences with a male therapist, and Nicolas describes feeling "weird" discussing his reactions to the client's stories with a female supervisor. Nicolas is having a difficult time finding words with both his client and his supervisor (both women) when discussing sexuality issues. Nicolas's reactions to his client may give important information about how the client uses her sexuality to protect herself or to gain power in her relationships with men. His ability or inability to articulate these reactions in supervision will play out similarly in the relationship with his client. If Nicolas and his supervisor are able to move beyond the "weirdness" to an honest conversation about salient feelings and important boundaries, Nicolas may in turn have the skills and maturity to deal therapeutically with his client.

Regarding Rosie's behavior, Dr. Vasquez suggests an underlying sexual addiction based in part on Rosie's history of chemical dependency. The fact that she has historically used substances addictively may predispose her to using relationships addictively as well. Rosie's relapses appear to be strongly related to relationship break-ups, and her binge episode resulted in multiple sexual encounters. She seems to use stories of her sexual exploits as a way of relating to Nicolas in counseling and is pulling on him for approval. These behaviors, combined with her use of Internet pornography, are enough to suggest that Rosie is developing a sexual addiction. It will be important to continue to assess the interactions between Rosie's chemical dependency and her relationship behaviors.

In conclusion, it will be invaluable for Nicolas to learn as much about himself as he can through the unique opportunities presented in this situation. Gaining insight into his reactions and the way people may use sexuality in relationships will only serve to make him a stronger counselor in the future. In addition, as he works through this particular issue in supervision, it will strengthen his understanding of the supervisory process and supervisory relationship, making future challenging client issues more manageable in the context of the working relationship with his supervisor.

References

Aponte, H. J. (1994). How personal can training get? *Journal of Marital and Family Therapy, 20*(1), 3–15.

Borders, L. D., & Brown, L. L. (2005). *The new handbook of counseling supervision*. Mahwah, NJ: Erlbaum.

Bradley, J., & Post, P. (1991). Impaired students: Do we eliminate them from counselor education programs? *Counselor Education and Supervision, 31*, 100–108.

Searles, H. F. (1955). The informational value of the supervisor's emotional experience. *Psychiatry, 18*, 135–146.

Chapter 3

Dealing With Supervisee Countertransference Toward Addicted Clients

Joseph P. Jordan

Topics

- Personal history of counselor interfering with counseling practice
- Refusal to use best practices or standard referral protocol
- Power struggles in supervisory relationship

Background

Chris is a 35-year-old White man who is a managing partner for a large counseling practice in a moderately sized southeastern city. In this firm Chris sees clients and provides supervision to some of the independent contractors for his counseling practice. Additionally, Chris is providing supervision for a master's-level community counseling intern from a nearby university.

Sylvia is a 46-year-old White woman enrolled in a master's degree community counseling program as a second-career student. She is divorced and raising two children, both of whom are teenagers and attend a nearby high school. Sylvia applied for an internship at Chris's practice after hearing from previous interns of the diversity of experiences available there. Sylvia is in her second internship semester with Chris, and during her first semester of internship she worked primarily with child and adolescent clients with behavioral and mood disorders.

Incident

As part of his supervisory duties, Chris reviews the client charts of his supervisees, checking for appropriate documentation and interventions. During a review of Sylvia's client charts, Chris became concerned about a particular client. In his chart review, Chris found documentation of attendance at group counseling and psychoeducational sessions, as well as therapy notes discussing client responses to group counseling sessions. Chris also found documentation of several individual sessions during the initial weeks of the client's substance abuse treatment, but no recent notes detailing client progress on an individual basis. Additionally, there is no documentation of referral to community support meetings for persons recovering from alcohol or drug dependency.

The client is a 50-year-old White man employed at a nearby manufacturing job. He was referred for substance abuse assessment and follow-up counseling after a supervisor smelled alcohol on his breath when he showed up for work on a Monday morning. The client reported during the initial assessment that he had taken a couple of shots that morning to "take the edge off" after a weekend of partying with a couple of friends who were visiting from out of town. The client reported a number of symptoms of alcohol dependence from the *Diagnostic and Statistical Manual of Mental Disorders* (4th ed., American Psychiatric Association, 2000) specifically slight withdrawal, tolerance, drinking more alcohol than intended, unsuccessful attempts to control his use of alcohol, and recreational activities (fishing with friends) given up or reduced in order to use alcohol instead.

Chris staffed this case with Sylvia prior to assigning it to her, explaining the usual course of treatment with this kind of client, which includes individual and group counseling, psychoeducational classes, and referral to outside support meetings of some type. Chris had noticed some reluctance on Sylvia's part to engage in their usual active discussion of client issues and needs but had attributed it to nervousness about dealing with an addiction client for the first time. After reviewing the chart and discussing this situation with another supervisor in the firm, Chris decides to bring this up in supervision with Sylvia.

In the supervision session, Sylvia confirmed Chris's perception that she was not requiring outside support group attendance nor was she requiring the client to keep the regularly scheduled individual counseling sessions. Sylvia described her own experiences at the self-help group meetings in negative terms: meeting rooms filled with smoke and the smell of coffee, and people looking bad and possibly still using. Also, the client reported that it was difficult to get away from work to make individual sessions, so Sylvia decided not to press the issue with him. As the conversation progressed, Chris asked whether Sylvia had known anyone in her past who suffered from an addiction. Sylvia described her ex-husband as having a drinking problem and that the self-help group meetings were of no help to him or to her and the family. In fact, Sylvia stated that her ex-husband lied about regular AA attendance and ended up living with a woman that he met at a meeting after Sylvia's marriage was over. At the present time, Sylvia's former husband was not paying child support, and she did not know if he was sober or where he lived. Sylvia stated that she had seen a counselor after the marriage ended, but that it was difficult financially as a single parent.

As the supervision session progressed, Sylvia came to the conclusion that she was not the best person to work with this client and that maybe referring him to another counselor was for the best. Sylvia stated that she was not that familiar with this type of client problem, that maybe she was more comfortable working with children and adolescents. Chris indicated that he would discuss a referral with his colleagues but that for now Sylvia would continue to see this client in group and in the psychoeducational classes.

Questions

1. What do you think Chris could have done differently to deal with Sylvia's resistance to providing counseling services to this client? Was Chris correct in supporting the idea of referring this client to another counselor?
2. How should the supervision of this intern be structured to address possible countertransference issues? What specific recommendations would you make for future supervision sessions with Sylvia?
3. Do you think any specific requirements should be in place for counseling trainees prior to seeing substance abuse clients (e.g., a course in basic substance abuse counseling concepts, mandatory self-help group attendance)?

Reference

American Psychiatric Association. (2000). *Diagnostic and statistical manual of mental disorders* (4th ed., text rev.), Washington, DC: Author.

Response

Geri Miller

Overall, Chris did a number of things correctly in his supervision of Sylvia: He gave her appropriate guidance for working with substance-abusing clients, thoroughly reviewed the charting of ongoing treatment, and consulted with a colleague about the chart review prior to discussing the client with Sylvia. Finally, he must have established a trusting, comfortable relationship with Sylvia, as indicated by her honest responses. This is critical to effective supervision (Miller, 2003; Powell, 1993).

His supervision error was his assumption that Sylvia's reluctance to actively discuss this case with him was due to her nervousness about working with a new type of client. This allowed her countertransference with addiction to flourish in therapy with a substance-abusing client. The simple intervention of stopping the "content" aspect of supervision and going to a "process" mode about his assumption would have invited personal disclosures about addiction. Also, as an addictions professional, Chris can safely assume that his supervisees have been touched personally by addiction. Therefore, when interns are working with substance-abusing clients for the first time, they should be encouraged to discuss their personal experiences in supervision to minimize countertransference that can affect a client's welfare (Miller, 2005).

Regarding referral to another counselor, Chris needs to watch the same tendency to respond to the situation without processing first. Processing Sylvia's request (to refer to another counselor) with a colleague before making a final decision decreases the chance he is supporting her avoidance. However, in consideration of the client's welfare, he needs to have the consultation as quickly as possible. If the consultation leads him to decide to allow Sylvia to continue working with the client, he must monitor the case closely and set a limited time frame in which to evaluate the appropriateness and effectiveness of her therapy. Should the consultation result in a referral of the client because Sylvia appears unable to contain or work through her countertransference, the referral should be explained to the client. Ideally it would best be done in a session with Chris, Sylvia, and the client to ensure the clarity of the message and to provide role modeling for Sylvia on how to address such issues.

Chris's supervision structure with Sylvia needs to be done in a strategic manner—regarding this client and any others who struggle with substance abuse issues (Powell, 1993). There are a number of recommendations that could enhance Chris's future supervision. First, he needs to ask Sylvia appropriate questions about her experiences at self-help meetings and with her ex-husband to elicit information that can guide the processing of possible countertransference issues. Second, it would help to have only a small percentage of her caseload focus on primarily substance abuse issues to both protect the welfare of the clients and avoid overwhelming her with an area that is so difficult for her. Third, the treatment progress of her substance-abusing clients needs to be monitored each week in supervision to determine how Sylvia's countertransference may be affecting treatment and to make any necessary corrections to her therapy approach. Fourth, careful and consistent review of her chart notes is required. Finally, because addiction is a blind spot for Sylvia, Chris needs to monitor for its presence in her entire caseload, particularly in the areas of assessment, treatment, and aftercare (Miller, 2005).

Sylvia needs to be given a clear message that in order to develop professionally, which is a goal of internship, she needs to learn about her blind spot so that she does not harm substance-abusing clients or clients who have issues related to substance abuse. She can learn about her blind spot by processing her reactions to substance abuse in supervision. She also needs to be encouraged to seek outside counseling for these issues because supervision sessions cannot be counseling sessions. There may come a point in the supervision that such counseling is made mandatory for her to complete her internship, but that would result from her clients being negatively affected by her countertransference, an inability to recalibrate her clinical approach with clients as a result of supervision, or an unwillingness to seek counseling.

Because it cannot be assumed that trainees have accurate information about addiction, specific addiction training requirements need to be in place. It is necessary to ask what they know about addiction and where they learned it. Then it is critical that trainees have exposure to the field of addiction in a formalized, educational format such as a basic substance abuse counseling course or appropriate readings and assignments so that they have a baseline of accurate information about addiction.

It can be safely assumed that most or all trainees have been negatively affected by addiction in their personal lives. Therefore, it may be appropriate for them to engage in experiential activities, such as attending self-help meetings (MacMaster & Holleran, 2005). However, such experiences need to be processed with trainees to determine what they learned and what the experiences were like. Additionally, they need a chance to process their personal reactions to addiction in a safe, honest manner in supervision. Addiction leaves wounds in people's lives, and trainees need to learn to recognize and address these wounds, thereby learning to honor the wounds for themselves and the welfare of their clients (Miller, 2005).

References

MacMaster, S. A., & Holleran, L. K. (2005). Incorporating 12-step group attendance in addictions courses: A cross-cultural experience. *Journal of Teaching in the Addictions, 4*(2), 79–91.

Miller, G. (2003). *Incorporating spirituality in counseling and psychotherapy: Theory and technique.* Hoboken, NJ: Wiley.

Miller, G. (2005). *Learning the language of addiction counseling* (2nd ed.). Hoboken, NJ: Wiley.

Powell, D. J. (1993). *Clinical supervision in alcohol and drug abuse counseling.* New York: Lexington.

Response

Louise Napolitano

The incident involving Chris and Sylvia invites analysis of a number of behaviors and circumstances. First, Chris's conduct as supervisor comes under scrutiny. Instead of helping Sylvia explore her reluctance to discuss the client's case, he made an assumption that she was nervous about her first counseling experience with an addiction client and apparently turned her loose with the case. Until this time, it appears that Chris and Sylvia enjoyed a productive supervisor–supervisee relationship, so it seems that the change in Sylvia's style of interacting would have prompted a response from Chris that would have helped her to grow in her understanding of herself as a counselor as well as in her knowledge of her client's needs and her ethical responsibilities.

Before assigning the addiction client's case to Sylvia, it would have been helpful for Chris to invite her to rate her competence to work with addiction issues, to discuss circumstances and experiences that might influence her ability to work with these issues, and to talk about what she was feeling and thinking as she anticipated working with this particular case. By allowing this opportunity for exploration, Chris could have cultivated a more supportive and trust-based relationship with his supervisee. Also, with the information Chris would likely have gathered through such a conversation, it is possible that he would have decided not to assign this case to Sylvia, or he may have chosen to adopt a very different supervisory style in his work with her on this case. Perhaps he would have been more involved, acting as a model and providing direction and structure as he acknowledged that she was at a different developmental stage in her work with this client than in her work with children and adolescents. Certainly, it would have been in the best interest of all concerned if his supervisory role had involved encouraging and guiding Sylvia rather than merely reviewing her charts.

It seems Chris's response to Sylvia's reticence parallels Sylvia's response to her client's resistance to complying with his treatment plan. Both the supervisor and the supervisee took a course of nonaction based on an assumption—Chris, that Sylvia was dealing only with nervousness; Sylvia, that the standard of practice for addiction clients is ineffective. In his future work with Sylvia, it may be productive for Chris to address how acknowledgement of this parallel can contribute to the professional growth of both supervisor and supervisee.

Given the laissez-faire pattern that was allowed to develop in Sylvia's work with this addicted client, it is arguably for the best that the client be referred to another counselor for continuing work. However, as Sylvia at least temporarily continues to work with him in group and psychoeducational classes, it behooves Chris to help her explore her countertransference issues, her ethical responsibilities to the client, and ways she may uphold these responsibilities. Continued work with the client as a transfer takes place will also allow Chris to further monitor Sylvia's handling of this client situation and possibly provide more examples and issues to bring into the supervision session for Sylvia to examine and address.

Certainly, it is still possible to redeem this experience—to assist the client as well as the supervisee. Sylvia can be encouraged in her self-exploration and can come to see that her pain and apparent anger associated with addiction issues and treatments represent a growing edge for her as a counselor. Awareness of her countertransference issues can help her understand herself, her needs as a counseling student, her ethical responsibilities, and the direction she wants to take as a counseling professional. Ultimately, this incident can help her to define her limitations and areas of expertise as a counselor and to make professional, ethical decisions accordingly.

Of course, if counselor trainees had to meet at least minimum requirements before seeing substance abuse clients, this incident may have been avoided altogether. On the one hand, assuming that Sylvia did not have substance abuse training, Chris and Sylvia would not have had this opportunity to see that they must gain a greater understanding of the ethical execution of their roles; on the other hand, the client certainly would have been better served, and after all, that is the most pertinent concern. Growth of supervisors and counselor trainees is important to the counseling profession, but it is imperative that this growth not occur at the client's expense. Requiring counselors to complete a substance abuse specialization prior to seeing addiction clients can help counselors cultivate expert skills in this area and can go a long way toward protecting the integrity and ethical delivery of counseling services.

Chapter 4

Mandated Supervision: Trouble for an External Consulting Clinical Supervisor

Gerald A. Juhnke

Topics

- Addressing mandated attendance and supervision requirements
- Responding to differing personalities and conflict between departments
- Managing a minimally invested supervisee

Background

Jim is a 46-year-old Caucasian man. He received his counselor education and supervision doctorate in 1991, has counseled addicted persons and their families since 1985, and has provided clinical supervision since 1987. Among his licenses and certifications, Jim is a Licensed Professional Counselor, Certified Clinical Addictions Specialist, Master Addictions Counselor, Approved Clinical Supervisor, and an American Association for Marriage and Family Therapy Clinical Member. He enjoys supervising counselors who facilitate family counseling sessions with addicted adolescents and their families. Approximately 5 months ago, Jim began working as an external clinical addictions supervisor to a hospital system and their community addictions centers.

Natalie is a 38-year-old single Caucasian woman who recently graduated with a master's degree in social work. She has worked for less than 1 year as an addictions counselor in her current place of employment, a community addictions center affiliated with a hospital system. During this time, Natalie gained a reputation among staff and supervisors as being "demanding," "irritable," and "overly confident in her clinical skills." As a result of reoccurring arguments with clients, staff, and her clinical supervisors; Natalie's failure to attend clinical supervision sessions; and her voiced complaints about clients, colleagues, and supervisors, Natalie was encouraged to transfer from the intensive outpatient addictions team to the adolescent and family addictions team.

Despite strong objections by the less senior Adolescent and Family Addictions Operations manager and his staff, the move was fully supported by the seasoned and senior-ranking Intensive Outpatient Addictions Team Operations manager and the hospital's Human Resources manager. The less experienced Adolescent and Family Addictions Operations manager determined that he did not have sufficient qualifications or time to address Natalie's supervision needs. Thus, he hired Jim as an external consulting clinical supervisor.

Incident

During the first 2 weeks of Natalie's clinical supervision, she and Jim mutually identified short- and long-term supervision goals and "concrete, baby-step" objectives relevant to Natalie's skill level. She further reported her perceived family addictions counseling strengths and deficits. Natalie was also encouraged to identify the family counseling model that she most regularly used with her recovering adolescent clients and their families. Natalie reported that she tended to use a structural family systems theory, but also used techniques from cognitive and behavioral theories. Jim commended Natalie on knowing the theories that she most frequently used. Then, Jim reported that structural family therapy and many of the cognitive–behavioral therapy techniques worked well with substance-abusing adolescents and their families. The two scheduled regular weekly sessions. Natalie indicated that she felt "relieved" that Jim knew these theories and reported that her previous clinical supervisors had not appreciated her family work. During the first supervision session, Jim described the policies and procedure requiring entry-level clinical employees to secure a minimum of one family counseling session per week. Natalie agreed with this requirement.

No remarkable events occurred within supervision for approximately 2 weeks. During the first two sessions, Natalie and Jim reviewed her videotaped sessions and role-played potential responses to family behaviors and statements. Jim encouraged Natalie to become more active in sessions. In the 3rd week, Natalie missed her scheduled supervision appointment. When contacted by Jim, Natalie reported, "I'm too busy helping needy kids to get supervision." Jim reminded Natalie of the agency's supervision requirements and informed Natalie that he would need to report any further absences to the Operations manager. Natalie was 15 minutes late for the next scheduled supervision session and reported that she was unable to videotape any of her family sessions because of her clients' videotaping concerns and their parents' refusal to sign necessary releases.

Jim reminded Natalie of the agency's videotaping requirements and encouraged Natalie to videotape client families that had previously signed consent forms. Jim further asked Natalie what he could do to make the supervision "better" or "more helpful" for her. Natalie curtly replied, "Nothing. Supervision is really stupid. What I really need is time to learn on my own. I don't want anybody observing me, not you, not my former supervisor, not anyone." Jim discussed the potential benefits of supervision and encouraged Natalie to consider participating. He also attempted to reframe the supervision process as a costly benefit the agency was paying for.

Natalie failed to attend the next scheduled supervision session. Jim then met with the Adolescent and Family Addictions Operations manager (Natalie's direct supervisor), who reported Natalie's failed supervision attendance to the Human Resources manager. Jim was encouraged to make the best of the situation Later that week, the Human Resources manager, Natalie's manager, Natalie, and Jim met. At the meeting, Natalie was informed that she had two choices, either attend weekly supervision sessions with Jim or be terminated.

Since the meeting, Natalie has complied with the weekly supervision session order and has provided family counseling videos as prescribed. Concomitantly, she has completed each recommendation that Jim has made during the clinical supervision sessions. However, Natalie self-reports she is uninvested in supervision and states, "Supervision is a waste of my time and talents."

Questions

1. How might Jim have been able to do things differently at the onset of the supervision process to promote Natalie's clinical supervision interests?
2. What suggestions might you have that could be used to develop Natalie's desire to more actively participate in the supervision process?
3. What could Jim have done differently to address Natalie's failure to attend the agency-required weekly supervision? Was it wrong for Jim to report Natalie's failure to attend supervision to Natalie's direct supervisor, and if so, what might Jim have done instead? Should Natalie be assigned a new clinical supervisor?

Response

Virginia A. Kelly

Clearly, Jim is faced with a difficult supervision situation. Resistance to clinical supervision may be the most challenging issue facing supervisors. In this case, the typical resistance that might be anticipated within the initial stages of any new supervisory relationship was exacerbated by the series of incidents leading to the relationship between Jim and Natalie. The fact that Natalie had already been identified as difficult to supervise, the fact that she had actually been moved from one unit to another because of issues that related directly to her ability to openly receive supervision, and the fact that she was "forced" into the supervisory relationship with Jim constitute a combination of circumstances that helped to create an initial barrier within the supervision relationship.

"Supervisory relationships are characterized by a power inequality" (Bernard & Goodyear, 1998, p. 72). Supervisees are understandably anxious and under stress related to the notion of being observed and possibly criticized (Borders & Brown, 2005). In Natalie's case, however, this seems exacerbated. Natalie seems to have retained a high level of anxiety associated with the supervision process despite the fact that she is not new to this role.

With respect to whether Jim might have been able to do anything differently at the onset of the supervision meetings to promote Natalie's investment in the process, I do not believe that there were any specific behaviors or interventions that Jim could have initiated that would have made a substantive difference in Natalie's response to the supervision experience. I believe that the issues that emerged were Natalie's and would have emerged regardless of what any supervisor may or may not have done.

That being said, the only thing that Jim might have been able to do was to anticipate Natalie's response to supervision given the circumstances that led up to the formation of this particular relationship. This may have enabled Jim to develop a plan for dealing with Natalie's resistance. Because Jim knew the history of Natalie's experience at this agency, he was most likely anticipating some level of resistance. It was fairly inevitable given Natalie's responses to supervision in the past. There would be no reason to believe, based on what Jim knew, that Natalie would remain open to supervision and fail to display the behaviors and attitudes that she had displayed within previous supervisory relationships.

In terms of suggestions that I might make to encourage Natalie's desire and commitment to the supervision process, I would most likely want to view Natalie's behavior from a somewhat psychodynamic perspective. I might suggest to Jim that he consider that Natalie is experiencing a transference relationship with him and that she may be projecting onto him attributes and expectations that she has consistently projected within past supervisory relationships. What is evident is that Natalie's response to Jim's supervision is not rational in the sense that Jim has clearly been supportive, nonconfrontational, and eager to assist Natalie in her development. Therefore, we might assume that her irrational response is based on previous experiences she may have had with individuals in positions of authority.

Although Jim must be sure to maintain his role as supervisor and not slip into a therapist role, perhaps it could be helpful to the supervision process for Jim to frame Natalie's behavior within this theoretical context. In doing this, Jim may be able to consider different options for helping Natalie move beyond her resistance. Perhaps from this perspective Jim could attempt to join with Natalie and empathize with her difficulties pertaining to openly receiving supervision. If Jim were to attempt to explore with Natalie some past supervisory relationships where she also felt resistant, he might be able to assist her in identifying her own issues related to authority.

Simultaneously, it was extremely important for Jim to maintain his boundaries as a supervisor. Part of doing this involved taking responsibility for addressing Natalie's failure to attend the agency-required weekly supervision. Setting clear limits and consistently adhering to preestablished guidelines with supervisees with a history of resisting supervision is paramount. Natalie's behavior in missing supervision and arriving late is clearly manipulative. If she were permitted to continue to behave in this manner without being confronted, she might never be forced to deal with the issues that are so clearly affecting her ability to develop within her professional role and act as a desirable colleague.

Jim absolutely did the right thing in reporting Natalie's behavior to her supervisor. It would not benefit Natalie in any way if she were permitted to split Jim and her agency supervisor. I believe that in order for Natalie to move beyond the beliefs, behaviors, and attitudes that seem to get in her way, she would need the individuals who might represent authority in this situation to work as a team. Again, Jim may have framed this issue in a manner consistent with joining with Natalie. For example, he could suggest that they tell her supervisor together so that he could support her as she attempts to work through this issue.

Finally, for many of the same reasons I have referred to above, I do not believe that it would be in Natalie's best interest to be assigned a new clinical supervisor. This could serve to reinforce Natalie's manipulative behavior and make movement through her issues with supervision ultimately more difficult. The most desirable outcome would most likely result if Jim can stay present for Natalie and continue to support her while simultaneously remaining clear and steadfast in maintaining the boundaries and expectations that have been established. If Jim can maintain this stance, and if Natalie can move through the process to a point where she can become more open to addressing her own issues as well as to receiving supervision from Jim, Natalie will benefit tremendously from this supervision experience.

References

Bernard, J. M., & Goodyear, R. K. (1998). *Fundamentals of clinical supervision* (2nd ed.). Boston: Allyn & Bacon.

Borders, L. D., & Brown, L. L. (2005). *The new handbook of counseling supervision*. Mahwah, NJ: Erlbaum.

Response

Joseph B. Cooper

Jim should be commended not only for his willingness to take on such a difficult case but also for his continued efforts to provide a productive supervisory working environment in the face of repeated resistance from his supervisee. I believe this case highlights a fundamental issue pertinent to those engaged in the practice of clinical supervision of addiction counselors: supervisee resistance (Culbreth, 2003). Although many factors have been cited as cause for such resistance (Bernard & Goodyear, 2004; Bradley & Gould, 1994; Liddle, 1986; Masters, 1992), supervisee anxiety seems to be one of the primary feelings that underlie resistant supervisee behaviors. Such anxiety may arise for a number of reasons, the most conspicuous being related to supervisee performance and evaluation, developmental level, and role conflict and ambiguity (Ladany & Friedlander, 1995; Muse-Burk, Ladany, & Deck, 2001).

However, with the case of Natalie, it would seem a different, although nonetheless pertinent, display of resistance vis-à-vis anxiety is at work, which Reifer (2001) identifies as the narcissistic vulnerably of the supervisee. The primary reason for such vulnerability is the fact that the supervisee's instrument of practice is, in large part, the personality of the supervisee. Thus, both success and failure are often experienced by the supervisee as a reflection of his or her own self and its functioning. Furthermore, within supervision, the supervisee's self—skills, intuition, clinical abilities, feelings, and blind spots—are all open to exposure and may potentiate the supervisee's vulnerability to narcissistic injury, which is often compensated for by the development of a grandiose professional self-identity (Gill, 2001). Natalie's behavior seems to exemplify such a protective grandiose self-expression. By understanding Natalie's resistance as a compensatory and protective reaction to her experience of anxiety and vulnerability, we can begin to develop interventions aimed at both protecting her fragile self and contributing to the building and repair process of the damaged supervisory working alliance (Bordin, 1983).

Although Jim did a thorough job of providing Natalie with an overview of the process of supervision and developing specific goals and tasks to be accomplished, it would have been important for Jim to have addressed some critical supervisory issues. First, I would have discussed with Natalie her feelings and thoughts regarding her previous experience in supervision. With respect to her prior supervisors, what did she find to be helpful, and what did she find to be unhelpful? What frustrations did she experience and how would she have liked supervision to have proceeded differently? If she experienced any counterproductive events in her supervisory relationship with her former supervisors, how did she respond? This would have given Jim a better understanding of Natalie's response pattern to the supervisory relationship, and with this understanding, he might have avoided recreating any future dysfunctional patterns. Second, I think it would have been important to process with Natalie any anxiety, vulnerabilities, or feelings of inadequacy she is having in her experience as a supervisee, especially concerning the evaluation of her therapeutic skills by her supervisor. Because these feelings are common to beginning supervisees, I would both normalize and empathize with these feelings and encourage their honest expression. By providing a safe environment for Natalie to voice her vulnerabilities, both the power of these feelings and her compensatory need to act out and defend against such feelings would be diminished (Gill, 2001).

Although we can only infer as to the cause of Natalie's resistance to her supervisor and the supervisory process, it would seem Natalie experienced one or more negative supervisory events over the first 3 weeks of her supervision. A frequent cause of such counterproductive events is the supervisor's failure to be empathetic toward the supervisee's thoughts, ideas, and feelings (Gray, Ladany, Walker, & Ancis, 2001). Possibly Jim's directive and teaching role was perceived by Natalie as dismissive of her own skills and abilities, and she responded to this empathic failure by acting out to defend her vulnerable self. Thus, I would suggest Jim first attend to the damaged supervisory working alliance by recreating a secure base (Pistole & Watkins, 1995) from which the supervisory process may be rebuilt. Supervisees who have experienced a counterproductive event with their supervisors often wish their supervisor had acknowledged the counterproductive event and processed it with them (Gray et al., 2001). With this in mind, Jim could gently begin to explore with Natalie his experience of her "pulling away" from the supervisory process, and ask for her feedback as to what changed or happened that may have led to this. In this way Jim can both rebuild the supervisory alliance and model to Natalie an appropriate here-and-now experience of congruence, communication, and trust for her to use in her own therapeutic work.

Finally, to regain Natalie's trust and confidence within supervision, I would adopt more of a consultant supervisory role (Bernard & Goodyear, 2004) with Natalie, taking a less directive and instructive position and using positive reframes to help increase her sense of power and self-esteem and to model how she may more effectively deal with her feeling, thoughts, and behaviors (Masters, 1992). Following Masters's example of positive reframing, Jim might say to Natalie: "I am struck by how perceptive and attuned you are to your client's needs during your sessions together and your supportive efforts at helping your client develop an abstinence plan. I am now wondering what you think is next. What might you do to continue to help your client achieve his or her goals?" Such an intervention both empowers supervisees and encourages them to explore and develop their therapeutic skills.

When caught in a power struggle, no one wins. However, it is the supervisor's ethical obligation to ensure that supervisees are able to function competently in their role as a counselor and do no harm (American Counseling Association, 2005). Although Jim was caught between the difficult tasks of managing his deteriorating supervisory relationship with Natalie and maintaining his ethical responsibility to ensure she functions competently, it was premature for Jim to report Natalie's failure to attend supervision to her direct supervisor. This action may have further eroded any remaining sense of trust or feelings of safety for Natalie within their supervisory relationship. Furthermore, I would not rush to assign a new supervisor to Natalie, as she and Jim would lose an opportunity to work through this impasse and experience the building and repair of the supervisory working alliance (Bordin, 1983). This would only model avoidance when one is confronted with interpersonal conflict and reinforce Natalie's self-protective defenses.

Keeping in mind that the relationship between supervisee and supervisor often parallels the supervisee's counseling relationship with his or her client, and vice versa (Morrissey & Tribe, 2001), it would be more appropriate for Jim to explore with Natalie her concerns about their relationship and to identify what needs to happen for her to experience the relationship as not only productive but also supportive and trusting. As opposed to listing the benefits of supervision, which might have come across as patronizing at best, or asking what could make supervision "better" or "more helpful," Jim might have explored with Natalie her feelings about their relationship and been open to the feedback he received from her. This is congruent with the recommendations of Ladany, Friedlander, and Nelson. (2005), who asserted that focusing on the supervisory working alliance is crucial for working through a supervisee's defensive behaviors. Once the supervisee feels safe enough to identify, acknowledge, and explore the problem in the context of a safe and trusting supervisory working alliance, then the supervisor can focus on the development of an agreed-on remediation plan.

References

American Counseling Association. (2005). *ACA code of ethics*. Alexandria, VA: Author.

Bernard, J. M., & Goodyear, R. K. (2004). *Fundamentals of clinical supervision* (3rd ed.). Needham Heights, MA: Allyn & Bacon.

Bordin, E. S. (1983). A working alliance based model of supervision. *Counseling Psychologist, 11*, 35-41.

Bradley, L., & Gould, J. (1994). *Supervisee resistance* (No. EDO-CG-94-12). Greensboro, NC: ERIC Clearinghouse on Counseling & Student Services.

Culbreth, J. R. (2003). Chemical dependency counselor supervisors' perceptions of supervisee anxiety and resistance in clinical supervision. *Journal of Teaching in the Addictions, 2*(1), 39-49.

Gill, S. (2001). Narcissistic vulnerability in supervisees: Ego ideals, self-exposure, and narcissistic character defenses. In S. Gill (Ed.), *The supervisory alliance: Facilitating the psychotherapist's learning experience* (pp. 19-34). Northvale, NJ: Jason Aronson.

Gray, L. A., Ladany, N., Walker, J. A., & Ancis, J. R. (2001). Psychotherapy trainees' experience of counterproductive events in supervision. *Journal of Counseling Psychology, 48*, 371-383.

Ladany, N., & Friedlander, M. L. (1995). The relationship between the supervisory working alliance and trainees' experience of role conflict and role ambiguity. *Counselor Education and Supervision, 34*, 220-231.

Ladany, N., Friedlander, M. L., & Nelson, M. L. (2005). Addressing problematic emotions, attitudes, and behaviors: Counseling in versus counseling out. In N. Ladany, M. L. Friedlander, & M. L. Nelson (Eds.), *Critical events in psychotherapy supervision: An interpersonal approach* (pp. 183-210). Washington, DC: American Psychological Association.

Liddle, B. J. (1986). Resistance in supervision: A response to perceived threat. *Counselor Education and Supervision, 26*(2), 117.

Masters, M. A. (1992). The use of positive reframing in the context of supervision. *Journal of Counseling & Development, 70*, 387-390.

Morrissey, J., & Tribe, R. (2001). Parallel process in supervision. *Counselling Psychology Quarterly, 14*, 103-110.

Muse-Burk, J. L., Ladany, N., & Deck, M. D. (2001). The supervisory relationship. In L. J. Bradley & N. Ladany (Eds.), *Counselor supervision: Principles, process, and practice* (3rd ed., pp. 28-62). Philadelphia: Brunner-Routledge.

Pistole, M. C., & Watkins, C. E. (1995). Attachment theory, counseling process, and supervision. *Counseling Psychologist, 23*, 457-478.

Reifer, S. (2001). Dealing with the anxiety of beginning therapists in supervision. In S. Gill (Ed.), *The supervisory alliance: Facilitating the psychotherapist's learning experience* (pp. 67-89). Northvale, NJ: Jason Aronson.

Chapter 5

Balancing Multiple Issues in Treatment

Pamela S. Lassiter

Topics

- Past sexual abuse issues in early treatment for chemical dependency
- The supervisory relationship

Background

Michelle is an experienced, Hispanic female substance abuse counselor and group leader working in an inpatient treatment setting. She holds a master's degree in professional counseling and has been in recovery from chemical dependency for 10 years. Michelle prefers working with male clients but is now assigned to work exclusively with female clients for the next year. Michelle works with a caseload of all female clients, providing primarily group counseling services with individual counseling as indicated. She has been working with her current supervisor Tom for approximately 1 year. Tom is a White male clinician with many years of experience working with substance abusers and their families. Although they occasionally disagree theoretically and philosophically concerning treatment approaches, Tom and Michelle have begun to develop a positive supervisory relationship, and both are dedicated to high-quality clinical care.

The agency has a long-standing "cultural" belief that counselors should discourage clients from delving into their trauma histories in the inpatient or initial phase of treatment because there is not ample time to explore these issues and it would be prematurely opening the proverbial can of worms. The philosophy is that clients should instead be encouraged to focus on obtaining and maintaining abstinence and that these deeper issues should be addressed in long-term, follow-up outpatient care. Tom disagrees with this philosophy in general and suspects that some counselors subscribe to it because they actually feel unprepared to deal with the trauma issues of the population being served.

Incident

Recently, an African American female client, Danielle, has come to Tom requesting a new counselor. Danielle complains that her counselor Michelle will not allow her to work on issues that she feels are crucial to her recovery. Danielle has been addicted to alcohol and cannabis for 10 years. She has completed inpatient treatment two times in the past 5 years but reports that she has never discussed her childhood sexual abuse history. She now feels ready to do so. Her longest sobriety has been 5 months. Although she responds well to 12-step support groups, Danielle usually drops out of aftercare counseling after only a few sessions each time. She reports that this is due to her fear of confronting her sexual abuse issues and the lack of available female counselors in her aftercare setting. She states that she has heard all the initial recovery information many times before and has identified her primary relapse triggers as grief and anxiety related to memories of childhood sexual abuse. Danielle, who is bisexual, has a history of unstable and emotionally abusive romantic relationships with both men and women. Her counselor and treatment team describe her as intelligent, insightful, and highly motivated.

Tom agrees that Danielle needs to address her sexual abuse issues if she is going to gain long-term sobriety. His approach to counseling includes empowering clients to be active in their own treatment and encouraging them to explore solutions and competencies. He decides to address this issue in his weekly individual supervision session with Michelle and is concerned with balancing the need to maintain a positive working relationship with his supervisee with that of attending to quality-of-care issues for this client. Michelle, the supervisee, believes that because the supervisor is both male and nonrecovering, he cannot fully understand the potency of sexual abuse issues for women or their impact on recovery. Tom suspects that Michelle has difficulty dealing with grief in her own life and has noticed that she avoids this with clients repeatedly. He has occasionally observed her shutting clients down when they want to deal with grief or other strong emotions, although he has not yet addressed the issue with her.

Questions

1. How should the supervisor handle this situation given his desire to continue a positive relationship with the counselor and his obligation to ensure quality care? Should the supervisor risk the supervisory relationship for the sake of the client's needs?
2. What are the ethical issues involved in this situation? What are the possible multicultural issues and how might the supervisor work within a multicultural context?
3. Are there parallel process issues, and if so, how might the supervisor negotiate them given the newness of his relationship with the supervisee?

4. What options exist for assisting and empowering this client and this supervisee given the existing circumstances?

Response

Kevin Doyle

Danielle's request has given Tom an excellent opportunity to address a number of issues with Michelle. Generally, substance abuse treatment programs have resisted client requests to change counselors, as doing so can cause chaos and staff splitting in a program. In this case, Tom has a chance to work with both Michelle, the counselor, and Danielle, the client, in a way that can help each to grow.

Given that Tom meets with Michelle each week for supervision, the weekly meeting would be the logical place for him to introduce and address some of the issues about this case. First, Tom should be sure that he is clear about the agency's belief regarding the inadvisability of clients' addressing trauma histories early in treatment. He should be clear as to whether this is a formal policy or a general guideline that might be interpreted on a case-by-case basis. He can begin his session with Michelle by clarifying just what the agency's stance is, so that both he and Michelle are clear on what is permissible. Tom may want to address this question in supervision with his supervisor as well.

Once the issue is clear for Tom, he can then proceed in providing Michelle with the supervision she needs. If the agency's stance is not a firm policy, he and Michelle can discuss Danielle's case in order to determine whether the client's desire to address her childhood sexual abuse issues might be clinically appropriate. Mitigating factors that might support this approach include the fact that Danielle has expressed the desire to do so, her two previous inpatient treatment failures, and the treatment team's description of her as highly motivated and insightful. These may be sufficient to allow Michelle to proceed cautiously in exploring these issues with Danielle, taking care to watch for any signs of decompensation or distress. If the agency indeed has a firm policy against addressing these issues, Tom faces a difficult dilemma. He should begin by making sure that Danielle's request is addressed and that the agency policy is explained to her. If this does not appear to be sufficient to resolve Danielle's complaint, Tom and the program should consider either referring Danielle to another program or using a consultant who can address her issues in a manner that is consistent with her treatment in the program.

In general, the supervisor's highest priority remains the client, as opposed to the supervisee. While being respectful of Michelle's opinion and experience, Tom needs to keep Danielle's treatment and recovery as his primary objective. As a supervisor, he has the obligation to challenge his supervisees' beliefs, styles, and philosophies in a manner that allows them to grow and improve as counselors. This may not always be comfortable, for either himself or his supervisees.

There are several ethical issues that manifest themselves in this case. First is the issue of client autonomy. Although clients do indeed have the right to autonomy, this does not extend to the point where it might be considered as dictating treatment. In an inpatient substance abuse treatment setting, it is not unusual for clients to want to dictate who their counselors are, what rooms they sleep in, or even what the daily schedule is. Such issues are not generally seen as appropriate for client decisions and would cause havoc in programs if clients were allowed to do so. A second issue related to autonomy revolves around the client's right to be involved in determining his or her goals. This can be complex in that clients may want to work on things (e.g., personal relationships) that are not the most pressing issues when a serious safety issue such as addiction is at hand. A skilled counselor must work with the client—often using the power of the treatment group or community—to help the client focus initially on more pressing issues. Finally, the issue of referral could be part of this case. If the program cannot address Danielle's issues relating to her childhood sexual abuse, and if these issues continue to interfere with her treatment, the program will need to consider referring her to a program where these issues could be better integrated into her treatment.

Multicultural issues may also be at work in this scenario. Danielle is a bisexual African American woman, whereas Michelle is a Hispanic woman who has been in recovery from her own addiction for 10 years, and Tom is a Caucasian man who is not in recovery. It is unclear from the information given exactly how these issues are playing out in the counseling and supervisory relationships; however, it would be advisable for all parties to address them. Michelle might ask Danielle what it is like for her to be counseled by a Hispanic woman. Similarly, Tom should ask Michelle how she feels about being supervised by someone who is not personally in recovery from addiction, as well as by a man. These questions will, if nothing else, lead to positive discussion and understanding, if not outright resolution, and put the issues on the table for ongoing consideration in the counseling or supervisory relationships.

Parallel process issues might also be occurring in that difficulties that are occurring in the counseling relationship might be concurrently happening in the supervisory relationship. Again, the supervisor would be well advised to raise this issue during his sessions with Michelle, leading her to consider how the counseling and supervisory relationships might be affecting one another. Addressing parallel process issues may open several doors of discussion between Michelle and Tom, possibly leading to resolution of this issue also (Bernard & Goodyear, 2004).

Several options exist for assisting and empowering the client and supervisee, some of which have been noted earlier. Because of Danielle's request for a change in her counselor, a staff member needs to respond to her and address her request, as well as her desire to explore her sexual abuse issues. This can be done by Michelle with close supervision, by another staff member or consultant, by referral, or later in Danielle's recovery if her treatment is progressing well and she is willing to work with staff on more immediate issues until that time. Validating Danielle's concern that these issues are important to her will be extremely important, particularly given her two previous treatment failures, and continuing to check in with her around them will help reassure her that her concerns have been heard and taken seriously by staff.

References

Bernard, J. M., & Goodyear, R. K. (2004). *Fundamentals of clinical supervision* (3rd ed.). Needham Heights, MA: Allyn & Bacon.

Response

Kenneth M. Coll

This incident presents a complex set of issues. The question of whether to deal with past sexual abuse early in treatment for chemical dependency arises, as do concerns about the supervisory relationship, including parallel process matters and ethical, gender, and ethnic issues. This supervisor and supervisee bring key strengths to resolving this dilemma. They have been working positively as supervisor and supervisee for 1 year and both are experienced, successful substance abuse counseling professionals. Michelle, the supervisee, is an experienced substance abuse counselor who prefers to work with men. However, she now finds herself working exclusively with women. Tom, her supervisor, also an experienced substance abuse counselor, disagrees with the agency belief that sexual abuse treatment early in substance abuse recovery is not beneficial to the client. The current dilemma is that Michelle's client Danielle would like to address sexual abuse issues and Michelle is reticent to do so.

Regarding Question 1, Tom clearly needs to continue his positive supervisory relationship with Michelle while also ensuring quality care for Danielle. This is a core component of clinical supervision (Bernard & Goodyear, 2004). In this case, it may be useful for Tom to consult Bernard and Goodyear's (2004) discussion about interpersonal triangles in supervision. If Tom enters into a supervisor–client coalition against Michelle, however unwittingly, damage will be done to the supervisory relationship. Bernard and Goodyear noted, "It is essential for supervisors to be aware of interpersonal triangles and their effects. With this knowledge, supervisors are better equipped to avoid problematic triangles and to manage others in a strategic manner" (p. 144). Therefore, Tom may want to call on Michelle's experience as a counselor (Bernard & Goodyear, 2004). Often, an effective strategy with an experienced counselor is to assume the consultant role and ask Michelle what she makes of the client's request and possible triangulation. It may be that Danielle has a history of triangulating, and this can become a therapeutic issue and goal for her.

Question 2 addresses possible ethical and multicultural concerns. The most prominent ethical issues for this incident per the *Ethical Guidelines for Counselors and Supervisors* (Association for Counselor Education and Supervision, 1993) include Tom's obligation to monitor Michelle's professional actions, Danielle's welfare, Michelle's clinical performance, and Tom's duty to help Michelle become aware of any personal or professional limitations. If Tom were to "order" Michelle to grant the client's request to deal with her sexual abuse, and to then go into counseling herself to explore personal issues without any discussion or consultation, he may be adhering to the letter of these ethical guidelines but violating the principles of informed consent and supervisee participation. These principles are also outlined in the ethical codes for clinical supervisors. Tom has an opportunity to address and help Michelle remediate potential personal and professional limitations, yet he needs to provide opportunities for Michelle to gain insight given her experience and the potential for cultural misunderstandings.

It is very important for Tom to be aware of the multicultural issues present, including gender and ethnicity. It is highly recommended that Tom, if he has not already done so, query Michelle's opinions about him as a Caucasian supervisor specifically related to any unintentional racism in his behavior, power dynamic problems, and trust and communication issues (Bernard & Goodyear, 2004). He may then want to ask Michelle (as a Latina counselor) if addressing these issues with Danielle (an African American woman) would be useful.

Question 3 addresses parallel processes—defined as "supervisees unconsciously presenting themselves to their supervisors as their clients have presented to them. The process reverses when the supervisee adopts attitudes and behaviors of the supervisor in relating to the client" (Friedlander, Seigel, & Brenock, 1989, p. 149). One potential parallel process involves Danielle disagreeing with Michelle's belief that sexual abuse should not be directly addressed in the inpatient phase of treatment, Michelle disagreeing with Tom's belief that sexual abuse should be directly addressed, and Tom disagreeing with the agency's belief that sexual abuse should not be addressed. Each party is pushing against authority, and this dynamic provides a potential impasse for therapeutic and supervisory progress. It is crucial for Tom as the supervisor to identify this process and take measures to stop it, for the good of the supervisory relationship, for the welfare of Danielle, and for his own benefit as a supervisor.

Question 4 asks about Tom's options for resolving this incident. Several have been mentioned. To summarize, it is recommended that Tom become aware of and discuss a potential interpersonal triangle at work against Michelle, explore with Michelle any ethnic or gender issues at work, and identify and explain to Michelle his part in a potential parallel process. It may be best for Tom to address these issues with Michelle from a consultant stance, respecting her many years of professional experience. It is suggested that Tom use facilitative interventions; that is, emphasizing the belief that with support and reflective activity, the supervisee can learn and change (Bernard & Goodyear, 2004).

It is essential for Tom to resolve his belief, counter to that of the agency (and Michelle), about addressing childhood sexual abuse in substance abuse treatment. Although there is no "right" answer, he may want to gather information from the professional literature and use this incident as an opportunity for rethinking his and the agency's stance, so that counselors and supervisors in the agency have clear ideas about the rationale for the stance taken. The issue of Michelle's preference for working with men and now working with women also needs to be explored with Michelle and perhaps with the agency administration. It may be that Michelle could be effective with both genders and the agency is underusing Michelle's skills and abilities. Michelle could also increase job satisfaction with such an arrangement. Finally, it is likely, given Tom and Michelle's strong working relationship, that through Tom's actions based on the suggestions provided, Michelle will identify and work to remediate any current personal and professional limitations.

References

Association for Counselor Education and Supervision. (1993). *Ethical guidelines for counseling supervisors*. Alexandria, VA: Author.

Bernard, J. M., & Goodyear, R. K. (2004). *Fundamentals of clinical supervision* (3rd ed.). Needham Heights, MA: Allyn & Bacon.

Friedlander, M. L., Seigel, S. M., & Brenock, K. (1989). Parallel process in counseling and supervision: A case study. *Journal of Counseling Psychology, 36,* 149–157.

Chapter 6

Confronting the Reality of Relapse

Todd F. Lewis

Topics

- Supervisee frustration with client relapse
- Supervisor suggestions for how to handle relapse with clients

Background

Doug is a White, 32-year-old male counselor at a local community agency. Doug recently earned a master's degree in counseling and has been working primarily in addictions and general mental health counseling. In graduate school, Doug became interested in addictions work after taking his first substance abuse counseling course. As a long-term goal, he is interested in pursuing the master of addictions counselor certification along with his general counseling license. Despite Doug's enthusiasm and interest in working with addictions cases, he sometimes has a tendency to adopt a "just say no" philosophy with his clients. From Doug's perspective, those who are addicted should be able to use willpower to overcome their problem. A hard worker by nature, Doug places great value in disciplining the body and mind to overcome obstacles and achieve good health.

Supervision with Doug was usually an upbeat, positive experience. Doug's supervisor Tom repeatedly commented to others about the positive attitude that Doug displayed and how he appreciated his developing skills as a counselor. In the back of Tom's mind, however, he sometimes wondered if Doug realistically understood the challenges of working with clients severely addicted to substances. Tom realized that discussing these challenges would only go so far. Doug would have to experience them firsthand so that they could be addressed directly in supervision. Indeed, Tom knew that sooner or later Doug would have to confront some of his cherished beliefs about how and why people, especially those addicted to substances, change.

Incident

During their weekly supervision session, Tom began in his typical fashion by asking how things were going and if there was anything pertinent on Doug's mind to discuss. From the start, Doug seemed very discouraged and was more reserved in his responses than usual. Tom's initial impression was that something was not sitting well with Doug. It turns out that Doug was concerned about his client Ray, who recently experienced a severe cocaine relapse while under Doug's care. To date, Doug has seen Ray for four sessions. The following discussion between Doug and Tom ensued:

Doug: Ray relapsed.

Tom: I am sorry, Doug, I did not quite hear you. Could you repeat what you said?

Doug: Ray relapsed. He told me yesterday that he returned to cocaine use and was devastated. I felt really awkward and struggled to find the right words.

Tom: How do you feel about that?

Doug: I feel like a failure. All this work, all this effort, for nothing! I thought we had made some progress. I thought he was strengthening his willpower to remain clean. What is the use of all this work if clients are not going to change?"

Discussion

Doug has clearly come face to face with the reality of his client's struggles in comparison with his own personal worldview of how people change. Doug's rather concrete view of a very complex human condition, human behavior and change, does not appear to serve him well as a counselor for this client. In addition, he is struggling with personalizing his client's progress, viewing relapse as a reflection on himself, as well as viewing his client's overall change process in a very simplistic and concrete way. This incident also appears to be providing Doug with an opportunity to learn about addiction and to learn about his role in the therapeutic process.

Questions

1. How should supervisors respond when supervisees become discouraged because a client has relapsed? What would you specifically say to Doug?

2. Doug revealed that Ray's disclosure about relapsing was awkward. What suggestions would you offer Doug as a way to appropriately respond to clients who reveal they have relapsed? What relapse prevention strategies might you offer Doug for use in future sessions?

3. It has been argued that relapse is now considered the rule rather than the exception in most cases of addiction. If this is true, how

might this message be communicated to supervisees who want immediate results?

4. How would you handle Doug's feelings of failure in this case? Considering your own views and experiences with clients who relapse, would disclosing some of your experiences be appropriate? If so, what would you share? If not, why?

Response

Simone Lambert

In first responding to Doug, it seems important to acknowledge his disappointment that Ray relapsed. Being empathetic with the supervisee can help positively affect the parallel process that seems to be in place, as Ray also seemed quite disappointed in himself. Doug would also benefit from examining what interventions were helpful and what he would have done differently in session. Examining what could have been done differently in counseling to prevent Ray's relapse would allow Doug to see what could be improved with the counseling work and what may have been beyond Doug's influence.

It would also be imperative to focus on what Doug did well. For instance, Ray returned to counseling despite his devastation. This indicates that after only four sessions there was an excellent rapport established. Doug should be commended for developing a safe environment for clients to work on their presenting issues.

Because Ray's disclosure about relapsing was awkward, it would be helpful for Doug to respond in a nonjudgmental manner. This client seemed to have already beaten himself up over the relapse, and it is unlikely that continued condemnation would assist Ray in his recovery process. However, Tom has the challenge of working with a supervisee who believes that willpower alone can help one to "just say no."

Tom could assist Doug first by finding out what prevention strategies were already in place and by reminding him of additional strategies to implement in future sessions. For instance, having a support network, changing environments or former associates, removing accessibility to substances, and having a specific plan of action in place when the urge to use arises are all preventative measures that can be implemented. Furthermore, it would be helpful for Doug to see what helped Ray maintain his sobriety between the first session and the relapse. By reframing the relapse, Doug can also suggest to Ray that he has had some level of success and that this can be achieved again. In fact, the time between the first session and the relapse may have been the longest period of abstinence Ray has had. This positive reframe would also encourage Ray to continue his treatment.

Often supervisees are as anxious as clients to have a quick fix. It is important to acknowledge that relapse is a normal part of recovery. The addiction did not form overnight, nor is it likely to be resolved in four sessions. Recovery from addiction can be a lifelong process. Having a realistic expectation of the timeline for treatment sets both the client and the counselor up for success. In this case, Doug reported feeling like a failure because of the client's relapse. Tom needs to ensure that Doug understands this was Ray's relapse, not Doug's. One of our guiding principles is to have clients be autonomous (Kitchener, 1984). Therefore, clients are entitled to make their own decisions, including whether or not to use.

By Tom's self-disclosing a number of cases and their outcomes, Doug would benefit from understanding the range of possible treatment results. Tom could share various experiences with past clients, illustrating key points that may be similar to Doug's current client situation. Tom could also demonstrate, from past cases of his own, how a multitude of factors are involved in the recovery process for clients that are completely out of the control of the counselor. In fact, this may be an important opportunity for Doug to learn that the recovery process is based on clients' therapeutic goals, social supports, their overall mental health, and most important their commitment level to change (Prochaska, DiClemente, & Norcross, 1992), not merely the commitment and enthusiasm of the counselor. Given the vast array of background experiences that clients bring to treatment, counselors need to have a multitude of strategies available to work effectively with clients.

Other salient issues include identifying triggers in relapse by exploring the context of the use and assessing possible dual diagnoses that may need to be addressed concurrently (Bradizza, Stasiewicz, & Paas, 2006). In addition to examining client and contextual factors, it is important to explore Doug's reaction to his client's relapse. Have there been other times when Doug has felt like a failure? If so, how is Doug's emotional trigger, possibly even countertransference, affecting his interactions with the client?

Tom can help Doug to identify strategies to deal with such disappointments as a counselor. Educating Doug about the role of relapse in the recovery process is paramount to preventing counselor burnout. In addition, Tom can encourage him to rely on his value of using mind and body to overcome obstacles and achieve good health (i.e., to take care of himself physically, emotionally, and spiritually). Finally, Doug should know that he can continue to obtain supervision to address his emotions and how they affect his effectiveness as a counselor.

References

Bradizza, C. M., Stasiewicz, P. R., & Paas, N. D. (2006). Relapse to alcohol and drug use among individuals diagnosed with co-occurring mental health and substance use disorders: A review. *Clinical Psychology Review, 26,* 162–178.

Kitchener, K. S. (1984). Intuition, critical evaluation, and ethical principles: The foundation for ethical decisions in counseling psychology. *Counseling Psychologist, 12,* 43–55.

Prochaska, J. O., DiClemente, C. C., & Norcross, J. C. (1992). In search of how people change: Applications to addictive behaviors. *American Psychologist, 47,* 1102–1114.

Response

Gerald A. Juhnke

Given the probability and frequency of relapse among my counselors' recovering clients, I have found it helpful to portray relapses as an expected stage within the recovery process. Once relapses occur, counselors and their clients can better identify ways to navigate the newly discovered triggering traps and maintain abstinence via cognitive, social, familial, and behavioral abstinence enhancers. When supervising, I attempt to inoculate entry-level counselors from experiencing "relapse tragedies." This is done by asking what their clients' relapses would mean to them. More often than not, entry-level counselors like Doug personalize their clients' relapses and misperceive relapses as their failures, not their clients'.

In Doug's case, it is crucial to move beyond the common, entry-level perception that willpower creates abstinence and promotes long-term recovery. Specifically, I would ask Doug five sequentially posed questions. The sequence starts with questions designed to promote supervisee introspection and moves toward enlarging the supervisee's perceptions of the recovery process. These questions include (a) What does Ray's relapse mean to you? (b) what does Ray's relapse suggest about you as an entry-level addictions counselor? (c) tell me how you are going to effectively resolve your frustration about Ray's case so your feelings won't contaminate other cases where clients are depending on you? (d) help me understand the differences between a "slip" and "relapse," and (e) because clients' recoveries are not always identical, tell me how you see Ray's slip or relapse as part of his ongoing recovery process? Based on Doug's response to the first question, relevant follow-up questions would be asked. Only when it was evident that Doug had gathered sufficient insight from his individual question responses would the next question in the sequence be used.

Doug's indication that it was awkward to discuss Ray's relapse is common. Many times these awkward feelings are related to supervisees' perceptions that they failed their clients, or even the novelty of such frank discussions. Supervising Doug, I would first validate him without validating his belief that relapse discussions must be awkward. I would do this by saying something like, "I hear you, Doug. Especially when first gaining addictions counseling experience, it may sometimes feel awkward to talk about relapse. However, you'll find this awkwardness dissipates as you gain more experience and understand that relapse itself is an important recovery stage."

Next, I would discuss how medical students may initially find certain patient discussions awkward. Yet, over time, as students progress from residents to physicians, they learn to become comfortable with patient-presented symptoms. Thus, I might say, "Have you ever thought about how awkward it might initially feel for a medical student to ask questions about a patient's symptoms to ensure the best treatment? Frankly, I anticipate that most medical students find it awkward to discuss bladder control problems. Later, however, as experienced physicians, such patient conversations are likely so focused on patient needs and so common that no awkwardness is experienced." The intent here is to suggest that relapse discussions are vital to effective treatment and awkwardness disappears with experience. Given Doug's stated feelings, I might further ask, "I wonder how physicians handle their feelings when patients who adamantly refuse to follow prescribed interventions such as losing weight or starting blood pressure medications later experience a stroke?" Again, this question would hopefully engender continued new insights for Doug about his feelings regarding Ray's relapse.

Related to prevention strategies for Doug, I would encourage him to seek his clients' permission to add familial components to their prevention programs. Family members can have a commanding effect on clients' recovery. Learning how these important people are triggering relapse behaviors and inviting them to participate in joining the treatment process increase the probability for effective recovery.

I typically find life stories and metaphors important to supervision. As a former chef, I readily use cooking metaphors. Supervisors can draw from their life experiences and discuss hastily implemented behaviors that lead to failure. I constantly tell supervisees about increasing oven temperatures or hastily creating a dessert only to experience an embarrassing kitchen disaster. Such stories portray counseling as a slow and arduous process and accentuate the fact that healthy, long-term life changes rarely occur quickly. However, I self-disclose counseling experiences only when such disclosures will promote supervisees' growth and development. Most often, as I mentioned, these disclosures revolve around my mistakes and blunders. It is my intent that such disclosure models opportunities for frank discussions and suggests to supervisees that every counselor will occasionally err. More important, it suggests that errors provide important learning opportunities that make us better counselors.

More often than self-disclosure, however, I usually describe in very general and nonsupervisee-identifiable ways how my previous supervisees experienced situations. Here, for example, I might state, "Doug, if I could introduce you to every counselor I have supervised, all would say at one time or another that they have felt like a failure because of a specific client's relapse. Most often this happens when counselors overidentify with a specific client or when counselors are relatively new to the process. However, my bet is that they would also tell you that over time, you will find that some who relapse will return to treatment, and in the long run these addictions counselors have enjoyed working in a profession that truly helps many recover despite overwhelming odds."

Chapter 7

Caught Between a Rock and a Funding Source

Jeremy M. Linton

Topics

- Funding source issues
- Conflict caused by counselor recovery status
- Traditional versus research-based treatment approaches

Background

A few years ago, Jim became clinical supervisor for an outpatient substance abuse treatment center that was administered by a large agency. As the clinical supervisor, Jim oversees clinical operations, reviews records, and provides clinical supervision. Jim also works closely with the agency's director to ensure that counselors are providing quality treatment services to clients. Most of the treatment provided by the agency is funded by several large grants from one organization. A major stipulation of these grants is that they be used to fund only research-tested treatment approaches. The agency selected cognitive-behavioral therapy (CBT) as its treatment paradigm, and counseling services are informed by a set of CBT manuals. Counselors are expected to use these manuals as the basis for all of the treatment they provide.

Recently, Jim was asked to be a part-time clinical supervisor at the therapeutic community (TC) administered by the agency, taking over for a supervisor who had been terminated. The TC serves 250 clients and employs 15 counselors, an administrative supervisor, and a clinical supervisor. The TC was funded by the same grants dictating the use of research-based treatment approaches, and a set of CBT curriculum manuals had been adopted for use.

Incident

In recent months several problems had developed at the TC. Because of a dispute with a publisher, the agency decided to change CBT curriculum manuals for the program. The staff was unhappy with the change and felt that the new curriculum did not provide enough direction. There had also been significant staff turnover, making the TC environment less stable. Finally, in the stressful environment of the TC, a conflict between counselors of recovering and non-recovering backgrounds was beginning to develop, and each group began to question the other's competence. The grant provider learned of the conflict and the ramifications it was having in the TC, and gave the agency 2 months to fix the problems or have its contract terminated.

Once Jim began working with the clinical staff, another more salient treatment issue became apparent. In recent weeks two of the senior counselors, Robert and Leo, decided without administrative approval to change the format of their treatment groups to a 12-step-based approach and actively eschewed the CBT model of the program. Within the TC, counselors followed the same group of clients throughout the program, and clients did not experience more than one counselor while in treatment. As a result, Robert and Leo's clients received entirely different treatment than the rest of the clients at the TC. The paradox of this change was that Robert and Leo's clients were the best performers in the TC after the change. Their clients showed the best progress, were the most active in the TC, and were always willing to work with their peers in resolving community issues. Although Robert and Leo's clients were clearly making better progress after the change, they were also speaking a different language within the TC. Jim even heard rumors of these clients speaking negatively of CBT in favor of the 12-step approach. Clearly the divisiveness among the staff was affecting the clients.

As Jim began to address the issues at the TC, he experienced much resistance from the staff. First, Robert and Leo were dead set against changing back to CBT. Second, the rest of the staff was split into two camps, recovering versus nonrecovering counselors, and neither camp had any interest in working on a resolution. Third, the administrative supervisor of the program provided little support. He was also new to his job, worked hard to appease everyone, and thought Jim should do the "dirty work" because he was with the program on an interim basis. Finally, Jim received little support from the agency's director. The director stated that this was clearly a clinical issue and was therefore Jim's responsibility. With all parties firmly ensconced in their positions, Jim saw little hope for improvement, and time was running out.

Jim became frustrated almost immediately on his arrival at the TC, and it was his opinion that the problems had gone on for so long that there was little hope of resolving them. However, Jim made a commitment to the agency, the program, and the clients to provide his best effort. Numerous questions nagged at Jim. How would he feel as a counselor if he were constrained by treatment manuals, had his abilities aggressively questioned by coworkers, and had the possibility of losing his job in the near future looming over his head? How open would he be to a new clinical supervisor's assistance? How would he feel if a funding source dictated what he did in treatment?

Questions

1. Which of the issues in this incident should be handled by a clinical supervisor and which by the administrative supervisor? What

could Jim have done to more clearly delineate the supervisor's and administrator's roles and responsibilities within supervision?

2. What techniques could have been used to prepare the clinical staff for some group and team-building interventions?

3. How should Jim have approached Robert and Leo? Is there a potential ethical problem inherent in the situation with Robert and Leo? Is it possible that working with them to change their treatment approach could have a negative effect on their clients' progress?

4. What are the ethical concerns of allowing treatment and clinical supervision to be dictated by funding sources? What could Jim have done in this situation to address this issue?

Response

Jill Russett

Consistent with research on supervision, this scenario demonstrates the lack of consensus and resulting role confusion that exists surrounding the distinction between administrative supervision versus clinical supervision (Henderson, 1994). Without administrative support, including that of the agency director, Jim is caught between the awkward roles of carrying out administrative responsibilities and providing supportive clinical supervision to the counseling staff. Jim must insist that the administration provide a clear delineation of responsibilities to prevent the risk of clinical supervision blending into administrative responsibilities.

Clear distinctions regarding the role and purpose of the two types of supervision exist. Administrative supervisors are tasked with overseeing, directing, and evaluating the work of staff members within an organization. Part of the defined responsibility is to delegate and monitor the work of the staff and ensure the agency is running smoothly (Holloway, 1995). In this case, the administrative supervisor needs to set clear procedural guidelines for all staff to follow, specifically emphasizing the expectation for staff to adhere to the prescribed treatment selected. In particular, Robert and Leo's decision to change programs needs to be addressed from an administrative perspective.

In the role of clinical supervisor, Jim's primary focus is on skill acquisition, professional development, and consultation. Ultimately, clinical supervision is oriented to the needs of the client (Holloway, 1995). Given the dissension among the staff and the limited time frame to adjust the program, it is imperative that Jim build a relationship with the staff, provide them with needed support, and begin to make the necessary changes in programming.

Of major contention among the staff are differences in theoretical orientation and treatment modalities, resulting in unresolved internal conflict. Twelve-step and cognitive–behavioral interventions are the two models most widely used in substance abuse treatment. Research on 12-step facilitation and studies on cognitive–behavioral interventions demonstrate comparable improvement and treatment outcomes for substance abuse (Ouimette, Finney, & Moos, 1997). Additionally, a study by the National Association of Alcoholism and Drug Abuse Counselors (NAADAC) in 1995 indicated that approximately 58% of its membership was recovering from a substance abuse addiction (Doyle, 1997). Considering that more than half of addictions counselors are in recovery, it is important to recognize their contributions and gain insight from both perspectives. By working together, staff recognize an opportunity to incorporate 12-step programming and cognitive–behavioral and other treatment modalities while meeting the grant-funding requirements of research-based treatment.

Jim can make use of team-building efforts to assist staff to bridge their differences, work effectively together, and focus on program development, an area of concern for all staff. A suggested team-building activity is to mix the staff of recovering and nonrecovering backgrounds into two groups, asking them to brainstorm programming alternatives. This approach will not only allow staff to work together but also provide them with a sense of empowerment and increased commitment to the program. Continued group work and collaborative team-building efforts between the counselors of recovering and nonrecovering backgrounds have the potential to lead to more comprehensive programming and less resistance between professionals, ultimately benefiting the client.

Although partly an administrative matter, Robert and Leo's decision to change programming without prior approval also needs to be addressed through clinical supervision. Although change in clinical treatment has initially yielded positive results, it is inconsistent with current programming and could potentially adversely affect client treatment. Jim needs to approach Robert and Leo with care and concern and in a genuine manner. The recently revised *ACA Code of Ethics* of the American Counseling Association (ACA, 2005) helps guide this interaction. Sections A and D of the *ACA Code of Ethics* are particularly relevant.

In Section A (The Counseling Relationship), four standards should be considered. Standards A.1.a. (Primary Responsibility), A.4.a. (Avoiding Harm), and A.4.b. (Personal Values) are codes that in essence address the welfare of the clients, minimize unavoidable or unanticipated harm, and consider the counselor's awareness of his or her own values, attitudes, and beliefs. Of particular note is Standard A.1.d. (Support Network Involvement), which indicates that counselors need to recognize support networks and the meaning they hold in client's lives. Historically, the principles of Alcoholics Anonymous and other 12-step support groups have been an integral part of treatment and recovery.

Three other ACA standards are applicable as well. Within Section D (Relationships With Other Professionals), Standards D.1.a. (Different Approaches), D.1.g. (Employer Policies), and D.1.h. (Negative Conditions) specify respect in working with other professionals, adherence to general policies and procedures of an employer, and the addressing of change through constructive action. Similarly, NAADAC (2004) provides ethical guidelines that apply in this situation also. Principle 9 (Duty to Care) outlines a counselor's responsibility to maintain a working–therapeutic environment and to strive for understanding and establishing a common ground rather than the ascendancy of one opinion over another. When Robert and Leo accepted employment, under these two codes of ethics they agreed to the employer's policies. Their current clinical behaviors could be considered in violation of these codes and should be addressed.

Although the ACA and NAADAC codes of ethics provide guidance to counseling professionals, the standards leave some areas unaddressed. In this scenario, treatment is primarily prescribed by an outside funding source, an arrangement not outwardly specified in the codes but still with ethical implications. Several ethical codes should be considered, including ACA Standards B.1. (Respecting Client Rights), C.2. (Professional Competence), D.1.g. (Employer Policies), and G.1. (Research Responsibilities).

Grant-funded projects often require reporting on treatment outcomes, such as the number of clients served and progress, and are often used for research purposes. Maintaining client confidentiality is imperative, and care should be used to ensure reports to funding sources do not violate client confidentiality. To limit the risk of conflict, staff needs to be trained and competent in the selected treatment modality. Jim needs to incorporate an evaluative component to assess the efficacy of treatment and to ensure it promotes the welfare of the client. By accepting the conditions of grant funding, the institution agrees to its policies and procedures.

References

American Counseling Association. (2005). *ACA code of ethics.* Alexandria, VA: Author.

Doyle, K. (1997). Substance abuse counselors in recovery: Implications for the ethical issue of dual relationships. *Journal of Counseling & Development, 75,* 428-432.

Henderson, P. (1994). *Administrative skills in counseling supervision.* Washington, DC: Office of Educational Research & Improvement. (ERIC Document Reproduction Service No. ED372356)

Holloway, E. (1995). *Clinical supervision: A systems approach.* Thousand Oaks, CA: Sage.

National Association of Alcohol & Drug Abuse Counselors. (2004). *NAADAC code of ethics.* Retrieved June 5, 2006, from http://naadac.org/documents/index.php?CategoryID=23

Ouimette, P. C., Finney, J. W., & Moos, R. H. (1997). Twelve-step and cognitive-behavioral treatment of substance abuse: A comparison of treatment effectiveness. *Journal of Consulting and Clinical Psychology, 65,* 230-240.

Response

Michael J. Taleff

Traditionally, administrative supervisors are accountable for an entire program. They are the person at the top, and the buck stops there. Clinical supervisors, on the other hand, manage clinical problems (e.g., client issues, professional development). Arguably, there is overlap between clinical supervisor and administrative supervisor duties. Yet, the final arbiter of personnel problems (e.g., destructive divisiveness among staff) is often the responsibility of the administrative supervisor.

The lack of clarity and delineation of job duties in this case is noteworthy. For one, Jim did not do his homework prior to taking the part-time position. He seems not to have asked exactly what his supervisory duties were, or the duties of those around him were. To differentiate between those duties, Jim needed to do two basic things: (a) Read the agency policy and procedures manual and (b) professionally encourage the administrative supervisor to do the "dirty work," with support from Jim, if the policy and procedure manual indicates this is an administrative, not clinical, area of responsibility.

From the unilateral changing of the parameters of a grant, chronic staff turnover, conflict between counselors, and years of appeasement to the consequent implications for client treatment, this program is a mess. To simply apply techniques (e.g., team-building exercises) to this situation has a high probably of failure. Simple techniques have been shown to be of minimal benefit to clients (Lambert & Bergin, 1994). There is no reason to believe they would be any more effective with counselors. The recommendation, in this case, is to dispense with the techniques for a bit and focus on trust building and respect. Given the condition of this program, that is going to take time.

There is not a potential ethical problem with Robert and Leo but a very real one. Counselors cannot, of their own accord, breach the conditions of a grant despite their assumed success. That is unethical. Moreover, the ramifications of such actions have the potential to cut needed program funds and jeopardize the livelihood of other staff. In addition, fermenting discontent among fellow staff certainly has ethical overtones. Such actions are disrespectful and uncivil, if not callous. In particular, these actions cannot help but be transmitted in some small (or large) way to clients. And that is definitely unethical (American Counseling Association, 2005).

A solid ethical core calls for respect and understanding of others. Essentially, that message needs to be delivered to Robert and Leo, preferably in private. While in this setting, the question "What is to be gained by your continued divisive behavior and unethical action?" needs to be asked. An accounting of actions is needed. Not excuses, mind you, or the shifting of blame, but a deep reflective analysis of how Robert and Leo's actions have contributed to the present state of affairs. This touchy issue should not be presented in an accusatory manner but with all the professionalism Jim can muster. Certainly, this could all backfire, and Robert and Leo could take this encounter as an insult and retaliate by undermining the program even more.

Ethical concerns for service programs do arise if funding drives treatment (e.g., drug companies funding a program only if it uses their product). Yet, the grant-funding scenario outlined here does not seem to be of this nature. Moreover, there may not be ethical concerns if, ahead of time, all staff were informed and agreed to use a certain treatment contingency. If, however, an empirically supported treatment was dictated by a funding source and, without consent of the staff, was implemented, then an interesting ethical situation arises. In such a scenario, the question becomes "Does refusal to use empirically supported treatments, and instead use empirically unsupported treatments, constitute an ethical concern? If so, what is it, and what are the parameters?"

If Jim has developed a modicum of trust with this staff, he needs to walk into his next staff meeting prepared to ask one searing question, "Given all the trouble this program has experienced, what small step are you prepared to make today that will improve *our* situation? Then, what small step will you make tomorrow, then the next day?" Jim should encourage the staff to apply a great deal of deep critical thought to their answers.

References

American Counseling Association. (2005). *ACA code of ethics.* Alexandria, VA: Author.

Lambert, M. E., & Bergin, A. E. (1994). The effectiveness of psychotherapy. In A. E. Bergin & S. L. Garfield (Eds.), *Handbook of psychotherapy and behavior change* (4th ed., pp. 143–190). New York: Wiley.

Chapter 8

I Am More Than Just Their Counselor: Counselor Boundaries and Limitations

Virginia Magnus

Topics

- The supervisory relationship
- Supervisor ethical responsibilities
- Supervisee boundary issues

Background

Grace is a 48-year-old White licensed professional counselor with an addiction specialty license. She provides supervision services for interns and acts as a consultant for a community addiction treatment agency. The agency provides inpatient treatment services for male and female adolescents, outpatient services for male and female adolescents and adults, and family counseling for the families of adolescents in inpatient treatment. Grace also has a private practice and works with a variety of clients. Her interest in the addiction field stems from her experience with alcoholism on both sides of her family, but not among her immediate family members. Grace is not a recovering alcoholic or addict.

The agency has been in existence for 3 years, and Grace has been providing supervision for interns since the inception of the agency. Some of the interns working at the agency are completing either practicum or internship requirements for a master's degree, and some are working toward a specialty license in addiction counseling. Grace meets with the interns once a week for the first 3 weeks of each month on an individual basis and as a group on the 4th week of each month. Topics of discussion include individual cases, ethical situations, and personal observations. Grace completes all the required paperwork for each of the interns, which will be part of their official professional development records. She also documents the number of internship and supervision hours completed by interns in the chemical dependency certification program.

Rachel is a 30-year-old Caucasian woman who works with both inpatient and outpatient male and female adolescents, and at times works with adults in the outpatient treatment program. She has been working for the agency for the past 2.5 years in a noncounseling capacity and as a result has decided to go back to school to complete an authorized certification program in chemical dependency counseling. Although Rachel admits to drinking too much at times, she is not an alcoholic nor is she in recovery. She has a bachelor's degree in psychology and believes her education has helped prepare her for the work she has been doing as an employee of the agency and also her recent work as an intern at the agency. Currently, she is completing her second internship with adolescents in the inpatient program in the morning and working as an employee for the agency in the afternoon.

Rachel enjoys working one on one with the adolescents and prides herself on being their "buddy." There have been times when she has bent the rules a little for what she deems to be good reasons. For example, when facilitating group as an intern, she ended a group session 30 minutes early because the clients were tired and did not have the energy to participate that day. Another time she cancelled an individual session with a client because the client was having a bad day and did not want to attend the session. In addition, Rachel has occasionally allowed clients to skip Alcoholics Anonymous or Narcotics Anonymous meetings, has neglected to follow treatment plans, and has not enforced program rules. Grace has discussed these occurrences and several other similar ones with Rachel in individual supervision sessions. On a number of occasions, Grace has also talked with Rachel about ethical standards, boundaries, and the responsibilities of an intern at the agency in comparison to the role of an employee. During group supervision, some of the other interns have objected to Rachel's behavior because it has been making it harder for them to do their jobs with their respective clients. Grace has also had several discussions with the director of the agency regarding Rachel's behavior and has expressed misgivings related to the appropriateness of keeping Rachel on as an intern.

Incident

Todd, a male adolescent, was placed in the inpatient treatment program by his parents 3 weeks ago. Typically, new clients begin to adjust to the treatment program within this time period; however, he has not. Rachel was the next intern in line for a new client, and therefore Todd was assigned to her. Over the course of the 3 weeks, Todd has had individual counseling sessions with Rachel, and she had facilitated group once since his arrival. Rachel has concerns about Todd's adjustment and has expressed feelings of deep sympathy for Todd during individual and group supervision. Several times she has referred to Todd's lack of adjustment, loneliness, and sadness. During group supervision, some of the other interns stated that their impression of Todd's behavior and adjustment problems were related to his unwillingness to take treatment seriously and to take responsibility for his own recovery. They also believed that he was trying to manipulate agency employees, and Rachel in particular, in order to get his own way and avoid treatment.

At different times during the following week, Todd told Rachel that he thought she was the only one who understood him and that he was very happy that she was his counselor. He also said he knew he could adjust to treatment and feel better if he could just talk to his girlfriend. In their next individual session, Rachel decided to let Todd telephone his girlfriend, thinking it would help alleviate some of his sadness and loneliness. She stepped out of the room for about 3 minutes to give him some privacy, and when she returned to the room he was hanging up. Todd expressed his appreciation to Rachel for letting him make the call and stated that he felt much better. That same evening, when the 2:00 a.m. bed check was done by one of the agency employees, Todd's bed was empty. Agency protocol for emergencies was activated, and the agency director, Grace, and Rachel were all called in to the treatment center.

Todd's parents were called after agency employees had carefully searched the center and grounds to make sure that he had in fact left the premises. The police were called, and Todd was reported as a runaway. His parents were very upset because they were worried that Todd would be looking for drugs and alcohol, and at the same time they were furious with the director for letting this happen while their son was in his care. The director blamed Grace for not supervising Rachel carefully enough. Grace responded by telling the director that she had warned him about having Rachel as an intern, but he had not taken her warnings seriously. Grace subsequently refused to supervise Rachel. When confronted, in tears, Rachel admitted to letting Todd call his girlfriend during a session earlier in the day and that this call may have been part of his plan to leave the center.

Questions

1. Did Grace respond appropriately to Rachel's feelings toward Todd? Did Grace facilitate Rachel's personal and professional growth in relation to self-awareness and her counseling role?
2. Discuss how you would help Rachel cultivate sufficient self-esteem and self-worth to be able to develop and maintain appropriate professional boundaries with clients.
3. Was Grace right in refusing to supervise Rachel after this incident? Why or why not?

Response

Kathleen M. Salyers

In reviewing the critical incident involving the clinical supervision of an intern student who is also an employee in an addictions treatment community agency, the first issue that arises is whether or not the supervisor Grace has received education and training in supervision and ethics. She is said to be a licensed professional counselor with an addiction specialty, but there is no indication that she has received supervision training or is endorsed to provide supervi-

sion. This is an issue that may well be prevalent in counselor education programs in states where supervision and ethical education and training are not required for state licensure as counselors, yet practicum and internship students
are placed in the field and receive field supervision. This may also be an issue
even in those states where supervision and ethics are a requirement for continuing education and there is a supervisory endorsement. Unless supervisors
have received training in these areas that is inclusive of all the components of
supervision and have an understanding of the developmental process of counselors-in-training, their education and training may still be lacking and thus lead
to situations such as the one described in this critical incident.

One issue surrounding this situation is that Rachel has been employed at
the agency for the past 2.5 years. It is mentioned that she has worked in various settings, but it is not stated in what capacity. Rachel has a bachelor's degree in psychology and is working on an authorized certification program in
chemical dependency counseling. There is no mention as to whether Rachel
has received education and training in ethics or professional behaviors. A concern in many states is the inconsistency between requirements to practice
clinical counseling and to provide treatment as a counselor in substance abuse
treatment facilities. Training requirements for these two areas can be quite different. This may have led Grace to assume that Rachel has more education and
training as a counselor than is the case, thus leading to difficulties in the supervisory relationship and Grace's inability to provide appropriate clinical supervision to Rachel.

It becomes clear that the supervisor was unable to provide clear and direct
supervision as required for a counselor-in-training. Grace discussed the issues
of "ethical standards, boundaries and the responsibilities of an intern at the
agency in comparison to the role of an employee," but it is apparent that
Rachel was not as developmentally progressed as the other interns, as they too
were aware of and concerned about her behavior. Grace failed to take remedial action that might have fostered Rachel's personal and professional growth
in relation to her self-awareness and her counseling role. Rachel's discussion
of Todd during individual and group supervision provided indicators that she
was not being objective in her response to her client. Awareness of the developmental stage of a counselor-in-training, such as proposed in the Integrated
Developmental Model (Stoltenberg, McNeill, & Delworth, 1998), might have
alerted Grace to the need to develop a supervisory relationship that was sensitive to the supervisee's developmental stage as a counselor.

The critical incident that is described actually began during internship
group supervision when Rachel's inappropriate boundary issues with clients
were not addressed in a manner that would resolve the problem. There clearly
were systems issues that may well have addressed the concerns with Rachel
before they reached the point of a critical incident. This would include the supervisor having the appropriate knowledge of her ethical responsibilities to
her supervisees, which would have resulted in her addressing the supervisee
boundary issues in a very clear and direct manner, possibly including a written remediation plan. Grace's refusal to continue to work with Rachel as a supervisee also indicates Grace's possible discomfort as a supervisor and lack of

awareness of the developmental process of the supervisory relationship. This manner of response would indicate that Grace's developmental stage as a supervisor was not a good match for Rachel's developmental stage as a counselor-in-training, thus creating conflict. Again, this would indicate a need for supervisory education and training for Grace. Also of concern is whether or not Rachel is receiving the same standard of education and training in her educational program as the other interns and the effect that this is having on her relationships with those around her, including her supervisor, fellow interns, administrators, and most important her clients. There is no mention at all of a consultation or intervention by the educational program who has placed her at this agency as an intern. Is Rachel having difficulties in her educational program as well as her internship site?

Apparently there were no clear directions about what was to transpire if an intern was having difficulties at the internship site. This was complicated by the fact that the supervisor was acting in a dual role with Rachel, as both an employer and an internship supervisor. Dysfunctional system interactions were the result of the lack of clear remedial plans for students who experience difficulties at their practicum or internship sites. Supervisor and student orientations to field experiences are an absolute necessity as the profession moves to more field experiences in practicum and internship. This also necessitates the development of supervision education and training opportunities for counseling field supervisors, as well as supervision education and training in counselor education programs for master's students.

Reference

Stoltenberg, C. D., McNeill, B., & Delworth, U. (1998). IDM Supervision: *An Intergrated Development Model for supervising counselors and therapists.* San Francisco: Jossey Bass.

Response

Geri Miller and Catherine Clark

There are numerous problems with the supervision provided in this scenario. Before examining the supervisor's behavior, Rachel and Todd's contributions to this difficult situation need to be examined to clarify how the lack of accountability for behavior ran through the agency, the supervisor, the counselor, and the client.

Rachel had a number of problems in how she related with the adolescents in general. In her individual meetings she focused on being their buddy and bending rules for them. These behaviors may be indicative of a number of issues that Rachel has, including low self-esteem, difficulty being an authority figure, a tendency to overidentify with client needs, and not holding clients responsible for behavior. This combination of issues laid the groundwork for her struggles counseling Todd and the difficulties that arose in supervision with her.

Although Rachel had been given feedback on her inappropriate behavior by her supervisor, she did not appear to act on the feedback. It is difficult to know if this is due to her own issues or if Rachel is using her behavior to meet her own needs rather than the needs of the client. Nonetheless, her inability or lack of desire to hold clients accountable for their behavior is a significant problem with adolescents who need to learn to be responsible and with addicts who tend to blame others for their behavior (Miller, 2005). Addicts need to be held accountable for their behavior within a spirit of compassion (Miller, 2005). Rachel's counseling approach was flawed by her being "too compassionate" and avoiding holding clients accountable for their behavior. Her counseling approach encouraged the adolescents to continue their dysfunctional behavior by remaining childlike and irresponsible rather than encouraging them into responsible adulthood and addiction recovery.

Rachel's behavior was combined with Todd's manipulative tendencies toward employees, especially Rachel, for his own personal interests. He did that by communicating a message to Rachel that she was the only one who understood him and that she was special to him. This manipulation was a perfect match for Rachel's need to be special to her clients and resulted in her decision to let him be alone during a call to his girlfriend, a decision that resulted in his leaving the facility.

Examination of Grace's mistakes of supervision needs to be put in the context of what Rachel and Todd brought to the table as well as the dysfunction of the agency. Rachel's boundary issues, her need to be special, and her difficulty holding clients accountable needed to be documented carefully in supervision (American Counseling Association [ACA], 2005). Although Grace informed the agency's director of her struggles with the supervision of Rachel, it is unclear if she documented those concerns in an appropriate manner. Grace needed to monitor Rachel more closely to make sure that the welfare of the client was the primary concern (ACA, 2005). For example, after repeated confrontations by Grace and Rachel's colleagues, it would have been appropriate to refer Rachel for counseling for her self-esteem and boundary issues as well as pull her off of individual counseling assignments until it could be demonstrated that she would set better boundaries and hold clients accountable.

In supervision, the focus could have been on Rachel's difficulty setting boundaries and holding clients accountable in order for her to learn about focusing on the welfare of the client. When Rachel was able to clearly see how her behavior directly affected the welfare of the client, she could be allowed to work with clients individually. In this way, Grace did not respond appropriately to Rachel's feelings toward Todd or facilitate her self-awareness in her role as a counselor. Culbreth (1999) indicates that substance abuse counselors prefer supervision that is "more proactive and intentional than reactive" (p. 8). Early intervention with Rachel could have promoted a more healthy development as a counselor.

The client was vulnerable to harm and the agency possibly open to legal liabilities when supervision did not focus on Rachel's problems as a counselor or limit the type of client contact she had (ACA, 2005). Focusing on Rachel's difficulty assuming the counselor role would have helped her develop self-esteem and maintain professional boundaries with her clients. A core of a healthy supervisory relationship is a mutually clear understanding of the expectations of the supervisory relationship and the evaluation process of supervision (Miller, 2005).

In all fairness to Grace, however, she tried to work within the agency by telling the director of her concerns about Rachel. Grace needed to make sure that she documented her reporting of behaviors to the director and that she made clear to the agency how not holding Rachel accountable for her behavior as a counselor had the potential to harm clients. She needed to document any barriers she believed the agency presented for her to effectively supervise Rachel. Grace's documentation of barriers would have allowed her to suggest that Rachel have a different supervisor. Refusing to supervise her after the situation with Todd makes her decision look punitive. At this point, it would probably be more beneficial to refer Rachel to another supervisor or to renegotiate the supervision contract with Rachel in collaboration with the agency director.

References

American Counseling Association. (2005). *ACA code of ethics.* Alexandria, VA: Author.

Culbreth, J. R. (1999). Clinical supervision of substance abuse counselors: Current and preferred practices. *Journal of Addictions & Offender Counseling, 20,* 15–25.

Miller, G. (2005). *Learning the language of addiction counseling* (2nd ed.). Hoboken, NJ: Wiley.

Chapter 9

I Am Not the Counselor for This Client: Building Competence and Confidence

Sullivan Moseley

Topics

- Substance abuse with a pregnant teen
- Counselor competence
- Supervisor assurance

Background

Mary is a White 50-year-old counselor working in a residential maternity home. At the age of 45 and after the death of her only child of 24 years, Mary returned to school and earned both her bachelor's and master's degrees. Subsequent to completing her counseling degree, Mary was hired as a full-time counselor by a maternity home that provides intensive therapeutic programming to pregnant residents who have been identified as needing acute treatment for themselves and their unborn infants.

One of the first clients assigned to Mary was Ginger, a White 17-year-old who was 5.5 months pregnant. She was admitted to the maternity home from lock-up after it was discovered she was pregnant. On admission to the maternity home, Ginger had received no prenatal care and tested positive for both cocaine and marijuana.

During the initial assessment, Ginger described her family history as intense chaos that included poverty, substance abuse, domestic violence, child abuse, and neglect. Ginger had been living in a car with the biological father of her baby until he abandoned her at a gas station. Shortly after, she met Antonio, an 18-year-old Latino from Central America, who wanted to take her back to his country, Guatemala, to live with his family and raise her baby. Ginger expressed that she had no interest in having the baby without the help of Antonio.

Ginger disclosed in the third session that she abused alcohol and smoked pot despite the consequences to her unborn child and that she had no interest in the child. Antonio had not called her in 2 days, and her wish was that she would lose the baby. If Antonio did not come to take her away, she would release the baby for adoption at birth.

Mary was struggling with prioritizing the multiple issues Ginger presented in session. Mary felt her first responsibility was to the unborn child by means of Ginger's prenatal care and sobriety. In counseling sessions, Mary was aware of her own varying levels of anxiety associated with questions of competence and a strong focus on self rather than the client. Mary was becoming frustrated, confused, and disabled by doubt. She urgently needed to confront her own feelings toward Ginger. She made an appointment for individual supervision with Stan, her supervisor.

Incident

The following is an exchange that occurred during individual supervision between Stan and Mary:

Stan: Hi, Mary. You said you desperately needed to talk to me?

Mary: Yes, I have a client that I need to refer. She possibly wants to release the baby for adoption, or needs to release the baby for adoption, or at least I think she needs to release the baby for adoption. I don't know what she needs. She needs more than whatever I have to offer [Mary's eyes tear, and she feels betrayed by her own emotions].

Stan: One minute you feel certain and the next you feel doubt about how to support this client. Tell me more about what is going on.

Mary: [She proceeds to give Stan the client's background along with all protocol concerning social services and child protective services.] So you see, this is why I need to refer this client to you.

Stan: You have worked successfully with other difficult clients. Describe some weaknesses you have working with this client.

Mary: I'm not sure what it is. I don't feel empathy for her. I don't know . . . I am always focused on the wrong thing, like when I corrected her for referring to Antonio as a Mexican . . . that just because he speaks Spanish doesn't make him a Mexican. That seemed like the one thing I knew for sure about this client; Guatemala is not in Mexico!

Stan: With all the ambiguity and uncertainty, you focused on the one thing you know for sure. What about you either contributed to or detracted from your ability to demonstrate empathy?

Mary: I'm not sure. I feel so sad [tears run down Mary's cheeks]. I grieve for the baby. How will Ginger ever give this child what Ginger herself has never had? [Mary openly weeps.] I am angry at Ginger for not knowing what she does not know; that is, how to value her life and the life of this unborn child.

Stan: You value life. You value both Ginger's and her unborn child's life. Your values are different from the values of your client. Who better would assist Ginger in finding her value? I believe your client is with the counselor she needs.

Questions

1. Discuss how Stan made a cognitive shift in supervision, moving from a client focus to a supervisee focus. If Stan had maintained a client focus, what possibilities may have resulted? Was it reasonable for Stan not to refer the client to another counselor? Explain.
2. Values and biases can affect supervisors' work with supervisees and counselors' work with clients. What kinds of strategies are helpful when supervisors work with clients and supervisees whose values are significantly different?
3. Do you agree with Stan's assessment of Ginger in supervision? Why or why not?

Response

W. Bryce Hagedorn

This incident highlights one of the critical differences between counseling and supervision, most notably the focus of intervention. In counseling, the obvious focus is on the client, whereas in supervision, the focus is on the supervisee, while at the same time remaining cognizant of the needs of the supervisee's clients. Oftentimes, supervisees will come into supervision with specific client needs, which mirrors those clients who come to clinicians with specific personal needs. It is the supervisor's job to impart this important tenet to supervisees: We are in the facilitating not the fixing business. The best way to teach this important principle is to mirror it in the supervisory relationship by focusing on the here-and-now with the supervisee's concerns.

In keeping the focus on Mary's thoughts and feelings as she experienced them and not providing the "quick fix" answer that she was likely seeking, Stan helped Mary to recognize the most important piece of her dilemma, which in this case was her own reaction to Ginger rather than Ginger's personal dilemma with her pregnancy. Had Stan focused solely on Ginger and helped Mary to resolve this particular situation, or had he readily agreed with her need to refer, he would likely have stunted Mary's growth as a clinician. Putting it another way, instead of giving Mary the fish she was seeking, he taught her how to fish in such a way that she can apply the learning to work with future clients with whom she struggles.

Finally, in terms of deciding whether or not to refer, Corey, Corey, and Callanan (2006) offered some concrete guidelines to aid in this decision. These authors assert that referrals are appropriate when moral, religious, or political values are centrally involved in a client's presenting problem. But that's not all. In addition to the presence of these central values, referrals are also appropriate when the counselor's (a) boundaries of competence have been exceeded, (b) discomfort with the client's values is extreme, (c) ability to remain objective is compromised, or (d) concerns with imposing his or her own values onto the client are severe.

Before getting into specific strategies, it is important to first recognize the effect of one's values and biases on the therapeutic/supervisory relationship. It is well known that therapeutic and supervisory relationships are, by their very nature, hierarchical. Clients and supervisees are the initiators of seeking assistance; they reveal their concerns, secrets, hopes, and failures, often in a unilateral direction, which results in their being placed in vulnerable positions. Early in the history of the helping professions, therapists were instructed to act as blank slates (Grimm, 1994), avoiding all disclosure of personal values and beliefs (McLennan, Rochow, & Arthur, 2001; Sacks, 1985). The practice was first advocated by Freud, who noted that "psychotherapy is a technical procedure, like surgery, that does not involve the values or life-style of the treatment agent" (Bergin, 1991, p. 396). This lack of personal feedback was infused into the supervisory relationship as well, and it perpetuated the hierarchical nature of that relationship.

With the advance of humanistic theory, counselors and supervisors were encouraged to be both authentic and genuine and to approach the relationship from a more collaborative perspective, which resulted in the use of self-disclosure. As self-disclosure tends to be the most widely used (and abused) technique, it must be tempered with intentionality. When working with clients or supervisees whose value systems are significantly different from the supervisor's, recognition and acknowledgment of these differences is crucial in establishing authentic relationships that foster positive change. This recognition happens on several planes: the counselor/supervisee, the client, and the supervisor must all recognize his or her values and biases and how these will likely affect the various relationship dynamics. There are several methods to foster this recognition for supervisees, such as candid discussions of values, the completion of any number of value exercises commonly used in counselor training programs, the reading of books and articles that express values contrary to the norm and discussion of these works, and encouraging experiential activities (e.g., visiting various religious institutions, seeking consultation with organizational leaders who represent nonmajority value systems).

In terms of the supervisee's specific work with clients whose value systems are significantly different from his or her own, it can be very therapeutic to highlight these differences during the session and discuss what these differences mean. If a supervisee fosters such a discussion of value differences, he or she must be clear that values have no inherent "rightness"; that is, each person's ownership of his or her values should be validated, even if these values are significantly different from the norm. Granted, values that advocate harm to others should be challenged in such a way that the client (a) does not feel attacked for expressing said values and (b) has the opportunity to reevaluate their appropriateness. Ultimately, clients should be encouraged to come to their own conclusions as to what their values are and understand where these values originate—it is usually at this point that these values can be evaluated by the client to see if they apply to the current life circumstance.

As can be surmised by my responses to the first two questions, I believe that Stan handled Ginger's dilemma appropriately in the supervision session. Through a here-and-now focus on Ginger's thoughts and feelings, coupled with an intentional "fishing" technique (i.e., "How can you work with this client—and clients like her in the future?"), I believe that Ginger will become more aware of her own values and biases and how these will affect her work with future clients.

References

Bergin, A. E. (1991). Values and religious issues in psychotherapy and mental health. *American Psychologist, 46*, 394–403.

Corey, G., Corey, M. S., & Callanan, P. (2006). *Issues and ethics in the helping professions* (7th ed.). Pacific Grove, CA: Brooks/Cole.

Grimm, D. W. (1994). Therapist spiritual and religious values in psychotherapy. *Counseling and Values, 38*, 154–164.

McLennan, N. A., Rochow, S., & Arthur, N. (2001). Religious and spiritual diversity in counseling. *Guidance & Counseling, 16*(4), 132–137.

Sacks, J. M. (1985). Religious issues in psychotherapy. *Journal of Religion and Health, 24*, 26–30.

Response

Laura J. Veach

The counselor in this incident, Mary, is clearly facing many of the issues inherent in counseling. Her significant concern about the health of the unborn child and her role and responsibilities as a counselor to both the 17-year-old, pregnant, drug-abusing client and her unborn child cause significant professional and personal stress for Mary. This stress has created a significant struggle for her in providing effective client treatment.

First, it is important that Mary's supervisor, Stan, respond quickly in the supervision session to the complex emotions arising in Mary. He astutely shifts the session from a primary focus on the client to the counselor. If Stan maintains focus solely on the client problems, a covert message is conveyed to the counselor to avoid examining and exploring her own inner struggles and emotions. Avoidance fosters a pattern of silence, insecurity, and secrecy with negative implications when Mary faces future challenging client issues. Often those issues that are most troubling in counseling work are the very issues most worthy of open discussion in supervision sessions. Stan's encouragement to identify key emotions and insecurities to this new counselor working with her first clients is an important model for her growth and development.

Next, the difficulty and insecurity Mary voices in supervision do not indicate a need for Ginger to be referred to a different counselor. Counselors' challenges and struggles with objectivity as their own competing values differ from clients' values in and of themselves are insufficient reason to refer—if so, clients would be hard-pressed to find any suitable counselor. That Mary recognizes these differences, is concerned about imposing her own values onto the client, and openly wrestles with this in supervision indicates Mary is caring for the client with professionalism. Additionally, Stan challenges Mary in another important way as he asks about her ability to demonstrate empathy, and with that challenge thus emphasizes an important therapeutic factor as a main focus for her current counseling. Stan stresses that Mary's role is to help the client, Ginger, identify her own value while caring for the therapeutic relationship. Weekly tape reviews of counseling sessions with Ginger can be added as opportunities for Mary to ensure her personal issues and values are not impairing her effectiveness. It is also important that a counselor's own unresolved issues be evaluated by the supervisor if they might interfere with his or her ability to work effectively. For example, it is valuable to explore whether unresolved grief related to the loss of Mary's only child is further complicating her objectivity. If so, Stan would be advised to also refer Mary for personal grief counseling as he continues supervision.

One additional component to add to Stan's supervision includes addressing Mary's feelings of urgency. The concern is underscored by the health risks to the client's unborn child. Stan and Mary both face an important responsibility and challenge. Ginger's self-report of alcohol and marijuana abuse in her first trimester of pregnancy combined with the positive findings for cocaine and tetrahydrocannabinol in the urine drug screen at the maternity home are serious. Prenatal alcohol use puts the unborn child at risk for one of the leading causes of birth defects, fetal alcohol spectrum disorder (FASD; Doweiko, 2006). One option, obtaining an evaluation by an addiction counselor specializing in FASD, can enhance the outcome for both the pregnant teen and her unborn fetus. The recommendations may further help the work that Mary is doing with Ginger and can provide additional resources as numerous decisions, especially pertaining to alcohol and other drug use affecting the fetus, are made.

Finally, a significant issue of counseling this client can be further complicated by the duty of the counselor to report abuse or neglect if state child protective laws include prenatal alcohol and other drug use resulting in damage to the unborn child. The FASD Center for Excellence within the Substance Abuse and Mental Health Services Administration (SAMHSA) noted that 31 FASD-related bills were introduced or passed in a number of states in 2005 (SAMHSA FASD, 2005). Virginia, similar to some other states, enacted legislation in 2005 to clarify reasons for a health professional to report child abuse or neglect. Reportable violations now include "a diagnosis by an attending physician made within seven days of a child's birth that the child has fetal alcohol syndrome attributable to in utero exposure to alcohol" (SAMHSA FASD, 2005, p.19). Fourteen states consider prenatal substance abuse regulated within their child protective laws and "therefore prenatal drug exposure can provide grounds for terminating parental rights because of child abuse or neglect" (American Pregnancy Association, 2006, p. 4). South Carolina further determined that prenatal substance abuse is a criminal act of child abuse and neglect (American Pregnancy Association, 2006). It becomes critical, then, for this supervisor and counselor working with any substance-abusing pregnant clients to consult with a specialist knowledgeable about child protective laws pertaining to prenatal substance abuse as beneficial supervision and effective counseling continue.

References

American Pregnancy Association. (2006). *Using illegal street drugs during pregnancy.* Retrieved August 25, 2006, from http://www.americanpregnancy.org/pregnancyhealth /illegaldrugs.html

Doweiko, H. E. (2006). *Concepts of chemical dependency* (6th ed.). Belmont, CA: Brooks/Cole.

Substance Abuse & Mental Health Services Administration, Fetal Alcohol Spectrum Disorder Center for Excellence. (2005, October). *Fetal alcohol spectrum disorders legislation by state: 2004-2005 legislative sessions.* Retrieved August 24, 2006, from http://www.fasdcenter.samhsa.gov/documents/FASDLegislationByState1005.pdf

Chapter 10

It's Not a Relapse, Just a Slip

Riley Venable

Topics

- Recovery issues among supervisees
- Dual relationships
- Professional ethics

Background

Tom is a 22-year-old White male counselor-in-training for his substance abuse credential. He graduated with an undergraduate degree in psychology from a local university a few months earlier, with a minor in substance abuse studies. He is currently working at an inpatient treatment center and has just begun to have his own caseload. He has been in recovery for 2 years and picked this career path because he wants to make a difference. He hopes to attend graduate school after he has a few years of experience. He picked John as a supervisor because he had seen him at 12-step meetings.

John is Tom's clinical supervisor and has been in private practice for more than 5 years. He is a 55-year-old White man and has been in recovery for 27 years. He initially became a substance abuse counselor through a hospital-based training program after being sober for 1 year. Several years ago he completed a master's degree and obtained his professional counseling license, and later his supervisor's certificate.

Incident

During his weekly individual supervision session, Tom relates the following experience from work:

"I was doing a discharge with one of our patients the other day. He is a dentist and completed the inpatient program almost 6 months ago. He has completed his aftercare, and I was just finishing up his paperwork with him on his way out. When he started treatment he had to surrender his license. When he started aftercare, he got his license back, and has been volunteering 2 days a week at a homeless clinic doing free dental exams. He is a really nice guy.

"The problem is, I saw him last night at a 12-step meeting that I had taken our patients to. His drug of choice was cocaine, and he shared in the meeting that he drank a beer at a ballgame over the weekend, so he was picking up a 'desire chip.' The ballgame would have been before I did his discharge paperwork."

"I know that if I tell the people at work that I saw him, I've broken his anonymity. I also think if word got back to the state dental board, he would probably lose his license, maybe permanently. I'd hate to see that happen, because he really seems to be turning his life around. I guess I'm telling you because I really don't know what to do. It seems like this wasn't a relapse, it was just a slip. But then again, he could have told me about it when I was going over his discharge paperwork."

"John, what do you think I should do? I don't want to get him in trouble when he was honest about his slip, but I really don't want to jeopardize my job either. If I let this go, do you think this guy will be okay? If I tell them at work, can I get in trouble for revealing what happened at a 12-step meeting? How about the other patients? Do you think they will trust me if they find out I told the staff what I heard at a meeting?"

Questions

1. How could John help Tom with his professional growth in this situation? Should he answer Tom's questions directly?
2. Does Tom have any ethical responsibility to tell anyone about what he saw and heard at the 12-step meeting, or does he have an ethical responsibility not to tell? Does his being in recovery make a difference? Does John have an ethical responsibility in this situation based on his knowledge of the incident? If so, what is it and how should John proceed?
3. Do you think that John's recovery status complicates his supervision of Tom? Why or why not?
4. What suggestions or guidance would you have for Tom? For John?

Response

John R. Culbreth

Tom is at an important juncture in his development as an addictions counselor. Either this incident can help Tom define his role as a professional counselor and as a member of the recovery community or it can create a belief system in Tom that relegates all addiction issues to simple, concrete terms that are not reflective of the real world. John, as Tom's supervisor, has a unique opportunity to help Tom move in a more open and accepting stance as a clinician, a stance that is not mired in rigid or absolute thinking.

As mentioned, a significant danger not stated in this incident is the promotion of a rigid mind-set in Tom toward his clients and their addictive behaviors. Substance abuse counselors with a personal history of addiction recovery have been shown to be (a) more dependent and conventional and less flexible in their viewpoints on addiction (Hoffman & Miner, 1973); (b) more concrete in thinking patterns and more likely to be considered "tough-minded" (Shipko & Stout, 1992); and (c) more rigid in beliefs around the disease model, less flexible in how this translates to treatment goals, and more likely to impose their own recovery and treatment values on clients, thereby minimizing client development and ownership of treatment goals (Moyers & Miller, 1993). Hopefully John will be able to help Tom move away from these concrete thinking processes and more toward an open and accepting approach to how addiction, and specifically this client situation, is viewed and managed. However, in this incident, John could be struggling with all of the same personality characteristics listed above because he is also in recovery. Therefore, John's recovery is as much a part of this incident as Tom's, making this incident all that much more complex and challenging.

It is important for John, at this point, to listen to what Tom is struggling with and support him as he works to reach a clinical decision. As he facilitates Tom's work through this process, John must remember that he is not working as the counselor by proxy, meaning that Tom's work is not John's work. John must remember that his work is with Tom. He cannot drop his work with Tom to "save" the client by being directive with Tom. If he does, then he sets several bad precedents. First, John would be telling Tom that his decision-making skills are not adequate for this type of issue. Second, John would be repeating, in a parallel way, the same process were Tom to report the slip. John learns of a difficult issue, then goes forward with a course of action that is not the best, that of intervening when it may not be warranted. Another potential outcome with this action is that Tom may be much less likely to disclose these types of difficult situations with John in future supervision sessions. This sets a very dangerous stage for John, as he is responsible for Tom's professional behavior. Yet, how can John monitor Tom's professional behavior when Tom is screening that behavior in a self-protective way?

Tom is right to be concerned for his client. However, he must also observe and work within his dual relationships in this situation. Tom is struggling with developing a clear understanding of where his role as a counselor stops and his role as a member in the recovery community begins. This is a clear dual relationship ethical issue. If Tom violates the client's anonymity from the meeting, then he puts into jeopardy his standing as both an AA member and his role as a trustworthy counselor. Right or wrong, it will be viewed as if Tom goes to his meetings, in part, to listen for clients who admit to slips or relapse, and then reports that behavior to the appropriate authorities. Many recovering communities are small, close-knit groups. Word travels fast once this "narc" behavior becomes evident. Tom will no longer be considered safe to talk with for clients or members in the recovery fellowship for fear of shared information being used against them. This is the counselor–client half of the parallel process issue mentioned above.

I think that Tom's concerns and ambivalence about whether to report this slip are legitimate. There is a significant clinical difference between a slip and a relapse. The client's behavior suggests that this is a slip. Treating this as such is warranted. Also, another aspect of this incident is the reality that Tom may not have much contact with the client once he is discharged, which is imminent. Counselors need to understand their limitations and also realize that they cannot control their clients and make them do right. Clients need to own their actions and behaviors, which based on the client having picked up a new desire chip, suggests that this client is doing just that. As mentioned in the beginning, John needs to monitor Tom's clinical decision-making process closely, work with and support Tom's attempts to sort through this difficult clinical issue, and identify areas for future discussion within the supervisory relationship. John can also provide Tom with examples and information about the differences between a relapse and a slip, as well as direct Tom to pertinent research on these topics. If John is uncomfortable with this approach, then maybe he will take the opportunity to learn and adjust his mind set based on his own reading of the research on this topic.

References

Hoffman, H., & Miner, B. B. (1973). Personality of alcoholics who became counselors. *Psychological Reports, 33,* 878.

Moyers, T. B., & Miller, W. R. (1993). Therapists' conceptualizations of alcoholism: Measurement and implications for treatment decisions. *Psychology of Addictive Behaviors, 7,* 238–245.

Shipko, J. S., & Stout, C. E. (1992). A comparison of the personality characteristics between the recovering alcoholic and nonalcoholic counselor. *Alcoholism Treatment Quarterly, 9,* 207–214.

Response

Charles F. Gressard

Tom's professional growth is an important issue in this situation. Tom is in an early stage of counselor development, which is probably consistent with Stoltenberg, McNeill, and Delworth's (1998) Level 1 counselor. In this level, counselors tend to view complex issues from a dichotomous perspective, and they experience anxiety in dealing with difficult clinical decisions. Powell and Brodsky (2004) viewed the Level 1 counselor as highly dependent on others, lacking in self and other awareness, thinking categorically, and being highly motivated and committed to work. Because Tom is probably just beginning to work through some of his dependency and categorical-thinking issues, this situation would be one in which John could help him begin to see issues in a more complex manner and in which he could help Tom begin developing some trust and a sense of autonomy in his approach to ethical dilemmas. Given these counselor development issues, I believe John should provide guidance and support for Tom with his decision making but that he should not respond directly to Tom's questions unless he believes that Tom may be moving in a direction that is not consistent with ethical standards. Instead, I would encourage John to model appropriate ethical decision-making behavior and to encourage Tom to work through an ethical decision-making model. This approach would allow Tom to see that there may be various solutions to ethical dilemmas and to see John working with complex issues in a nondichotomous manner.

I would also encourage John to provide a lot of support during this process. Tom is most likely going to be feeling insecure and threatened in dealing with this potentially troublesome ethical problem. Tom will only be able to grow in this situation to the extent that he feels that John "has his back" with this issue.

The second question hints at the complexity of this ethical and supervision issue and is what makes it so interesting. There are several ethical issues and a couple of legal issues that converge in this situation. One question relates to the fact that this information was shared at an Alcoholics Anonymous (AA) meeting. There are two important implications of the setting in which the information was learned. The first is AA's principle of anonymity, which is an essential principle for AA's effectiveness. The second is Tom's role when he heard the information. Tom was attending the meeting as an AA member, not a counselor. I believe this is an important point and one that John should help clarify with Tom, as it is relevant to the decision. The issue of boundaries also brings up the issue of dual relationships, which Tom should be encouraged to explore. It may not affect the outcome of this decision, however. When viewed from this perspective, it would appear that Tom should not disclose this information.

Another issue is whether the client is a danger to others. It could be argued that by having a slip and then omitting this information at the discharge meeting, the client is showing some strong signs of relapse, which because he is seeing patients as a medical professional could lead to an endangerment of his patients. I would argue at this point, however, that the danger is not imminent, and that there is therefore insufficient reason to break either confidentiality or AA anonymity and notify the licensure board, the homeless clinic where the client volunteers dental services, or anyone else.

There are two possible legal issues. Some states have laws or regulations that require certified or licensed professionals, or those under supervision, to report impaired professionals to the appropriate licensure board. John would have to be familiar with these laws and would have to help Tom explore these laws to see if this is a situation in which they would be required to report. As state requirements vary considerably, their actions would depend on either the existence or the wording of the law or regulation. The second issue would be the federal confidentiality law, known as 42 CFR (Fisher & Harrison, 2004). Assuming that John and Tom's program is covered by 42 CFR, they would have to sort out whether they can report this behavior if they decide that there is imminent danger to others. There is a possibility that a state law might conflict with 42 CFR, in which case I would encourage John and Tom to consult with legal counsel to determine which rules might take precedence in this situation.

Overall, it would appear to me that the best course of action is probably to take no action at this point, with a critical issue being the patient's likelihood of presenting a danger to patients. I think John's obligation is to assist Tom in thinking through this situation and in becoming familiar with the issues, the relevant ethical codes, and the relevant legal issues. I don't think Tom's being in recovery makes any difference in this situation other than his obligation as an AA member.

The main complication of John's recovery status in this critical incident is the degree of recovery. If there are still some unresolved issues in John's recovery process, it might lead to an emotional response on John's part that could cloud his judgment, or it could lead to an overprotective response toward Tom. It would be important for John to be clear about his professional role in this situation. Given his length of time in recovery, his education, and his experience, I would be optimistic that his recovery status would not complicate the situation. Overall, my main suggestion for both supervisor and supervisee is to take advantage of this potentially strong learning opportunity and to take a close look at how their recovery status interacts with their professional behavior.

References

Fisher, G. L., & Harrison, T. C. (2004). *Substance abuse: Information for school counselors, social workers, therapists, and counselors* (3rd ed.). Boston: Allyn & Bacon.

Powell, D. J., & Brodsky, A. (2004). *Clinical supervision in alcohol and drug abuse counseling: Principles, models, methods*. San Francisco: Jossey-Bass.

Stoltenberg, C. D., McNeill, B. W., & Delworth, U. (1998). *IDM supervision: An integrated developmental model for supervising counselors and therapists*. San Francisco: Jossey-Bass.

Chapter 11

Only I Can Save My Client: Boundary Issues for Counselors

David Whittinghill

Topics

- Practitioner limitations
- Countertransference
- Client–counselor boundaries

Background

Marlin is a 37-year-old White male professional counselor working toward state licensure and state certification as a professional addictions counselor. Marlin recently graduated from a mental health counseling program offered by a nearby university and was hired shortly thereafter by an outpatient substance abuse treatment provider. Over the past few months, several of Marlin's clients have exhibited increased depressive behaviors and expressed having suicidal ideations. As a result, Marlin has become excessively fearful his clients will follow through with disclosed suicidal plans and kill themselves. Even though he has demonstrated exemplary clinical knowledge and skills when working with suicidal clients (i.e., accurately assesses severity of client suicidal risk, conducts effective crisis intervention strategies including obtaining no-suicide contracts), Marlin feels solely and excessively responsible for his clients' welfare to the extent that he gives suicidal clients his home address and telephone number.

Marlin's obsession with "saving" his clients may stem from two areas. First, Marlin is in recovery from alcoholism through attending Alcoholics Anonymous and believes his sobriety is contingent on helping others to obtain and maintain sobriety. Second, while growing up, Marlin's father, the local school system superintendent, drank addictively for 20 or more years. His father was held in high esteem by his peers and the public he served, but behind closed doors he drank excessively, screamed insults, and threatened physical violence while drunk. Many times after a drinking episode, his father would experience a great deal of guilt and shame to the point of becoming suicidal and walking around the house late at night holding a loaded pistol to his head. From a young age Marlin took it upon himself to protect his family from his father's alcoholic rages and would spend hours talking his father out of killing himself.

Larry is a 53-year-old White man who sought counseling from Marlin following his arrest and conviction for drunk drinking. Larry began drinking addictively following a separation and divorce from his wife 3 years earlier. His wife left Larry to marry a much younger man. As a result of his drunk driving arrest, his wife has brought and won court cases citing Larry as an unfit parent and she has full custody of their children. Larry is very distraught. He tells Marlin his ex-wife will not allow him to see his children more than 1 day a month. Larry also believes his ex-wife and her new husband have turned his children against him. He has been seeing Marlin for 4 months. Larry attempted suicide 2 years prior to seeing Marlin by overdosing on pain medication and alcohol. Fortunately, a friend stopped by to check on Larry and found him lying unconscious in the kitchen and called for an ambulance and paramedics.

Incident

One particular morning, the clinical director for the agency overhears several clients in the hallway complaining about Marlin not showing up for their weekly group counseling session. The director investigates the allegations of the group members and finds Marlin has indeed telephoned and canceled his appointments for the day. Clerical staff and other counselors also disclose Marlin has established a pattern of calling the office to cancel morning appointments over the past few weeks.

The following day, Marlin comes to work and the director requests a private meeting. Behind closed doors, Marlin divulges he has been providing off-site suicide crisis counseling for his client Larry. Marlin explains that Larry's new wife often telephones after midnight to tell him that Larry is drunk and threatening suicide. The director asks for additional details, and Marlin says he usually can counsel Larry over the phone and, after an hour or so of conversation, is able to obtain a verbal contract not to commit suicide and a commitment for an office visit from his client. Marlin is quick to point out the telephone interventions do not interfere with his ability to come to work the next day. However, when pressed about his repeated absences from work, Marlin reluctantly admits that on several occasions Larry has been extremely agitated and refused to commit to a verbal contract and has fired his gun into the floor to indicate his suicidal intent to his wife and to Marlin on the other end of the phone. On these occasions, Marlin says he has traveled to Larry's house alone and negotiated with him for hours until Larry surrendered the firearm and agreed not to kill himself. Marlin explains the house calls last for many hours and are unusually intense. When he returns home, Marlin says he is emotionally drained and physically exhausted and calls the office staff to cancel morning appointments with clients to catch up on lost sleep.

Questions

1. What are the key supervision issues for Marlin? Are there safety issues to be addressed? How can Marlin's supervisor address the effects of Marlin's family-of-origin issues in how he is handling Larry's treatment?
2. Assume Marlin remains firm in his conviction that he is the only counselor who can prevent Larry from committing suicide. How should the clinical supervisor respond? Is Marlin engaged in any ethical violations?
3. What would be an appropriate supervisory model for working with Marlin? How could a supervisor help Marlin overcome his overly responsible reactions to suicidal clients?

Response

Wendy Charkow Bordeau

After reading the case of Marlin trying so hard to help Larry, I experienced several emotions, including fear for both the counselor and the client, sadness about the connection between Marlin's early life history and Larry's current situation, and anxiety regarding the urgency of the supervision needs. It was immediately obvious to me that Marlin, though well intentioned, was not only failing to help his client but was actually engaging in maleficence, an ethical term denoting "doing harm" to one's client. The maleficence I saw extended beyond Larry and his family to the other clients whose needs were going unmet when Marlin was physically and psychologically unavailable.

The first question posed relates to key supervision and safety issues. I am extremely concerned about counselor and client safety. It is not a far stretch to imagine the lethal damage that could occur while Marlin and Larry are negotiating over Larry's loaded firearm in Larry's home. I also wonder what Marlin does with Larry's firearm once it is surrendered. In addition, I do not believe that Larry's verbal no-suicide commitments made over the telephone in his late-night telephone conversations are to be trusted. To begin with, I am of the professional counselor contingent who disagrees with the use of no-suicide contracts in general. I do not believe that these contracts are clinically or legally valid, especially in that they can provide a sense of false security to the counselor. Rather, I endorse the use of a treatment and safety commitment (see Rudd, Mandrusiak, & Joiner, 2006) with all clients that specifically details what to do in an emergency situation, including but not limited to suicide, with current contact information for several trustworthy and immediately accessible referral sources.

Several immediate legal and ethical issues are also present in this case. First, Marlin is not promoting client welfare in terms of his treatment of Larry and other clients. Further, I question Marlin's professional competence though he has been reported to demonstrate good skills in other cases involving suicidal clients. Competence is not limited to only knowledge and skills; rather, it also entails that the counselor is personally able to cope with the issues presented by the client and intervene effectively. In this case, Marlin appears indisputably impaired. The American Counseling Association's *Code of Ethics* (2005, Standard C.2.g.) says the following about counselor impairment:

> Counselors are alert to the signs of impairment from their own physical, mental, or emotional problems and refrain from offering or providing professional services when such impairment is likely to harm a client or others. They seek assistance for problems that reach the level of professional impairment, and, if necessary, they limit, suspend, or terminate their professional responsibilities until such time it is determined that they may safely resume their work.

It is certainly understandable why Larry presents so many emotionally charged challenges for Marlin. As a supervisor, I would be empathetic to the merging of personal history with client dynamics. However, I would be much more confident about Marlin's abilities as a professional counselor if he would have taken it upon himself to ask for help. How long would this have continued if the clinical director did not happen to hear the other clients' complaints? Additionally, it seems that Marlin is not being honest in supervision and peer consultation regarding his involvement in this case.

A third ethical and legal issue involves professional boundaries. Marlin appears to be descending down the slippery slope, a phenomenon used to explain the downward journey professionals take when relaxing what may appear to be superficial professional norms toward more dangerous behavior. A counselor's giving suicidal clients his or her home address and telephone numbers is poor practice and could lead to harmful, nonprofessional interactions or dual relationships.

I have also been asked to address how Marlin's supervisor could address the family-of-origin issues. I use the Discrimination Model of supervision (Bernard & Goodyear, 2004), in which the supervisor alternates between the roles of counselor, teacher, and consultant to address the counselor's skills, self-awareness, cognitive conceptualization, and professional behaviors. According to this model, I would try to help Marlin identify his personal "hot spots" that are triggered by Larry and other suicidal clients. I would hope to facilitate Marlin's conceptualization of the linkages between the emotions and behaviors triggered by his client and his own personal history and coping mechanisms. Most likely, I would remove Marlin from Larry's case, and possibly other cases involving moderate to high suicide risk, while this supervision work was taking place. A referral for counseling would also be made; although I feel comfortable helping Marlin identify his issues and develop a plan for addressing the convergence of personal and professional material, the therapeutic work that needs to be done is far too complex and personal to be conducted only in a professional supervisory relationship. I feel a strong sense of responsibility to the counseling profession and client safety, particularly as Marlin is currently moving toward licensure and the ability to practice independently. Also, it is not fair for Marlin to be expected to completely "spill his guts" to a person who holds administrative and supervisory power over him. Therefore, I would need to know that he is addressing his problem areas using both close supervision and personal counseling. I would also want documentation of such and would only continue supervising Marlin if he would consent for his counselor to share Marlin's schedule and general progress in counseling.

Finally, how would I respond to Marlin's conviction that he is the only counselor who can prevent Larry from committing suicide? Issues related to counselor sense of power and control jump out at me. I would use cognitive–behavioral techniques, such as Socratic questioning and the downward arrow (see Beck, 1995), to question how Marlin has come to this belief, its validity, and its potential consequences. Despite all the problems discussed throughout, it does appear that Larry trusts Marlin and that they have established a relationship. I would hope that Marlin would realize the paradox that his efforts to control Larry and keep him safe are in fact leading to the opposite result. Perhaps Marlin could meet with Larry in the presence of a supervisor or trusted colleague to discuss his intentions to help but his inability to do so. It is even possible that Marlin's admission of his infallibility and humanity, along with the desire and commitment to work out his difficulties, might be therapeutic to a depressed and suicidal client.

References

American Counseling Association. (2005). *ACA code of ethics.* Alexandria, VA: Author.

Beck, J. S. (1995). *Cognitive therapy: Basics and beyond.* New York: Guilford Press.

Bernard, J. M., & Goodyear, R. K. (2004). *Fundamentals of clinical supervision* (3rd ed.). Needham Heights, MA: Allyn & Bacon.

Rudd, D. M., Mandrusiak, M., & Joiner, T. E. Jr. (2006). The case against no-suicide contracts: The commitment-to-treatment statement as a practice alternative. *Journal of Clinical Psychology, 62,* 243–251.

Response

Tyra Turner Whittaker
and Stephanie L. Lusk

The primary issues for supervision in this incident are the counselor's unresolved personal issues and a failure to adhere to boundaries within the counselor–client relationship. Marlin, like many new counseling graduates, had assumed the role of "savior" in the counselor–client relationship. Novice counselors often struggle with the need to rescue clients. However, the counselor's need to rescue his client stems from unresolved issues in his personal life. Marlin is obviously experiencing issues with countertransference. Unresolved issues with his father are causing him to spend an inordinate amount of time with the client, especially after business hours.

The importance of maintaining boundaries should be addressed in supervision. Not only is the counselor spending time with the client after hours but he has also released personal contact information to the client that may compromise his safety. The counselor appears to be unaware that he is endangering himself when he visits the client alone and without accountability. The term *accountability* is used here to address the fact that no one knows that the counselor is visiting the client in the middle of the night. The client is often armed and inebriated, which can lead to an unpredictable and potentially deadly outcome.

The final issue to address in supervision is the counselor's continued cancellation of appointments with other clients. The counselor is operating unprofessionally and is compromising the therapeutic process by canceling appointments and not being "present" during other sessions. In addition to being unprofessional, this behavior constitutes an ethical violation on the part of Marlin toward all of his clients and places the agency in jeopardy.

The supervisor plays an instrumental role in helping the counselor address the effects of his family history on his professional relationship with the client. The supervisor could address such issues with him by confronting the potential countertransference and the concept of being a wounded healer (Trusty, Ng, & Watts, 2005). The supervisor can also point out that the counselor feels that his sobriety is contingent on rescuing Larry, which stems from unresolved childhood issues with his father. The supervisor can further assist Marlin in seeing the connection between spending hours talking his father out of killing himself and his need to operate in the same manner with his client. Finally, the supervisor could also address the universal limitations of all counselors in that not every client will be responsive to treatment no matter what intervention is used. Although he has demonstrated exemplary knowledge and skills with suicidal clients, he may not be successful with every client.

Assuming that the counselor remains firm in his conviction that he alone can prevent the client from committing suicide, he is then in violation of the *ACA Code of Ethics* (American Counseling Association, 2005). Standard C.2.g. of the *Code* refers to professional impairment and specifically states that counselors should be cognizant of physical, mental, or emotional issues that could cause harm to clients. When such issues are recognized, the counselor should discontinue providing services to clients until it is safe for them to continue (ACA, 2005). Standard A.4.a. also speaks to avoiding harm to clients. The counselor is also compromising his ability to adequately serve all of his clients by being exhausted at work and failing to provide his clients with adequate notice prior to canceling appointments. Continual rescheduling and cancellation of services is not only unprofessional but also interferes with the therapeutic relationship.

According to the *ACA Code of Ethics* (ACA, 2005, Standard F.1.a.), the primary responsibility of the supervisor is to monitor the progress, performance, and professional development of the counselor-in-training as well as the welfare of the clients being served. The supervisor in this case should recognize the limitations of the counselor's performance and address them in supervision. The supervisor should also require the counselor to contact his agency's clinical director to transfer Larry, and possibly other suicidal clients, from his caseload. If the counselor fails to do so, the supervisor has an ethical responsibility to report the counselor to the ACA ethics committee and the state licensure board to prevent imminent harm to clients.

We believe that using the Discrimination Model of supervision would be appropriate in this incident. The supervisor could address Marlin's developmental and affective needs while also fluctuating between the roles of teacher, counselor, and consultant as Marlin addresses his affective issues (Bernard & Goodyear, 1992). In the role of counselor, the supervisor can facilitate Marlin's self-growth by assisting him in exploring and processing his thoughts and feelings during sessions with suicidal clients and how his unresolved childhood issues are affecting his counseling (Pearson, 2006). The supervisor can also assist the counselor in seeing the connection between his sobriety, his father, and his client, all dealing with issues of alcoholism. Furthermore, the supervisor may direct the counselor to seek personal counseling in addition to supervision and his Alcoholics Anonymous meetings. This approach will, it is hoped, facilitate the counselor's professional and personal development.

References

American Counseling Association. (2005). *ACA code of ethics.* Alexandria, VA: Author.

Bernard, J. M., & Goodyear, R. K. (1992). *Fundamentals of clinical supervision.* Boston: Allyn & Bacon.

Pearson, Q. M. (2006). Psychotherapy-driven supervision: Integrating counseling theories into role-based supervision. *Journal of Mental Health Counseling, 2,* 241–252.

Trusty, J., Ng, K. M., & Watts, R. E. (2005). Model of effects of adult attachment on emotional empathy of counseling students. *Journal of Counseling & Development, 83,* 66–77.

Part II

Community Counseling

Chapter 12

Duty to Warn: Who Ya Gonna Call?

Toni Roth Sullivan

Topics

- Duty to warn
- Breach of confidentiality

Background

Although law enforcement professionals are members of one of the most stressful occupations, they are often reluctant to seek mental health treatment (Anderson, 2002). This incident involves a mental health counselor, Jason, who has been receiving urgent telephone calls from Helen, a police officer's wife. Helen is a 38-year-old woman, married for 13 years to the officer. They have two elementary school–age children in the home. Helen has been calling on a daily basis for a week to report that her husband has been drinking heavily and is "abusive."

Incident

Jason has encouraged the caller to come into the clinic to meet face to face, but she has refused. Instead, the calls have continued and have escalated in urgency. Helen has offered very little information, but Jason has a first name and a place of employment. He has conducted a risk assessment each time Helen has called and has determined that there is no imminent danger to self or others. The abuse has been verbal, and their marital issues have been present for several years.

This week, however, Helen described her fears in detail. She admitted to having an affair with a coworker and reported that her husband confronted this man and threatened him with his service revolver. Jason discussed safety concerns, available options, and the importance of having a plan to protect herself and her children.

At this point, Jason advised Helen to seek safety. She immediately called back to say that she wants her friend (the coworker with whom she had the affair) to help her move things from the home. Jason tells her he will return her call and consults with me and the agency's clinical team to determine the best course of action.

Discussion

We are all feeling anxious about a potentially volatile situation. Children are involved, as well as a man with a history of threatening and angry behavior, a possible substance abuse problem, and a weapon. In addition, Helen is putting others in her workplace at risk for violence.

After consultation with a supervisor, Jason contacts Helen to reiterate the seriousness and dangers associated with family violence and reviews the safety concerns and escape plans with her. Helen's choices seem likely to fuel her husband's rage and his need for control. She seems both emotionally and economically dependent on her husband, yet is not willing to continue in the marriage or give up her other relationship. Instead, she has told her husband that she is moving out of the family home with the children and will not tell him where they will go.

In supervision, there is additional discussion about the counselor's own personal biases and values concerning Helen's choices. The counselor was unsuccessful in convincing the woman to follow her safety plan and to keep the situation from escalating. The decision is made to notify the security division at the woman's workplace of the potential for violence.

Questions

1. What are your reactions related to the case? Who is the client? Whose needs are being met? Did the danger presented reach the threshold of "imminent"? Was it enough to require breaching confidentiality? Are there special concerns in this case because the husband is in law enforcement? What kind of follow-up services can, or should, be provided? What? How? With whom?
2. Did transferential issues affect the decision making in some way? If so, how might the supervisor have responded to the counselor about these issues?
3. What is the burden of responsibility on the supervisor as contrasted with that of the counselor to take more directive steps in facilitating the woman's safety?
4. As a supervisor, when designing policies and standards for clinical care, how might you construct or recommend customary and standard minimum policies related to potential life-threatening situations and client care? What established resources and advocacy statements, for example, might be helpful to clinical supervisors and their agencies in designing emergency response care standards?

Reference

Anderson, B. J. (2002). Confidentiality in counseling: What police officers need to know. In *Gift from within*. Retrieved February 6, 2007, from http://www.giftfromwithin.org/html/confide.html

Response

Nancy G. Calley

This incident illustrates the many complexities involved in clinical work, drawing out issues related to legal mandates and the various dimensions related to interpretation of such mandates, ethical requirements, business relationships formed by mental health clinics, and the roles of the clinician and the clinical supervisor. Central to this incident is the issue of duty to warn, which constitutes one of the most challenging issues faced by mental health clinicians because it places the responsibility of taking action to protect an individual on the clinician and requires him or her to breach client confidentiality in such incidences.

The client in this case is the woman that has contacted the clinic for help. Having formed a therapeutic relationship with the woman, the clinician's actions are governed by the state and federal laws related to clinician–client relationships as well as to the ethical standards of the clinician's field. As a result of the alleged threats of physical harm by the client's husband, the clinician must determine if the information provided requires action. For guidance in making this determination, the clinician must examine the law related to duty to warn.

Broadly, duty to warn deals with the duty of mental health practitioners to use reasonable care to protect third parties against dangers posed by clients. The case of *Tarasoff v. Board of Regents of the University of California* (1976) established this legal precedent. Briefly, according to the Tarasoff case, a clinician has a legal duty to warn when there is (a) an immediate intent, (b) to inflict serious harm, (c) with the apparent ability to complete the intended act, (d) against an identifiable victim.

This case illustrates an interesting dimension of the concept of duty to warn as it focuses on disclosure about allegations of a third party's (the client's husband) potential harm to another third party (the client's coworker) as well as potential harm to the client, rather than the more straightforward scenario by which the legal precedent originated: disclosure by a client of potential harm to a third person. Following a liberal interpretation of duty to warn, the clinician has an obligation to make the coworker aware of the potential threat and to report the suspicion of potential harm of the client and the client's coworker to the local law enforcement agency.

Based on the information provided to the clinician, the husband had verbally threatened the client's coworker with his revolver. At this point in the incident, the case could be viewed as having met the criteria of imminent danger, as the husband has already made a verbal threat and has access to and has demonstrated a plan to use a revolver (by including it in the verbal threat). This type of information requires the clinician to breach confidentiality for the sake of the potential protection of others. If the identity of the coworker is not known, notifying the security team at the coworker's place of employment should demonstrate reasonable effort on the part of the clinician to fulfill this part of the legal mandate. However, if the identity of the coworker is known, notification to someone other than the intended victim (unless the intended victim is a minor or a vulnerable adult, in which case notification to the parent or legal guardian would be considered sufficient) may not prove sufficient. In addition to directly warning the client's coworker of the threat, the clinician must also make contact with the local law enforcement to report suspicion of potential harm to the client and the client's coworker. Simply because the clinic has a business relationship with local law enforcement does not exempt the clinician or clinical staff from compliance with state and federal laws.

However, to ensure that the police report is filed with someone other than a peer of the client's husband, the clinician should make a verbal report directly to a law enforcement supervisor followed by a written statement filed with the local police department as well as with the central administration. Such steps may ensure appropriate reporting and documentation to individuals in law enforcement with oversight responsibilities. Following the reporting of this incident, it is recommended that the clinic and the local law enforcement agency participate in a debriefing to review the reporting process and to determine if any alternate steps should have been taken.

Depending on the outcomes of the debriefing, new protocols may be established to guide the clinic in the future when reporting to local law enforcement (i.e., concurrent reporting to additional district). Follow-up services should be provided to the client by the clinician to continue therapeutic support, as she is the identified recipient of services. The client is the only individual with whom an identified therapeutic contract has been initiated. Follow-up services should include a continued focus on the client's ability to enact her safety plan. Additionally, the terms of the therapeutic relationship must be reviewed to articulate the inherent expectations and limitations. Such a discussion must include termination planning and a referral to another clinician if the client continues to be unwilling to implement the treatment plan despite disclosures that she or others are potentially unsafe as a result.

It does not appear that transferential issues affected the decision making in this case; however, whenever issues of protection arise, clinical supervisors must explore the possibility of transference to ensure that these are not affecting the clinician's perspective. Broadly, the clinical supervisor is charged with ensuring that supervisees provide effective and accountable counseling services that comply with ethical and legal standards. As a result, clinical supervisors assume legal liability for supervisees and thus may be held legally responsible for the inactions. With regard to duty to warn, the clinical supervisor has the legal obligation to ensure that when justification for fulfillment of the requirement exists, it is carried out. Therefore, if the clinician does not fulfill this responsibility, the clinical supervisor is required to do so.

Effective clinical supervision practice begins with the development of comprehensive protocols and policies that make up the administrative and operations aspects of the clinical practice. With respect to incidents related to emergency procedures, a specific policy identifying guidelines is a critical component to be included in the policy handbook. In constructing such a policy, state and federal law must be reviewed and reflected in the policy as well as information pertaining to the intersection of ethical codes. The policy should provide clear guidelines regarding the steps that must be taken upon the emergence of a critical issue. This should minimally include information regarding notification and methods of notification, documentation, consultation with a supervisor, and a guiding framework for decision making.

Additionally, telephone numbers of emergency contacts should be posted throughout the clinic, including local authorities, domestic violence organizations, psychiatric care facilities, and other such community resources. Clinical supervisors should partner with local and federal organizations dedicated to domestic violence as well as the professional associations of mental health practitioners for assistance in constructing emergency procedures.

Clinicians are charged with an immense burden to promote client welfare and to protect individuals from harm, and clinical supervisors are ethically and legally accountable for the abilities of their supervisees to fulfill these responsibilities. Incidents in which issues related to duty to warn exist serve to remind us of the breadth of such responsibilities.

Reference

Tarasoff v. Board of Regents of the University of California, 551 P. 2d 334 (Cal. 1976).

Response

Marjorie Baker

Domestic violence is a complex and multifaceted problem in all cultures, classes, and income groups. Women are at a significantly greater risk of intimate partner violence than men. Findings from the U.S. Department of Justice's National Violence Against Women Survey indicate that approximately 4.8 million American women are physically assaulted by an intimate partner each year (Tjaden & Thoennes, 2000). Domestic violence includes a wide range of abusive behaviors chosen by the perpetrator to achieve absolute control over all aspects of a victim's life. Not all domestic abusive behaviors are considered a crime, but any form of abuse has detrimental effects on victims and is unacceptable.

Each domestic violence case presents unique challenges that require individual responses specific to the dynamics of that particular situation. Effective solutions to domestic violence situations include a focus on enhancing the safety of victims and their children, holding perpetrators accountable for their abusive actions, and empowering victims to reestablish their lives without violence. We must address the issues of domestic violence in an efficient, effective, and safe manner. It is essential that we also remember the safety of the silent victims, the children, in these incidents. Any response to domestic violence should include an understanding of the cycle of violence, the controlling behaviors of perpetrators, and available resources for the family. Victims must be offered options, education, and information, and couples treatment should never be an initial recommendation in abusive situations. Victims are the experts of their own situation and must be treated with respect and equality when they reach out to the community for support and assistance.

This domestic violence case presents its own share of challenges in the counselor's attempts to assist this caller. Obviously, Helen was in a critical period of her life and developed courage to confide in the counselor on several occasions. She is not a client of this mental health center, but she is developing trust in Jason with the likely hopes that her information will be treated with confidence to protect her safety and well-being. The counselor's support and willingness to listen contributed to this victim's continued contact and self-disclosure.

Helen's danger level is high because of her husband's history of substance abuse, his access to a weapon, and his previous threats. She should be strongly encouraged to inform her employer of the situation, and if Jason establishes a duty to warn, the intended victim (the coworker) must be informed of this immediately. Helen was provided with a safety plan, which is an excellent first step.

Victims need for others to connect to them in a supportive manner. This can be done by focusing on the victim's ways of sharing her story and her strategies of ending the violence in her life. We must listen to the victim and be empathetic to her way of responding to her situation. She, better than anyone else, knows the intricate details of her situation. Also, counselors must not allow their transferential issues to take precedence over victim safety. Victims sometime make poor choices in their efforts to survive, but safety should never be compromised.

Additionally, it is vital for the supervisor to support and consult with the counselor and other experts in responding to this case. The supervisor should also review the contract with the law enforcement agency and the mental health center's policies that focus on responding to reports made about law enforcement officers who may or may not be receiving services at this mental health center. The law enforcement agency and the mental health center should continue to review and update their policies on issues of this nature, placing priority on victim safety.

Finally, the community must establish a coordinated community response involving various professionals, victims, and community members. It is imperative that professionals develop interrelationships between health, legal, and social service sectors, particularly local domestic violence programs. Our society must not dismiss or minimize this social problem, and victim safety must be the first priority in responding to families. We must offer a coordinated response that includes (a) careful assessment of safety and risk level, (b) proper intervention for children involved, and (c) emotional support and effective re-sources. We all must work to end this atrocity and protect the community.

Reference

Tjaden, P., & Thoennes, N. (2000). *Extent, nature, and consequences of intimate partner violence.* Washington, DC: U.S. Department of Justice, National Institute of Justice. (Available at http://www.ncjrs.gov/pdffiles1/nij/181867 .pdf)

Chapter 13

Methodological Approach in a Multicultural Setting: We're Not in Kansas Anymore

Krista Malott

Topics

- Duty to protect
- Selection of method of therapy
- Counseling in a multicultural context

Background

At the time of this incident, I was supervising counselors-in-training at a community clinic in an urban area in a Central American country, where I was charged with monitoring counseling practices from the tradition and perspective of family therapy. Rita and Elsa, the counselors, worked together as family therapists at the clinic. As their supervisor, I assisted in planning sessions and debriefed with them following observations of sessions. We began immediately with a challenging case involving allegations of domestic violence between a mother and her adolescent son. Related to this case were issues of client and supervisee safety, exacerbated by the isolated nature of the setting. As a supervisor from the United States, I struggled to comprehend the cultural manifestation of the topic. I had to decide if continued provision of counseling services would intensify the abuse and create a dangerous situation for the clients and supervisees, knowing that virtually no other services existed for clientele of average income.

Incident

Rita and Elsa's first clients, a son and his mother, presented with what appeared to be a feasible goal: to improve their communication. The first session went smoothly, or so we believed. However, shortly after, we received a phone call from the mother. She stated she had not been fully honest in the session. She had feared her son's reaction to her honesty.

The dramatic tone of her confession was dismissed by Elsa and Rita as a typical Latina overreaction. Too quickly, I accepted this explanation, with my own training in multiculturalism seemingly confirming this conclusion. I was also hesitant to investigate via telephone because of the family therapy belief that individuals must share information within the family context. Side consultations with the counselor could potentially fragment the family and create unproductive alignments.

Underestimating the extent of the mother's fear, we endeavored to address the phenomenon in the subsequent session. The mother was reticent in her son's presence. Following the session, she called twice. Her tone of urgency had increased from the initial call. We took notice and investigated in the next session, splitting up the counselors in order to speak privately with the mother. It was then that we learned that the son had been verbally abusive with his mother on a regular basis. Recently, he had also stated threats of physical violence.

Discussion

I was mortified to realize the vulnerable position in which we had placed the mother. Yet I was initially immobilized because of lack of resources available to the clients. Referral services in their country were nonexistent, and the mother had no family she could turn to for support. However, as the only trained supervisor of family therapy in the country—available for a few weeks only—I believed it was imperative that my supervisees continued as family therapists, rather than splitting the clients and working with them individually. The challenge was ensuring the safety of both the mother and my supervisees. The clients' isolation from environmental supports and their intense codependent relationship led me to believe that continued work with the two together might potentially exacerbate the son's abuse (Pagani, Larocque, Vitaro, & Tremblay, 2003).

Ultimately, we decided to continue, with a change in our format. We started and ended each session with the clients together as a family but worked with each on a principally individual basis. The supervisees interspersed family therapy with victim–perpetrator interventions. Even that reduced amount of time together proved anxiety provoking for the mother, me, and supervisees. We feared an increase of abuse following the sessions. The supervisees feared provoking the son within the sessions.

However, after six sessions, we agreed that progress had been made. The mother spoke in a more empowered manner. Both mother and son were communicating more honestly while demonstrating improved parent–child and adult–adult roles. They expressed a desire to return following the holidays. However, because of the risks and ensuing stress involved, we decided not to work in a family format with the two again.

Questions

1. Who was most vulnerable in this scenario and why?
2. What were the risks in choosing to continue working with the family as a unit, compared with the risks of working individually? What are the possible liabilities of either strategy?

3. Beliefs or assumptions concerning Latin culture prohibited me from initially recognizing a potentially threatening situation. What are ways to guard against such cultural bias in future cross-cultural work?
4. I recognize that I was responding to the needs of my supervisees (to experience live supervision with actual clients) as well as those of the clients in deciding to continue work with the family. As supervisors, how do we decide when one supersedes the other?
5. Although geographically and culturally isolated, with whom could I have consulted or what resources could I have used in an effort to augment support in addressing this situation?
6. What other thoughts or suggestions might you have related to this scenario?

Reference

Pagani, L., Larocque, D., Vitaro, F., & Tremblay, R. E. (2003). Verbal and physical abuse toward mothers: The role of family configuration, environment, and coping strategies. *Journal of Youth and Adolescence, 32*, 215–222.

Response

Consuelo Viteri

The most vulnerable person in this scenario is the mother. Many victims of abuse look for services for the perpetrator or family. The mother's call after the first visit reflected her discomfort. Her urgent tone indicated that she felt vulnerable and perhaps feared that the son had successfully manipulated the therapists to think that she may have overreacted. This is not unique to Latin culture. Most victims of abuse call because they fear therapists cannot see the whole picture. The mother may not have known how to express her concerns. Instead of looking for "typical" Latin cultural characteristics, it is important to understand that culturally an adult or even adolescent male assumes the position of head of household if another male figure is absent. This would be more reflective of the multicultural context that was missed. It is likely that when the mother got home, she was blamed and perhaps intimidated by her son to follow his lead in sessions. The mother continued to be at high risk because the perpetrator may have manipulated the information divulged in the session and used it against her at home. Typically the victim becomes afraid of not being believed. The perpetrator usually agrees to continue and commonly insists on family sessions rather than working on issues separately.

Continuing to work as a family in which one person verbalized discomfort is a clear liability because the therapists and abuser are victimizing the mother in each session. The mother asked for help but was put into an uncomfortable situation. This would increase her feelings of helplessness and hopelessness. But a victim will often defer to the experts. Individual assessments (psychosocial histories done separately) may have helped the therapists gain a clearer understanding of each person's perspective on the reason for therapy. Most likely, the therapists might have been able to identify the red flags of issues of power and control such as minimization, denial, and blame. Also, the therapists would have been able to identify separate goals for each client. In my experience, communication problems are often identified quickly by assessing whether the communication style of individual clients is passive, passive-aggressive, or aggressive. Individual work may have helped the mother, if only by validating her victim position in a domestic violence dynamic.

Although we often make broad generalizations about a given group or culture, we must acknowledge the limits of such "norms" as may be taught in classes or texts. To some degree, these teachings about ethnicities may be true, but the counselor should strive to understand each individual, family, or community with a respect for its cultural uniqueness. I assume that the therapists were also Hispanic and the best resource that the supervisor had at hand. Although the incident portrays the mother's presentation as "Latina overreaction," one may think of their feelings as anxious or fearful. As a supervisor, listening to the therapists' concerns might have been a way to understand their own issues or their knowledge about domestic violence (victim–perpetrator dynamics). Supervision designed to understand the parallel process, transference, or their reactions to the mother may have been important. Most victims present as desperate, and at times the therapist will doubt the reliability of the information the victim was trying to convey. The therapists' individual histories and personal reactions to the mother may have opened the door for the supervisor to explore their views on traditional cultural roles versus their intuition that the mother was in danger.

This scenario is an excellent teaching case to understand why family therapy is sometimes contraindicated in cases of domestic abuse. The supervisees' needs in this case, in my opinion, were to understand how not to further victimize a victim in family sessions. The supervisees may have an opportunity to recognize their limitations and be directed to educational training in identifying issues of power and control in relationships. In domestic violence one person is able to keep another in a submissive position. One therapist could work individually to validate and support the mother as she developed an understanding that her son's blame and threats were not her fault and that the responsibility of change fell on her son. The other therapist could focus on helping the son change his communication style with assertiveness training and time-out strategies. The son would be guided to talk about himself only, challenging him to take responsibility for his thoughts, feelings, and behavior. He could also learn about the effect of his verbal abuse toward victims. If the clients were seen together, a clear limit could be established to prevent either one of them from naming, complaining about, or blaming the other, hence avoiding revictimization. The abuser's target is the mother, and danger to outsiders is minimal.

The supervisor responded to the therapists' anxiety. By helping them to process their feelings, she may have helped them understand their limitations and perhaps even encouraged them to create separate psychoeducational groups in their country to respond to victim and perpetrator needs separately.

In summary, the client, as a primary resource, is the best supplier for understanding both the nature of his or her problems and cultural norms. Additionally, counselors and supervisors must have specific training related to domestic violence. To fail to do so might put clients at greater risk. A counselor should assess training resources based on accreditation and reputable status in the field. If one has access to the Internet, there are many additional reputable Web sites and books that are considered staples of the specialization within domestic violence counseling. Many of these sources have been translated into Spanish.

Response
Solange Ribeiro

In my opinion, the mother was most vulnerable, both emotionally and physically. Having found the courage to express her fear in private to the counselors indicates that she had developed at least some trust in the counselors and in the counseling process. She was then betrayed by having her fear discounted as overreaction and brought up for discussion in a conjoint session, which increased the potential for verbal and physical abuse by her son.

The reason why most family therapists refuse to work conjointly with victim and perpetrator is anchored in the do-no-harm principle. In this case, by choosing to ignore the client's concern for her own safety and to continue to work with the family as a unit, the counselors significantly increased the potential for harm. Risks that come to mind instantly include

- To the mother: risk of becoming a victim of physical abuse or of increased verbal abuse, risk of further isolation as a result of loss of trust in the counselors and the counseling process, and risk of escalation of victimization as isolation increases;
- To the son: risk of becoming a perpetrator of domestic violence, which might be avoided if tendencies were identified early and engagement in individual counseling and a domestic violence program (if available) started immediately, and risk of strengthening self-defeating private logic that will likely affect all his future close relationships with women;
- To the family: increased risk of fragmentation;
- To the supervisees: risk of finding themselves responsible for triggering or escalating domestic violence and risk of becoming careless in the investigation of any given situation as a result of poor supervision;
- To the supervisor: risk of heightened liability under the principle of respondent superior, scope of competence issues, and potential loss of credibility or other worse sanctions.

The possible liabilities of either seeing the clients as a family unit or seeing them individually would depend on the laws and the licensing rules in this Central American country. Independent of legal and professional liability, however, the failure to abide by the do-no-harm principle can always place a counselor in a position of ethical liability.

Generalized assumptions about any culture are most often likely to be simplistic and inaccurate when applied to any given client. Global, national, and local cultural beliefs and traditions tend to be only one of the components influencing a family's culture. Not all Latinos have the same cultural origins, religious beliefs, educational backgrounds, family traditions, or life experiences. Within each family, each individual has his or her own private logic. Therefore, textbook information about any culture should be used only as general guidelines to avoid obvious blunders when first meeting a client and as a starting point for a counselor's initial hypothesis, which must then be adjusted as more detailed information about clients is obtained. The client is the expert on his or her culture, and careful interviewing is the best strategy for obtaining accurate cultural information.

In my view, the client's needs always supersede those of the counselor (in this case, the supervisees), unless there are concerns about the counselor's safety while doing the work. In this case, counselor safety does not appear to be at stake, as there are two counselors involved, and the work is being done at the clinic, presumably with other staff and resources. In addition, by focusing on the supervisees' need for experience in family therapy, the supervisor may have overlooked the fact that a prerequisite for being a good family therapist is being a good therapist, which comprises the use of all core conditions of the therapeutic relationship.

The clinic, in an urban center, presumably with access to university and other resources, is not in a small village in the middle of the jungle. Moreover, the counseling center is part of a large community, near a large university, and the supervisor mentions that "virtually no other services existed for clientele of average income." This indicates the presence of other mental health professionals in the area. Regardless of the family's socioeconomic situation, geographical setting, nationality, or cultural setting, domestic violence is still a dangerous social ill, and consultation with other professionals in the area would have been a valuable tool in the decision-making process.

This is a good scenario on which to base further discussion of whom the focus of a supervisor's attention should be—the client or the supervisee. In this case, the supervisor's concern that the supervisees might not gain enough experience in family counseling in the short time available if family counseling were to be discontinued in favor of individual counseling resulted in a decision that increased the risk of harm to the client. Furthermore, the supervisor's concern for the supervisees' interests—coupled with rigid cultural assumptions—appears to have prevented the supervisor from using the opportunity to challenge the supervisee's dismissal of the mother's fear as "Latina overreaction" and to focus supervision on the counselor–client relationship and on case conceptualization. Ideas might include but are not limited to professional consultation with other specialists, even if they were not of a family therapy tradition (e.g., social work, sociology, law enforcement, government social service agencies). Additionally, research via books, professional associations' legal support, and Internet resources would be useful.

Chapter 14

Competence, Clinical Oversight, and Clarification of Roles: Whose Job Is It, Anyway?

Karen Eriksen

Topics

- Competence and clinical oversight
- Role and responsibilities of outside consultants regarding supervisees
- Clarification between supervisor, agency, and university

Background

Lucinda, a 45-year-old private practitioner, licensed as a professional counselor and marriage and family therapist, counsels clients individually, as couples, as families, and in groups. She uses MaryAnn Walters's competency-based contextual therapy, for which she has received advanced training. She has practiced for 20 years and is considered a master therapist, and thus is pursued as a supervisor. She is well known in her locale for her success with difficult families.

James, in his first semester of field work, works in a nonprofit agency that counsels low-income children and their families. The internship meets part of the requirements for his master's degree in counseling at a local university. His position requires counseling individuals, couples, families, and groups. His supervision at the agency (as it was initially set up) meets state requirements, that is, 1 hour per week of individual supervision and 2 hours per week of group supervision with no more than eight interns in a supervision group and each supervisor providing individual supervision for no more than three interns. James wishes to attend a supervision group that Lucinda is running out of her private practice in the hope that he will receive more, and perhaps better, supervision than he is receiving at his agency. James worked for 2 years following his bachelor's degree at a crisis hotline; is the president of the Connection, the student association for the counseling students at the university; and receives top grades at the university. He is 28 years old.

During the informed consent process, Lucinda informs James that she will not be legally responsible for his clients because she is not his site supervisor; therefore, her group would officially be consultation for him. This means that his supervisors would have the final word on any client issues. Lucinda discusses the boundaries between herself and his other supervisors. He understands these and agrees with them. He indicates his wish to learn more about Lucinda's particular school of family therapy and about how to apply the theory to the clients he is seeing; he feels he is unlikely to receive such information at his site or his university, which operate from a different theoretical orientation. Lucinda agrees to admit him to the supervision group. They sign her usual consents related to fees, schedule, cancellations, responsibilities for clients, and what to do in ethically challenging or dangerous situations.

However, Lucinda also asks for the phone numbers of his university and site supervisors and asks for permission to speak with them to clarify boundaries and responsibilities. Initially he is a bit reluctant because he does not want his site supervisor to feel insulted by his reaching beyond what she is offering him. Lucinda suggests that because ongoing professional development is expected of counselors, and because her group will not be supervision per se for him, she could propose their experience as a further learning and growth opportunity for him. He agrees to this.

Lucinda contacts both supervisors, explains that James is pursuing greater knowledge and understanding of competency-based contextual family therapy, and, if the supervisors agree, will be participating in her consultation group. She indicates her work with him will only be consultation, not supervision, and that in any conflict between her consultation and the supervision, the supervisors would have the final word because they are legally responsible for the clients and most aware of the specifics of the site and client needs. She also requests to consult with them if she has any concerns about what James relays during the groups. Both the site and university supervisors respond positively, adding that James is lucky to have a place in one of Lucinda's groups, as they know her reputation. They also voice relief to have another professional who they can trust helping them out, as the demands of the agency and university are often overwhelming.

Incident

During James's initial meetings with the supervision group, Lucinda discovers that the site has only one licensed supervisor, Gerry, with whom Lucinda had previously spoken. Eight interns from various universities work at the agency's three sites, and these interns provide all of the agency's counseling services. The supervisor is located and conducts supervision at the main site, 1 hour from James's rural site. James is the sole mental health provider at his site and works afternoons and evenings. The part-time receptionist at his site is not physically present during all of the hours he is counseling there. When Lucinda asks James during the 2nd week of the semester how many clients he is seeing, he tells her nine plus a group of eight women with domestic violence issues.

In initial discussions, Lucinda voices concerns about the lack of an on-site supervisor (to which he responds, "She is always available by cell phone") or the presence at his site of any other licensed or unlicensed mental health providers. She expresses fears for his safety at a rural location where the violent domestic partners of his group clients live. Lucinda also expresses concern about the number of interns this site supervisor is supervising, which could mean legal responsibility for upwards of 80 clients or families if each intern sees 10 clients. Finally, Lucinda worries about the number of clients referred to James at the beginning of his field work; she believes two or three clients would be more reasonable. When she gives voice to her concerns, James becomes defensive, indicating that he can handle it. He also tells her that this is a unique opportunity for him because unlike many of the other sites, this one is near his home. He worries that his internship situation will get "messed up." He feels pressured to finish his degree on time because he is about to have his third child and is bringing in less than adequate income while doing his internship. Of course, he isn't required to come to Lucinda's supervision group, and so could dismiss her concerns by terminating with the group. However, regardless of his available choices, she worries about his abilities this early to assess his capacities, to know when he is over his head, to be put in a position of so much responsibility when he is so green, and to navigate among the competing messages from Lucinda, the university, and on-site supervisors (who apparently have decided that this set-up is okay). Lucinda tells James that she will need to consult with his supervisors.

When Lucinda contacts the site supervisor, Gerry, she is quite sympathetic to Lucinda's concerns. She shares these concerns because she knows the site is out of compliance with state supervision requirements for interns. She informs Lucinda that the agency recently lost a large grant, and as a result had to lay off all of its paid and licensed professionals. The agency still has the same large number of clients in need, but they have to be seen by interns or not at all. She expresses anxiety about the interns, about the clients, about her job, and about what the owners of the agency are going to do to rectify the problems. In a second phone call, she sounds relieved that the owners have decided to pay licensed people hourly for their presence at the distant sites, which will assist her on a number of different levels.

Lucinda also contacts the university supervisor, who is shocked at her news, as this site has been approved for years by the university and had previously met all of the university's rather stringent requirements, as well as the state's Board of Behavioral Science training requirements. She clearly did not know that this problematic situation existed and indicates that she will "get right on it."

As a result of the supervisors' responses, Lucinda assumes that the problematic situation will be rectified soon. James does indicate that he has reduced his client load to five clients and a group, although he feels really torn because of the very needy clients who will now not receive counseling. Four months later, Lucinda discovers from James that he is still alone at his site with no licensed professional, and that aside from reduced numbers of clients, the same circumstances still exist. Furthermore, his site supervisor has not been contacted by the university. When Lucinda again expresses concern, James indicates that he has things under control, that he is doing fine, that he feels no undue stress, and that his clients are all getting better. He believes there is nothing to be worried about.

Discussion

This case contains elements that are related to working contracts among the various stakeholders, the counselor's rather youthful abilities to evaluate his capacities, the site's legal and ethical compliance with supervisory requirements, the lack of communication between the site and the university, and the very real needs of low-income clients who are unable to receive services anywhere else. Also a concern is the level of ethical responsibility shared by group members who have now also become aware of these situations. All of these will be concerns whether or not James decides to continue his participation in Lucinda's supervision group.

Questions

1. What do you think about students participating in consultation groups, where they will discuss clients from another site, concurrently with receiving onsite and university supervision? How successful would a beginner be at navigating among multiple role models, suggestions, or clinical models? What concerns might you have? What might you do to address these concerns were you responsible for the consultation group?
2. What red flag might pop up for you when James mentions the desire for "better" supervision outside of the agency? How might this have been addressed?
3. What might Lucinda have done differently before allowing James to enter the group to preclude the development of these concerns?
4. How might Lucinda address the student's inflated assumptions about his capacities in a developmentally appropriate way, and without discouraging him or leading him to believe that Lucinda does not have confidence in him?
5. What should Lucinda do with the information she has now, after 4 months have passed? If you were her, how would you keep from alienating James, given whatever you have decided to do? If Lucinda does alienate James and he decides to terminate with the group, what responsibilities does she still bear ethically and legally?
6. Will the hours spent in the supervision group meet Council for Accreditation of Counseling and Related Educational Programs or state standards for hours of supervision?
7. What gender issues might you be concerned about?
8. Any other thoughts about this case?

Response

Lori Ellison

At first glance, this appears to be a less-than-ideal situation even though Lucinda's supervision experience is well reputed. The fact that James feels the need to reach beyond his current level of supervision is telling. He wants to be a competent counselor and may be doing a fine job for a student at his stage of development. However, his lack of experience makes it difficult for him to assess his own level of skill. One cannot report what one does not know is wrong. No matter what level of skill he has, it is doubtful it is adequate for the load that he is being asked to shoulder virtually alone.

It is likely that the mixed messages, both practical and theoretical, that he is receiving from his site supervisor and his university supervisor versus what Lucinda is telling him also add to the confusion. Lucinda made it clear from the beginning that the site supervisor and university supervisor would have the final say, yet these two are leaving him in a dangerous professional position that she questions. The center's financial woes notwithstanding, this situation could have been corrected with the suggestion Gerry made to have a part-time supervisor located in their satellite clinics. Unfortunately, the center never followed through on this promise.

Another concern is that the clients James sees must have informed consent regarding the additional supervision James is getting from Lucinda's group. Many more people now will have access to his clients' confidential information. They have a right to decide whether they want their information shared with this group or not. Nothing at all was mentioned about this in the scenario.

An additional concern is the ethical obligation the school appears to be neglecting in providing sufficient supervision for this student counselor. The isolation of his work without a supervisor on the premises is asking for trouble. It would be risky for a seasoned professional to work under such circumstances; to ask this of a counselor trainee is unthinkable. Were a crisis of any sort to occur when James was there alone, particularly if Gerry could not be reached, he could be vulnerable, both personally and professionally.

His professor's and supervisor's dismissal of the concern Lucinda has voiced indicates there is a problem beyond the student's capabilities. It is the responsibility of the counselor educator to ensure that the counselor-in-training is receiving adequate supervision at his or her site. Once the situation at the site became clear to the university, action should have been taken. At the very least, the number of interns could have been reduced by reassigning them to other sites to make the supervisory relationship more manageable. This may greatly reduce the number of clients served, but it is the more responsible decision to provide adequate supervision for the protection of clients who are served.

The ethical codes are clear about counselor competence. Counselors are only to practice within the competence level their supervision has provided for them. James appears to be forced to practice above his skill level, and his supervisors seem to be okay with this. Lucinda's duty and that of her group members is to protect the clients whom she now knows may be at risk. The

ACA Code of Ethics (American Counseling Association, 2005) states that counselors should consult with those showing impairment "and intervene as appropriate to prevent imminent harm to clients" (Standard C.2.g.). Although Gerry may not have been able to control the decision of the owners, as a supervisor she did have an obligation to protect all clients seen by student counselors. Although she is trying to manage the situation, it is neither prudent nor effective to provide supervisory support for all eight interns at once by herself when the standard is no more than three. Regardless of James's response, Lucinda has a responsibility to report the egregious lack of supervision from which all of the interns at this agency are suffering. This agency is so heavily dependent on counselor interns that it is ill-equipped to supervise and manage them responsibly.

The hours accrued in Lucinda's group supervision should not be counted for Council for Accreditation of Counseling and Related Educational Programs or state standards, as the agreement with Lucinda clearly defined this relationship not as supervisory but as a consultant. Because the supervisor–student ratio at the agency does not meet state standards, it may be questionable as to whether those hours count. If they were deemed legitimate, then only the hours accrued by the site supervisor and the university supervisor should be reported.

That James sought additional help from a female supervisor might show that gender does not affect the dynamic of the relationship. However, the female-supervisor-to-male-trainee relationship has been shown to have some unique dynamics that can be potentially conflictual (Wester & Vogel, 2002). Perhaps his supervisors, at least one of whom is also female, decided that his skills were well enough developed to place him in such a vulnerable position. Perhaps it was merely the escalating voice of necessity that forced the choice. Either way, when Lucinda confronted the insufficient supervisory oversight, James bristled. Is it more a competence issue? Perhaps, but it may also reflect a gender bias or at the very least a communication difference.

Lucinda must encourage the skills that James is developing and affirm that he is progressing in his abilities, but also tactfully enlighten him to the truth that the more a counselor knows about the counseling profession, the more the counselor learns what he or she does not know. James must learn to accept that all counselors will need supervision from time to time; we simply can't know and be able to do everything. Purposeful and tactful instruction on the appropriate assessment of one's skills would go a long way toward helping James accept this about his own skill level. Lucinda must work to help him understand the importance of adequate care for the sake of his clients and for his own sake as a counselor trainee.

References

American Counseling Association. (2005). *ACA code of ethics.* Alexandria, VA: Author.

Wester, S. R., & Vogel, D. L. (2002). Working with the masculine mystique: Male gender role conflict, counseling self-efficacy, and the training of male psychologists [Electronic version]. *Professional Psychology: Research and Practice, 33*, 370–376.

Response

Warren Throckmorton

This situation, like so many in the helping professions, is a reminder that the road to ruin is paved with good intentions. Whatever Lucinda's motivations were, it is admirable that she would want to help a motivated young trainee. However, problems quickly arose despite her initial efforts to craft some boundaries.

Although I am sure that supervision from multiple supervisors has worked for some clinicians, I am skeptical that this is the optimal arrangement for most trainees at James's level of competence. The primary reason relates to theoretical and technique mastery. The case study noted that James felt he would be "unlikely to receive such information at his site or at the university, which operate from a different theoretical orientation." I see nothing in the case that explored what kind of theoretical or technical perspective the site or university supervisors provided. If the theoretical orientations are radically divergent, how will the trainee integrate the two? More practically, how will he decide what clinical strategies to implement? If his university and site supervisors direct him to make an intervention at odds with Lucinda's consultation service, then what will James do?

Generally speaking, trainees are not capable of integrating perspectives when they are not technically proficient in either two or more theories. This arrangement may serve to confuse James, erode his development as a counselor, and risk harming his clients. Lucinda should have addressed this straightforwardly with James. I would want to know what James believes is inadequate about his current supervision at the university and on the site. Like many trainees, James has many balls in the air and is juggling roles at home, work, and school. Trainees often feel they have to please everyone and that the chief end of their graduate experience is to finish without making a professor or supervisor angry. So instead of confronting a situation at school, students may try to get help in a variety of ways. I can't fault James for trying. Had I been Lucinda, I would hope I would remember to ask several questions, such as

- From what theoretical perspective do your current supervisors operate?
- What is your level of agreement and comfort with those theories and perspectives?
- How do you get along personally with the supervisors?
- Are you afraid for any reason to raise your concerns (as was implied in his initial reluctance)?

A difficult aspect of this case is how to address James' inflated assumptions about his capacities in a developmentally appropriate way. It would be optimal to do so without discouraging his enthusiasm for the profession. Self-disclosure from Lucinda about her own training experiences may help James integrate her concerns. Most master therapists have war stories to pass along, and I suspect it would have been helpful to James to hear that Lucinda's concerns derive in part from her own training process. I think Lucinda can make it clear that her extra care in deliberating over his involvement is not a personality issue. She wants him to get the best possible training experience given his circumstances, and being in her group may not be in his best interests at present. In thinking about how to resolve the case, several questions may be posed. What should Lucinda do with the information she has now, after 4 months have passed? If you were her, how would you keep from alienating James, given whatever you have decided to do? If Lucinda does alienate James and he decides to terminate with the group, what responsibilities does she still bear ethically and legally?

My primary concern would not be James's feelings, although I would try to handle the matter as sensitively as possible. I would also let James know that my calls to the university are efforts to model appropriate ethical responses to what is a complex but potentially harmful situation for all involved. I think James could actually learn much about how professionals handle real-world problems. Lucinda has a professional duty to advocate for improved conditions, not only for the sake of the trainee but also for the clients of that agency who are not being adequately served.

If James does decide to terminate from her group, or given the circumstances, Lucinda terminates his involvement, she still has a duty to advocate for the clients of the agency and the trainees who are placed there. She may need to indicate to the professors at the university that she is prepared to report her awareness to the appropriate state oversight agencies. As far as her legal exposure, I would immediately consult with both my personal attorney and professional liability insurer.

Chapter 15

Due Process Versus Duty to Serve: Three for the Road

Lyndon Abrams

Topics

- Due process
- Duty to serve clients
- Conflict of interest

Background

Marjorie is an administrative and clinical supervisor for a staff of eight counselors at a community mental health agency. The agency serves a fairly large geographical area, providing treatment and case management services. Marjorie has contacted the ethics instructor from the counseling program where she graduated for an ethical and supervisory consultation on the following situation.

Incident

Three of the counselors supervised by Marjorie decided to covertly establish a private practice in the community served by the agency at which they were employed. They concluded such a venture was necessary because of what they called "excessive clinical oversight and managed care" that often influenced their treatment decisions. Their plan was to see their clients at either location (i.e., the mental health agency or the private practice), with each client making the determination as to where he or she wished to be served. They would continue their employment with the mental health agency and work to develop the practice simultaneously. They would provide clients additional choices for treatment and offer a competitive fee structure.

On discovering this plan and after reviewing ethical standards and agency policy, Marjorie determined that the involved clinicians would be terminated based on a violation of counseling ethics and agency policy. After reaching the decision regarding termination of these staff members, Marjorie's concern shifted to the welfare of the clients of the dismissed counselors. Two of these counselors were engaged in some fairly specialized services that could not be readily supported by members of the remaining staff. Marjorie was also concerned about keeping counseling loads for the remaining staff at a reasonable level until replacement staff could be hired.

Discussion

This case raises issues related to due process, conflict of interest, communications breakdown, clinical coverage and potential abandonment of clients' care, effectiveness as both a clinical and an administrative supervisor, and the insight and forbearance of the counselors.

Questions

1. Are there any general ethical or legal supervisory principles that should influence the consultation offered to Marjorie in this case?
2. Is it within counseling ethics to use the newly established counseling practice as a referral source, particularly for the special-needs clients served by the departing clinicians?
3. What should be told to clients inquiring about why the counselors are no longer at the agency?
4. The dismissed counselors have asked for access to the clients' contact information. Should that information be granted? Similarly, should the clients be informed about the existence of the new practice and given contact information for the new practice group without a formal referral?
5. What personal or professional issues face Marjorie as a clinical and administrative supervisor accused of "excessive clinical oversight and managed care," now that she is without a staff and coverage for the agency's clients? What is your sense of how appropriate it was for her to fire the counselors given the potential conflicts of interest, due process issues, and clinical needs of the clients?

Response

Perry C. Francis

An often overlooked area of ethics and professional behavior is our relationships with our colleagues, supervisees (students, beginning professionals), and other mental health professionals from related disciplines (e.g., psychiatry, psychology, social work). This case is an example of what can happen when we are unwilling to go to a colleague, supervisor, or other professional and discuss problems or issues that are interfering with our work with clients, our growth as professionals, or the administration of an agency. Sadly, the consequences go beyond the mental health professionals and affect clients who often have the least amount of power in the triadic relationship.

From the supervisor's perspective, it is important to provide the supervisee with an open and supportive environment where issues can be identified and discussed based not only on the needs of the client but also on the developmental needs of the supervisee. This includes ensuring that the supervisee knows and complies with appropriate ethical and legal codes as well as any agency policies. This review is the responsibility of the supervisor as part of his or her agreement (informed consent for supervision) to provide supervision to the counselor. Also included in this review are any evaluation procedures as well as what to do in the case of a disagreement about an evaluation, treatment decision, or conflict with any agency policy (due process issues). As presented in the case study, there was a perceived environment of "excessive clinical oversight and managed care" that impeded the work of the counselor supervisees. This alleged excessive clinical oversight may also reflect the supervisor's failure to take into consideration the developmental level of the counselors or her own lack of training in supervision theory and counselor development. Our ethics (and many state laws) require us to have obtained appropriate education and experience in counselor supervision before providing supervision to other mental health professionals. These issues must be raised as one provides consultation services to Marjorie.

Although Marjorie will need to consider her actions and how they affected the actions of her counselor supervisees, this does not relieve the counselors of the responsibility to act in an appropriate and ethical manner. The *ACA Code of Ethics* (American Counseling Association, 2005) states that, "Counselors behave in a legal, ethical, and moral manner in the conduct or their professional work. . . . Counselors strive to resolve ethical dilemmas with direct and open communication among all parties involved and seek consultation with colleagues and supervisors when necessary" (Section H, Introduction).

Many private practice counselors get their start in agency settings, gaining valuable experience and training as well as the chance to specialize in a particular area. Agencies often provide a regular client base and counseling supervision. Once that experience is gained, counselors may expand beyond their agency and open their own practices. Balancing the role of agency counselor and private practice counselor can be difficult until one establishes a practice. This is one reason why the *ACA Code of Ethics* addresses this issue by stating that counselors do not recruit clients to their private practice through their employment in other settings (Standard C.3.d.). The interaction between the agency's needs, the counselor's needs, and the client's needs can become so tangled that each is damaged, and ultimately the client or potential client can be harmed. For example, who is to decide when a client's needs are beyond the ability of the agency to provide services? A counselor within that agency who is opening a practice specializing in that area? That evaluation and decision is tainted by the needs of the counselor to obtain clients, even if the agency cannot provide services. Additionally, former counselors of the agency (whether dismissed or not) should not have access to client contact information without the client's express permission. This, and other information, is confidential and not to be used for the building of a counselor's practice.

The counseling relationship can be very powerful and take time to build. When a counselor leaves a practice setting, an appropriate process should be designed to move current clients to other clinicians within the setting and to allow for termination with clients whose treatment is coming to a close (ACA, 2005, Standard A.11.). When a client asks the reason for the transfer, honest communication between the client and counselor is necessary. If the counselor is leaving to open his or her own practice, this can be shared with the client. This allows the client to make his or her own decision concerning treatment options. In this particular case, with the counselors' employment being terminated abruptly, an appropriate transfer or termination process was not allowed, and again, it is the clients who are unduly burdened. Allowing the counselors an opportunity to close or transfer active cases would have been a better clinical decision. If, as implied in this case, that opportunity is not allowed and questions arise about the counselors from their clients, honest communication that shares appropriate facts (and if asked for, professional contact information), not judgments, is in order. Additionally, that information should not place the client in a position of judging the counselors' behavior and thereby implying or explicitly demanding loyalty to one group over another.

Counselors are responsible for knowing and understanding their ethical codes. When counselors or supervisors behave poorly or unethically, it is incumbent on other professional counselors to work directly with each other, using the skills of open communication to confront each other in appropriate ways. This benefits the profession, the counselor, and ultimately the client. Providing due process also allows for the rights of each person to be protected and respected so that we can ultimately serve the greater good of the profession and our clients.

Reference

American Counseling Association. (2005). *ACA code of ethics.* Alexandria, VA: Author.

Response

Theodore P. Remley Jr.

A fundamental issue raised in this case study seems to be whether it is ever acceptable to terminate a counselor who has specialized areas of expertise needed by clients served by a counseling agency. The answer has to be that certainly it is acceptable. A counseling agency does not have an obligation to provide services to every client who seeks counseling. If an adult client is seeking counseling for sexual abuse experienced as a child and none of the counselors on the staff have expertise in that area, then the agency may not be able to serve that particular client. Counseling agencies sometimes lose staff members who have particular counseling skills. Counselors may quit their jobs, relocate, retire, or get fired. The agency then has to hire someone with similar skills to take that counselor's place, send a staff counselor to training to develop skills that were held by the departing counselor, or perhaps discontinue offering counseling services in that particular area. It would be unreasonable to determine that a counseling agency could not fire a counselor who had violated agency policies because that particular counselor has a needed counseling specialization.

An important principle that should be considered when discussing this situation with Marjorie is that employees agree to abide by agency policies when they accept employment with an agency, and agency supervisors must enforce those policies. Although the case discussion does not say this, I am assuming agency policy forbids counselors from opening private practices in the same community that would serve the same clientele as the agency.

I can think of no ethical standard that would be compromised if Marjorie's agency referred special-needs clients to the newly established counseling practice. However, the board of directors or the chief executive officer of the agency may decide to decline to make such referrals based on business principles. Agency officials may determine that it might encourage additional counselors to leave the agency and set up competing counseling practices in the community if the agency were to support such new practices by making referrals to them. On the other hand, if a client requested counseling services that the agency was not able to provide because no counselors on the staff had that expertise, and one of the counselors who departed did have that expertise, the agency would have an ethical obligation to inform the client that the agency could not provide the counseling services but that a counselor in private practice in the community might be able to do so.

I think an appropriate way to inform clients of the counselors' departure would be to say that the counselors had left the agency to establish their own private practices in counseling. No additional information would have to be provided.

Client contact information is the property of the agency, and the departing counselors have no right to that information. In addition, federal and state privacy laws would prohibit providing personal client information to third parties without the express written consent of the clients.

There would be no ethical principle that would prohibit informing clients of the existence of the new practice and giving clients contact information for the new group practice. However, a business decision could be made not to provide that information to clients unless necessary because the agency could not provide particular services that one of the departed counselors could provide in the new group practice.

I believe Marjorie should reflect on her administrative practices because three of her eight staff members were significantly dissatisfied with her management practices. She might even seek consultation in an effort to determine whether she was supervising in an inappropriate or ineffective manner. On the other hand, it is possible that the three departing counselors had unrealistic expectations, given the climate of managed care that prevails in mental health practices today. Marjorie could discover that her administrative practices are appropriate, and in the future she may need to provide a more thorough explanation to potential employees of job expectations, managed care, and clinical oversight requirements.

If agency policies prohibited employed counselors from opening private practices in the same community that serve the same clients as the agency (to avoid conflicts of interest), then Marjorie had no alternative but to address the issue with the three counselors. It is possible there could have been an alternative to firing the counselors. For example, if the counselors had agreed to close the practice they had opened, then perhaps they could have kept their jobs.

Due process issues were not raised in the facts of the situation. I would assume if the agency had procedures regarding terminating employees, Marjorie would have followed those procedures. Any procedures an agency has regarding disciplining or terminating employees must be followed by supervisors.

After the three counselors have left the agency, if clients need counseling in areas in which existing counselors do not have expertise, then the agency should hire a new counselor with such expertise, train an existing counselor in that area of expertise, or explain to the client that the agency cannot provide counseling in that area and refer the client to others in the community who might be able to help.

Chapter 16

Identifying the Repressed: Pushing the Public Envelope in Expressive Arts Therapy Training?

Michele P. Mannion

Topics

- Confidentiality
- Power differential between supervisor and supervisee
- License to interpret in expressive arts-based supervision
- Group versus individual burden of care

Background

A few years after finishing graduate school, I pursued additional certification in the area of expressive arts therapy in an effort to connect to a newly burgeoning passion for oil painting and bring a greater skill set to working with outpatient clients. Participants had heard horror stories of how intensely rigorous the training was in this particular program, with an emphasis on participant as client. The training emphasized a psychoanalytic approach emphasizing object relations theory, and participants held a particular concern over the "emotional stripping" of defenses and repressed material. The nature of the training tended to be highly experiential and process oriented.

Group supervision occurred in small groups of six participants. During these group meetings, the emphasis was on the processing of assigned art-making homework. During a group supervision session, a participant shared her artwork and conveyed her difficulties working with child oncology patients in a hospital setting. She was very descriptive in her reactions to the hospital setting and her artwork. My countertransference to her descriptions was fairly immediate. Three years earlier, I had needed emergency surgery because of substandard minor surgery that resulted in a perforated colon and a case of peritonitis. Because I was left alone overnight in the hospital, the diagnosis of peritonitis was not made for nearly 24 hours, and but for the advocacy of a dear friend who was a nurse, I likely would have died. I remained hospitalized for a week, and my recovery took nearly 8 weeks.

As I sat silently with tears streaming down my face, my supervisor used immediacy and redirected his attention. I conveyed the circumstances of my illness and the associated long-lasting, likely consequence: compromised fertility. Then my supervisor used a term that was curious to me at the time: *trauma*. "This was a trauma," he said. "You have been traumatized, and you need to address it." Trauma? Me, traumatized? I sat dumbfounded, shaken. I had not ever given this consideration, but having a label to apply to the experience did create a sense of relief.

Incident

Shortly after this personal revelation, my supervisor was a guest speaker in one of the other trainings I was taking. This training included individuals studying dance therapy, and the total number of students in the class was over 20. My supervisor asked if I would volunteer for a movement mirroring activity. I was assigned a partner who would mirror my movement. While this was occurring, 20 other participants sat in a circle around us. After approximately 1 minute of this mirroring exercise, my supervisor stopped me and my partner. He asked the group to provide feedback about my movements. "Lacking fluidity," "uptight," and "posturing" were general descriptors. My supervisor called attention to the stiffness I exhibited, primarily from the waist down. He noted that my hands kept moving in front of my abdomen, close to my body. He told the class of the knowledge that he had that most of them did not, that I had experienced trauma in my abdomen and that I was protecting this area of my body with my defensive posturing. As soon as my supervisor began to convey this, I burst into tears.

Discussion

I did not feel that my experience was validated; I felt raw, exposed. Additionally, I felt like I had been set up, and the information I had previously provided in a much more intimate setting, exploited. What was the compelling reason for this public disclosure? Was my supervisor only capitalizing on a teachable moment, one that fit within the model of training within expressive arts? I did not have the wherewithal to address my concerns about disclosure with my supervisor; in fact, I never brought it up with him. I was not ready at this time to participate on any level with this topic.

Questions

1. When might training in expressive arts justify the use of student disclosures made within a group supervision setting?
2. Therapeutic competence is enhanced when counselors address their own issues. Given the powerful reactions that can occur with the expressive arts process, where do supervisors draw the line in "processing" material with supervisees?

3. How should supervisors delineate between feedback that is necessary for professional growth and feedback that is harmful?
4. What obligation do supervisees have in letting supervisors know
   when they feel they have been harmed?
5. What additional thoughts or insights do you have about this situation, particularly about the perspectives of both the supervisor and
   the supervisee?

Response

LeAnne Steen

When I read this incident, I had several immediate reactions related to ethical
considerations when supervising students. Because of this, I decided to break
my response into three sections: (1) ethical considerations in supervision related to this critical incident, (2) my responses to the questions posed by the
writer not explicitly covered in the ethical considerations section, and (3) other
thoughts I have on critical incidents and supervision related to training in expressive arts therapy.

Ethical Considerations

Supervision is an interesting component of counselor development. The balance between exploring and encouraging personal growth and maintaining a
professional relationship that avoids engaging in therapy with supervisees is
often difficult to negotiate. In the beginning of the description, the supervisor
was able to maintain this balance, as reported by the writer. According to the
ACA Code of Ethics (American Counseling Association, 2005), he followed the
principles outlined in Standards F.5.c. (Counseling for Supervisees) and F.7.b.
(Self-Growth Experiences) in that he helped the student identify a personal
problem, a "trauma" that needed to be addressed and that could impede counseling in the future.

Unfortunately, he violated several standards of the *ACA Code of Ethics*
(ACA, 2005) when he decided to share information from a confidential group
supervision environment in a classroom setting. According to *ACA Code of
Ethics* Standards F.3.a., F.4.a., F.6.a., and F.7.a., he violated several standards of supervision that were developed to help supervisors maintain the balance between multiple roles. A counselor educator has a responsibility to set the
boundaries with the supervisee and minimize potential conflicts while working to not compromise the supervision relationship (Standard F.3.a.). In this
context, the supervisor also has the responsibility to incorporate informed
consent into the supervision process with supervisees (Standard F.4.a.).

Even if the supervisor had not specifically outlined the points of informed
consent and confidentiality, I believe that an expectation of confidentiality
about personal issues is implicit in the supervisor–supervisee relationship and
that such personal information would not be open to discussion in other fo-
rums without specific permission from the supervisee (exceptions are possi-

ble for cases in which counselor educators must consult with one another regarding the status of a student's growth as a counselor and the effect on the profession; Standards F.6.a. and F.7.b.). As a final note, the supervisor has a responsibility to adhere to ethical standards and model appropriate behavior with supervisees. It is inherent in the supervision process for supervisees to feel vulnerable; using their personal issues in a classroom context, without specific permission, is inappropriate (Standard F.6.a.).

Responses to Questions

When working with students using expressive arts materials in the supervision process, it is important to remember that expressive arts activities are designed to touch the deeper, subconscious realms of personal experience. Because of the nature of the experience, supervisees may "disclose" something personal through their artwork without realizing it until they begin to process it with the supervisor. I believe it is important for supervisors to find a balance in working through this process with the supervisee. There is a line, as the writer indicated, past which the supervisor should not push the supervisee through the processing stage. Although it is important to acknowledge some of the material, a supervisor should use his or her intuition and professional training to stop the processing and encourage the supervisee to continue processing with a therapist before the line between supervisor and therapist is crossed. In the context of group supervision, a supervisor must sometimes stop the processing even earlier in order to protect the supervisee. It is also important to encourage students while training and processing with each other through expressive arts activities to be careful and recognize each other's vulnerability in the situation while maintaining professionalism.

The supervisee has a professional responsibility and obligation to acknowledge problems in the supervision relationship. Supervisees may feel this part is very difficult, and it is important for the supervisor to encourage student feedback to the supervisor throughout the process of supervision. These boundaries should be outlined in the beginning of the supervisory relationship. If the supervisee feels threatened by potential ramifications from the supervisor for honest feedback, the supervisee should seek the assistance of another supervisor or senior faculty to facilitate the process.

Other Thoughts

In working with students and expressive arts materials through the process of supervision, there is something I feel is important to keep in mind that has not been specifically addressed yet in this critical incident. The supervisor needs to be aware of the relationship between the choice of materials and access to the subconscious. Expressive arts materials affect us more or less deeply in a continuum from pencil lead and crayons on one end to wet clay from the earth on the other. I would not advise a supervisor to work with supervisees in the beginning of a relationship with materials from the earth such as wet clay or even sand. It is important to allow the process to unfold and allow the supervisee to feel comfortable with the vulnerability and emergence of the subconscious before moving into the deeper realms of material use and, consequently, personal growth and understanding.

Reference

American Counseling Association. (2005). *ACA code of ethics.* Alexandria, VA: Author.

Response

Harriet L. Glosoff

I was incredibly moved by the incident described by this contributor. As I read her story, I could not help but think how her experience in her training program, in some regard, paralleled her medical experience. In both, she experienced trauma, and her trust was violated. In the hospital, she not only experienced the physical trauma of having her colon perforated but also a betrayal of trust. She trusted the medical staff members to first do no harm and then, when harm did occur, to at least accurately diagnose and treat her condition. In her training program, the contributor most probably expected her supervisor to respect the confidentiality of information shared within the supervision group, except under clearly understood circumstances. In addition, in the model described, if I were a student, I would expect the supervisor to have a certain level of clinical skill and be able to assess the benefits and risks involved with my working through my previous trauma. Once again, it might have felt as if her trust was betrayed and poor judgment exercised in "diagnosing" harm.

Whenever I am presented with an ethical, clinical, or supervisory situation, if I do not have the opportunity to actually talk with all parties involved, I try to at least imagine the scenario from the different perspectives of the stakeholders. I found the questions posed at the end of the incident helpful in doing this, and my responses follow.

Most counseling programs use experiential learning to help students understand the material being presented and to increase their understanding of themselves and how their personal issues influence their professional work. To me, a primary question is how students are prepared for this and how much they understand about how personal information will be treated within the training community. Because training in the particular expressive arts program described included a clear emphasis on student as client and tended to focus on the use of highly experiential and process-oriented activities, the process of informed consent is particularly critical. In fact, based on the foundations of the program, I would say all protections normally afforded to clients should be extended to the students, but I will speak specifically to students and supervisees. Based on the *ACA Code of Ethics* (American Counseling Association, 2005), supervisors are required to help students and supervisees understand possible ramifications of their self-disclosures. In addition, they are responsible for minimizing potential conflicts that may develop because they are serving in more than one professional role (in this case, as supervisor of a small group of students and as an instructor for a larger class) and for helping supervisees understand how supervisors may behave in their different roles. During the initial informed consent process, supervisors and supervisees should clarify expectations regarding how supervisees will be evaluated, what happens if the supervisor believes the supervisee is impaired or would benefit from counseling, and, of course, the parameters of confidentiality, including what will happen with any information shared.

Although I believe the supervisor breached confidentiality in this situation without justification, I can't help but wonder if the trauma experienced by the contributor would have been lessened if she knew in advance this would happen. For example, if students were told information obtained in one venue might be shared in other venues, the contributor may have chosen to not disclose intimate details of her medical experience or, at least, might not have felt betrayed or blindsided.

I strongly agree with the statement that "therapeutic competence is enhanced when counselors address their own issues." Because of this, I expect counselors-in-training, especially in the climate of an expressive arts experience, to engage in self-reflection. Counselors-in-training should expect to be encouraged by their supervisors and colleagues to explore issues from different points of view, from outside their own worldview. As counseling supervisors and counselor educators, we offer a variety of opportunities geared toward helping students do their work. Although varying aspects of the supervisory process and other components of counselor development may feel therapeutic, it is essential that supervisors not confuse therapy and experiential learning aimed at helping students grow. Neither supervisors nor counselor educators should "serve as counselors to current students unless this is a brief role associated with a training experience" (ACA, 2005, Standard F.10.e.). I believe the supervisor overstepped his bounds by sharing the information obtained in the supervisory process with the larger class, especially without first obtaining permission from the contributor. Separate from the issue of breaching confidentiality, it strikes me that if the culture of the program is to treat students as clients, supervisors must demonstrate strong "clinical" judgment about what might and might not enhance therapeutic competence and what might simply retraumatize someone. If I were the contributor, I would have felt blindsided in addition to having to deal with the original pain of my medical experiences. Although doing so in private with a counselor may be an important part of both a personal and a professional journey, I cannot imagine how it would increase therapeutic competence to be put on the spot to deal with such a painful memory in a public venue.

I would not use the term *feedback* to describe what occurred between the supervisor and supervisee. With that said, I do think helping the contributor consider what happened to her as being a trauma might be considered feedback by the supervisor in this case. Having a label did provide her with a sense of relief, and I have found this to be true with other supervisees as well. I do, however, think we walk some fine lines when giving feedback that is associated with what we believe is deep work to be done by our supervisees. This is where clinical judgment is important. Whether working with supervisees or clients, I do believe we are ethically bound to help them make informed choices about when and how they do their work and with whom. Informed choices include the possibility that if supervisees decide they are not ready to work through particular experiences or issues, they also may or may not be ready to go on to internship or to be endorsed for graduation.

I believe both parties in the relationship, as with all professional relationships, have obligations to own their thoughts and feelings. It is also important to consider the hierarchical nature of most supervisory relationships in training programs. I talk with supervisees about power issues, such as ways in which supervisees can empower themselves and their concerns about repercussions from supervisors. I also point out that if they find themselves in such a situation, it means that there is something amiss in the supervisory relationship. Although it might be empowering for supervisees to let their supervisors know they believe they were harmed, each supervisee must carefully consider the potential benefits and risks involved in confronting a supervisor. One thing I have found helpful is, at the start of supervision, to identify with supervisees a third party who might be called in to help work through challenging situations.

One thing I have not discussed is how the supervisor's breach of confidentiality might influence others in the program. In addition to harming the contributor, I find it sad that other colleagues who were in the class may have decided against disclosing information about themselves that may have, if handled properly, enriched their personal growth and their therapeutic competence. Obviously, I do not know what the supervisor may have been thinking when he choose to share personal information in the larger class. His intent might have been to help the contributor or to use the information to help her classmates understand a particular concept at a deeper level. Regardless, I would say that there are more respectful and effective ways to achieve either goal while allowing supervisees and students the prerogative to disclose personal information in a public venue. This is especially true when we know supervisees or students may be dealing with deep material better explored in a private and individual or small-group context. In such cases, when I know personal information from a supervisory context may come up in a larger class setting, I speak with the supervisee first to discuss possible ways to handle this. Modeling partnerships in growth processes can help supervisees learn to do the same with clients.

Reference

American Counseling Association. (2005). *ACA code of ethics*. Alexandria, VA: Author.

Chapter 17

Confidentiality: Casual, Comfortable, and Communal

James R. Ruby

Topics

- Confidentiality and dual-role issues
- Case presentation
- Appropriateness of group supervision

Background

This incident takes place in a community mental health center that serves two communities with a combined population of nearly 62,000 people. Residents of these communities come to the center for a variety of reasons including individual, family, and group outpatient counseling; psychiatric assessment and treatment; psychosocial rehabilitation; alcohol and drug treatment; and psychoeducational groups. Services are offered on a sliding scale according to the client's ability to pay. Clinicians and interns within the center receive both individual and group supervision from master's-level, clinically licensed persons. Many of the clinicians and supervisors are residents of the communities being served.

Incident

The incident occurs during group supervision sessions. A clinician or intern is routinely asked to take a turn presenting a case with which she or he is having difficulty. The goal of the presentation is to receive feedback from other clinicians, both supervisory and otherwise, in an effort to assist the presenting clinician with strategies for successfully serving the client. A presentation would typically include a detailed history of the client, including her or his history with the presenting problem. Historical information regarding education, family, medical treatment, mental health treatment, vocational development, and other personal matters is included in the presentation by the primary clinician serving the client.

Clients sign an informed consent statement indicating that they understand that their personal information will be discussed within the confines of individual and group supervision. However, it is not clear that clients understand that someone they know in a more casual manner might be working at the center. It is not unusual to hear another clinician say something along the lines of "I went to school with him," "She lives on my block," or "My kid goes to school with him." Thus, a clinician participating in the group supervisory session who is potentially offering clinical feedback often has knowledge of the client that may or may not be known by the clinician who is actually serving the client. Furthermore, the client intended to be served by the group supervisory process is unknowingly having personal information disclosed to classmates, neighbors, or others they may know casually or personally.

There appears to be no clinical supervisory intervention or management of this process, and there also appears to be no signs of any of the clinicians involved in the process viewing this as a potential violation of a client's confidentiality.

Discussion

The *ACA Code of Ethics* (American Counseling Association, 2005) speaks clearly to the issue of client confidentiality. Standard B.1.c. states, "Counselors do not share confidential information without client consent or without sound legal or ethical justification." Furthermore, Standard B.1.d. further states, "At initiation and throughout the counseling process, counselors inform clients of the limitations of confidentiality and seek to identify foreseeable situations in which confidentiality must be breached." Finally, Standard B.3.a. states, "Counselors make every effort to ensure that privacy and confidentiality of clients are maintained by subordinates, including employees, supervisees, students, clerical assistants, and volunteers."

Questions

1. Are the clients' confidentiality rights being violated when their cases are being presented and one of the clinicians recognizes them as fellow community members?
2. What is the supervisor's role in this situation?
3. In what way could a client's case be discussed in a group supervisory setting without a possible violation of her or his confidentiality rights?
4. What are some other potential confidentiality concerns posed by conducting clinical supervision in groups?
5. Are there times or situations when group supervision is simply contraindicated?

Reference

American Counseling Association. (2005). *ACA code of ethics*. Alexandria, VA: Author.

Response

Marc A. Grimmett

The client's confidentiality rights are not violated based solely on the fact that one of the clinicians recognizes the client as a fellow community member. It can reasonably be expected that a clinician who resides in the same community as the community mental health center might be familiar with some of the residents being served by the center. This is especially true in smaller communities that have a limited number of mental health service providers.

There are, however, conditions under which the client's confidentiality rights could be violated. One example pertains to the informed consent statement clients are required to sign. It is stated in the scenario that "it is not clear that clients understand that someone they know in a more casual manner might be working at the center." If the client does not know that a casual acquaintance is working at the center, they have no reason to expect this person would be participating in group supervision with direct access to their personal information. In this case, the client has not provided consent and confidentiality has not been maintained. Section F.1.c. of the *ACA Code of Ethics* (American Counseling Association, 2005) states that "supervisees make clients aware of who will have access to records of the counseling relationship and how these records will be used."

It is the role of the supervisor to demonstrate, maintain, and enforce the ethical standards of the counseling profession and to promote the welfare of the client. The group supervision environment described in this incident lacks professionalism and is conducive to casual and clinically irrelevant comments about clients. Such behavior does not respect the dignity of the client (Standard A.1.a.). The supervisor bears responsibility in the establishment of this environment. In this situation, the role of the supervisor is to address these behaviors in the process of group supervision. One approach would be to directly discuss the purpose of group supervision and the expectations for clinicians involved as it relates to this incident. An alternative approach would be to have the clinicians imagine and process the following situation: Following group supervision, they find themselves in a social situation (e.g., class reunion, neighborhood meeting, school play) with the client whose case was presented. Do they think their personal comments demonstrate appropriate professional and ethical behavior?

There are several precautions that can be taken to maintain the confidentiality rights of clients when their cases are discussed in group supervision. First, guidelines can be instituted that require clinicians familiar with the client to be discussed in group supervision, either by prior knowledge or relationship, to share this information with the group supervisor. The clinician and the group supervisor can then determine if their participation violates client confidentiality or is otherwise prohibitive. Second, every effort should be made to remove all identifying information from case presentations. Finally, clinicians involved in discussing the client case are not to ask for information intended to reveal the identity of the client.

Multiple relationships pose a confidentiality concern when clinical supervision is conducted in groups. The likelihood that clinicians may know the client under discussion is greater in group supervision. Again, this is particularly true in smaller communities. Additional information about a client, acquired outside individual counseling sessions (i.e., during group supervision) may be helpful in conceptualizing the client's problem. The acquisition of such information, however, potentially violates client confidentiality. It may also interfere with the therapeutic relationship, given that the client has yet to share the information with the counselor and that the information may be inaccurate. In addition, an inherent conflict of interest exists when multiple relationships factor into group supervision, because a clinician can potentially provide clinical opinions about a client with whom he or she has a preexisting, nonprofessional relationship. If a clinician already has a relationship with the client being discussed, he or she should not be involved in that aspect of group supervision because objectivity is compromised. If the presence of multiple relationships cannot be avoided or controlled, individual supervision should be used as an alternative.

Reference

American Counseling Association. (2005). *ACA code of ethics.* Alexandria, VA: Author.

Response

Lori L. Brown

Confidentiality can be a difficult issue to manage in any group situation. When dealing with group supervision of mental health practitioners in a community agency, one might assume that these professionals are aware of the ethical need to protect client confidentiality. Still, this does not excuse the supervisor from addressing dual-role and confidentiality issues as they become apparent in the group process.

In the setting where both clients and professionals are members of the same social community, there are bound to be some dual-role issues. That is, practitioners are likely to know some of the clients who frequent the mental health agency where they work. Clearly, it would be best to avoid serving as a clinician for one's next-door neighbor. Sometimes this kind of connection is unavoidable in group supervision. Thus, it is not a matter of a clear-cut ethical violation when a case is being presented and one of the supervision group members recognizes the client as someone he or she knows in the community. When it comes to professional consultation and supervision, sharing information about clients with other clinicians is within the limits of confidentiality. As long as the client is informed up front that his or her case may be discussed in group supervision, then confidentiality has not technically been compromised.

However, there is a definite possibility of a violation of confidentiality in this situation. At the very least, the practitioner who recognizes that she knows the client whose case is being presented in group supervision should acknowledge to the group that she has this awareness. This allows the group supervisor to monitor the situation in order to determine whether this group member should remain in the session. Because all clinicians are bound by client confidentiality, the supervisor should state that this client's confidence must be protected, despite any prior relationship. If the clinician feels she will be unable to remain objective during the case discussion, she should voluntarily remove herself from the group supervision session. Likewise, if the supervisor finds this to be true, he or she should ask the clinician to leave the room.

Even if cases were presented to the group under assumed names or using numbers or random initials, it is likely that any clinician who has a relationship with the client will recognize him or her from the demographic information alone. If the clinician in the dual-role situation only knows the client casually, then perhaps it need not interfere with the supervisory process, nor would it be a violation of the client's confidentiality rights. The greater the strength of the community relationship, however, the greater need for the clinician to leave the group during discussion of this case.

There may be other types of dual relationships that also pose confidentiality concerns. For example, if one of the group members is distantly related to the client's husband, it may not be appropriate for that person to learn certain confidential information about the client. Although there are no absolutes in these cases, it is the supervisor's job to monitor the group for such conflicts of interest. The supervisor should, at minimum, ask the group if anyone needs to remove him- or herself because of prior knowledge of the client's situation. In the end, the greater part of the responsibility for maintaining client confidentiality falls to the clinicians who make up the supervision group. As with any type of group, there is a greater risk of breach of confidentiality because of the larger number of people involved. As long as the dual relationship is minimal and the clinician guards the confidentiality of the client, there is no ethical violation.

Group supervision offers many unique benefits to group members, including multiple perspectives on cases, peer feedback, and normalizing of the clinician's experiences. These benefits are not available in individual supervision, which has much more of a relationship focus between supervisor and supervisee. Therefore, there would be very few times where group supervision in a community agency might be completely contraindicated. The pros nearly always outweigh the cons. Still, in some rare circumstances, it might be best for the supervisor to only meet individually with clinicians seeing particular clients. One example of such a circumstance might involve a client who is currently involved in a high-profile legal case. His name is in all the papers; everyone in the community knows generally of his legal battles. It might be unwise to divulge much of his confidential information to a large group of practitioners, as it could lead to subjective discussions of his very public situation, detracting from the value of the group supervision process. Instead, individual supervision sessions might be most constructive, keeping exposure to his story to a minimum of two professionals.

In summary, the supervisor's role within group supervision is to remind group members to guard the presented clients' rights to confidentiality. Having done this, the supervisor may still, on occasion, need to ask one or more group members to excuse themselves from certain case presentations because of said group members' dual relationships with the client being presented. In most instances, this action should be sufficient to protect the client's rights. However, in some rare circumstances, the supervisor may determine that certain clients' cases should never be discussed in group supervision, only in individual supervision sessions. Overall, group supervision is an excellent means of exploring cases among peers, as long as clinicians keep client confidentiality in the forefront of their minds.

Chapter 18

You and Your Contract Don't Mean Anything to Me!

Judith A. Harrington

Topics

- Contracts
- Dueling disciplines
- Off-site supervision
- Triangulation

Background

Audrey is in her first year of employment with a public mental health center. Because of recent changes in state billing and reimbursement standards, she and all counselors are required to become credentialed as licensed professional counselors (LPCs) in order to qualify their services rendered for billing. The agency has mandated that Audrey and the others seek licensure according to supervision regulations leading to LPC status. There are no approved supervising licensed professional counselors on staff or on-site who qualify with the Board of Examiners in Counseling requirements to provide Audrey with approved supervision. She and others are encouraged to seek supervision from an approved supervisor off-site, whose fees the mental health center agrees to pay.

Dr. Michaels, the clinical director of the mental health agency, is a clinical psychologist who has recently relocated from another state. Not only is he newly appointed in his position but he is also relatively unfamiliar with state LPC requirements (as a psychologist), mental health state regulations, and state billing procedures. He replaces a clinical director who shepherded the agency's response to these state mandates and who approved Audrey's selection of her off-site supervisor, Katherine.

Audrey is a 50-year-old woman who excelled in her graduate degree program, earned good grades, and succeeded in a full-time paid professional internship before her graduation. She had strong performance in graduate school, exhibits maturity, and served as a long-term volunteer with mentally ill persons prior to pursuing her graduate degree in counselor education.

Incident

Audrey entered into a Board of Examiners–approved plan of supervision with a supervising licensed professional counselor, Katherine. Katherine is also a mature counselor in her 50s with a long history of providing therapy and clinical supervision. At the outset of their supervision together, Katherine recommends that they draft a contract for supervision not only with each other but also with the mental health center. These documents supplement the official plan of supervision submitted to the board as a working contract and informed consent for all parties. Katherine has learned from past experience as an off-site supervisor that a working alliance is a valuable prerequisite with not only the supervisee but also the employing agency and its clinical director.

Katherine has written and secured many contracts before with her other supervisees and their employing clinical directors without incident. She maintains that an off-site supervisor is obliged to collaborate with and defer to in most situations the on-site supervisor, honoring agency policies and procedures while carrying out the terms of the plan of supervision with the counselor. She prefers a proactive and preventative working alliance in the event that a dispute or a clinical dilemma potentially divides or triangulates the supervisor, supervisee, and clinical director.

Katherine has generated a working contract for the three parties that has been signed by herself and Audrey. She has asked Audrey to present it to Dr. Michaels for review and his signature. She has even encouraged them to edit and redraft the document if he would like changes. Additionally, Audrey has signed a contract with Katherine that is a statement of informed consent, rights and responsibilities of each party within their dyad, and terms of their working arrangement.

Audrey has taken the contract to Dr. Michaels, who assures her that he will look it over "sometime." Because Audrey has been mandated to become licensed as soon as possible, she and Katherine embark on their weekly supervision meetings off-site and have met weekly for a couple of months. In the third month, Katherine met with Audrey at her place of employment in order to do live supervision and observation. When attempting to meet with Dr. Michaels during this site visit, he is unavailable and does not arrive at a prearranged meeting with Katherine and Audrey. Katherine and Audrey proceed with their supervision activities.

In the fourth month of the supervision arrangement, Audrey encounters a clinical dilemma involving a judgment call about whether to report to Child Protective Services recent abuse of a child admitted by one of her clients. After extensive discussion and review of the case, along with an anonymous consultation with the Child Protective Services help line, Katherine and Audrey agree that she must submit a report about the abuse. When Audrey informs Dr. Michaels about this decision, he yells at her, "Who the heck is Katherine, and why are you calling Child Protective Services? This case does not require reporting, and you will not call Child Protective Services. You report to me, not Katherine!"

Audrey calls Katherine immediately. She feels as if she is caught in the middle and does not know what is best for her client or her compliance with the duty-to-report statute. She feels that her licensure-seeking supervision has been invalidated and scorned, even though she has been mandated by the agency to pursue the credential. She becomes worried about the future success of her working relationship with both Dr. Michaels and Katherine and the possibility that her supervision may be "contaminated." When reviewing the breakdown of communication between the parties, Katherine and Audrey realize that Dr. Michaels has not signed the contract and appears to not fully understand the working alliance that Katherine had promoted with the agency. It should be noted that the agency has been paying Katherine's fees for supervision of Audrey.

Discussion

This case contains elements that are related to informed consent and working contracts between supervisee, an off-site supervisor, and a clinical director who is identified with another discipline in the mental health professions. Additionally, the relational dynamic of this case reflects an unresolved triangle of competing demands on Audrey, the supervisee. There is some question about whose burden it is to promote a working alliance between an off-site supervisor and an agency supervisor.

Questions

1. On whose shoulders did it fall to shepherd and facilitate a sound working contract between all parties?
2. When should clinical supervision have begun? Was it reasonable for Katherine and Audrey to begin their formal supervision meetings without the three-way contract being signed by an agency representative?
3. What do you think about Audrey being asked by Katherine to be responsible for getting the contract to Dr. Michaels? What do you think about Dr. Michaels admonishing Audrey for a clinical judgment for which Katherine was also responsible?
4. How might this breakdown in communication between the agency and the off-site supervisor be resolved? What strategies might these three persons pursue in order to prevent future conflict and invalidation of the supervision experience?
5. If the off-site supervisor is, in theory, loyal to the idea of working within the agency's method, how might (or should) Katherine continue her working alliance with the agency, especially because Audrey is "in her care" and she is paid her supervision fees by the agency?
6. What other thoughts or insights do you have regarding this vignette?

Response

Quinn M. Pearson

My reactions to the situation and my ideas regarding a satisfactory resolution were affected by several key elements within the case: (a) The supervisory relationship and choice of supervisor had been approved, (b) a formal contract was in place regarding informed consent, (c) a formal plan of supervision had been approved by the state licensing board, (d) the new clinical director may not be aware of the agency mandate or of the former clinical director's approval of Katherine to provide supervision, (e) the working contract with the three parties was not signed by the clinical director, (f) 4 months have passed without follow-up regarding this working relationship, and (g) Audrey's maturity and skill may belie the fact that she is a new, relatively inexperienced counselor.

I believe that the clinical supervisor, Katherine, was ultimately responsible for providing the structure for facilitating a sound working contract between the three parties and monitoring the situation to ensure that all parties were agreeable to the working agreement. Asking Audrey to present the contract to her clinical director Dr. Michaels seemed to give Audrey an appropriate level of responsibility for and autonomy in her own training. Additionally, Audrey would presumably have more access to Dr. Michaels, as well as more knowledge regarding agency policies and protocols. Giving Audrey responsibility for initiating discussions with the clinical director appropriately mirrors her responsibility of carrying out treatment plans and strategies with clients. Similarly, Katherine's responsibility to monitor Audrey's work with clients relates to Katherine's responsibility for ensuring that Audrey has followed through on initiating the discussion with Dr. Michaels.

Ideally, clinical supervision should have begun once all three parties had signed a final version of a working contract and each had been given a copy. In reality, however, it seems reasonable for formal supervision to have begun before the contract was finalized, especially because legal documents (i.e., plan of supervision and informed consent forms) had been formally approved and completed. As mentioned above, allowing 4 months to pass without any inquiry about the contract was a mistake. In hindsight, Katherine would have been wise to have used Audrey's desire to begin immediately as incentive for Audrey to get the clinical director's input, signature, and involvement in the supervisory relationship before beginning clinical supervision.

As stated above, I believe it was appropriate to ask Audrey to initiate communication with the clinical director regarding the supervision arrangement. After ensuring that Audrey initiated this communication, however, Katherine should have taken an active role in meeting Dr. Michaels personally and facilitating a meeting with all three parties. Because he had seemingly no awareness of who Katherine was, and given the likelihood that agency policy was not being followed, his reaction was not surprising. Such a decision to contact

Child Protective Services has potential consequences for the agency in terms of liability and client trust. His reaction was likely intensified given his own and the agency's vicarious liability as well as the fact that the need to report abuse was not clear-cut in this instance.

The first step involves Katherine privately reflecting on her own feelings about and reactions to the situation. This reflection and expression of feeling will allow Katherine to accept responsibility for her role in contributing to the incident and to stay calm while managing the intense feelings of Audrey and perhaps of Dr. Michaels. The next step involves meeting with Audrey to allow her to express her strong feelings, to review the events that led to the incident, and to work to understand Dr. Michaels' perspective. Without blaming Audrey, Katherine should state her regrets about her own role in not completing the contract or making contact with the clinical director. Finally, Katherine and Audrey should work together on a plan for repairing the relationship between Audrey and Dr. Michaels and forming a working relationship among the three individuals. In order to avoid usurping Audrey's autonomy and rescuing her, I believe that Katherine's overall approach should be to offer ideas and assistance to Audrey as she works to resolve this situation. Although some direct communication is needed between Katherine and the clinical director, it needs to occur after Audrey has begun to work through her problem with him, and as a part of an overall plan to form a solid working relationship among all three.

The critical incident provides the incentive for all parties to discuss and negotiate a working agreement as originally proposed by Katherine. As such, the abuse-reporting problem can be reframed as an opportunity to discuss agency policies, licensure requirements, and the resultant pressures on the supervisee, the on-site supervisor, and the clinical director. When framed positively, this dialogue could, one hopes, lead everyone to see the potential benefits to themselves, the clients, and the agency.

Communication is critical in supervision, especially when several policies, regulations, professional identities, and personalities are involved. In the absence of clear communication, each party tends to act on assumptions. When these assumptions are false or conflicting, problems arise. Katherine assumed that Audrey followed through with getting the clinical director's approval of the working agreement. Audrey assumed that the clinical director had read, understood, and agreed with the conditions of the working contract. Although Dr. Michaels' assumptions are less clear, he seemed to assume that he had ultimate authority over and responsibility for Audrey's clinical work. The abuse-reporting incident brought these false assumptions to light. The concept of responsibility keeps surfacing as a central theme in this case. Although it is clear that supervisors are legally responsible for everything their supervisees do, it does not mean the supervisor is responsible for doing everything for the supervisee. Figuring out who is responsible for doing what is sometimes complicated, especially when such factors as counselor development and client welfare interact with legal regulations and agency policies.

Response

Robin Wilbourn Lee

Given that *supervision* is defined as "overseeing" (Merriam-Webster, 1994), Katherine was responsible for controlling the process of contract negotiation. According to Bernard and Goodyear (1998), supervision is defined as "an intervention provided by a more senior member of a profession to a more junior member or members of that same profession" (p. 6). This definition of supervision applied to this case places Katherine in a position of power and influence, with Audrey as the junior member. Although there is little or no age difference between Audrey and Katherine, Katherine is considered the senior member because of her years of experience in the counseling field. Therefore, Katherine has the responsibility of assisting Audrey in securing a written and valid contract for supervision. Dr. Michaels will more than likely respond more favorably to Katherine as an experienced professional as opposed to Audrey, an inexperienced counselor. Given her experience, Katherine could have modeled appropriate professional behavior by approaching Dr. Michaels regarding the contract that had already been negotiated with the former clinical director. Katherine would have found more success in renegotiating the contract with Dr. Michaels than would Audrey.

Often times, counseling professionals find themselves on the low end of the totem poll, viewed by other helping professions with a degree of disrespect. This is due to several factors. First of all, the counseling profession is the youngest of the helping professions (approximately 40 years old), as compared with psychiatry, psychology, or social work. Second, the counseling profession has not secured the same support from third-party referred sources as other helping professions. Often, counselors are not approved by insurance companies as mental health providers who can be reimbursed for services rendered. Last, there is a certain "territorialness" that can exist between the helping professions. Given that the goal of all helping professions is the same (i.e., to help clients change), other, more well-established helping professions (e.g., psychology, social work) may think it important to maintain a certain level of perceived power. Therefore, the counseling profession often finds itself defining its place and purpose to other helping professions. Given that Dr. Michaels is a clinical psychologist, Audrey may find herself dealing with circumstances she is not only unaware of but also unfamiliar with. Katherine may have a deeper understanding of the dynamics of the helping professions and therefore should be able to help Audrey comprehend her place in working with clients as well as working with other helping professionals. Katherine, as a more senior member of the counseling profession, can use this situation as a learning opportunity to help Audrey understand professional issues related to counseling. It is unfortunate that Dr. Michaels may share the opinion of other helping professionals who view professional counselors as inferior. Dr. Michaels is not willing to afford Audrey, as a junior member of a helping profession, an opportunity to grow and learn her craft. Most professions have some degree of responsibility to teach younger, more inexperienced professionals. Dr. Michaels seems unwilling and untrusting of Audrey as a trained and competent helping professional in spite of the agency's mandate to get her licensed.

Because only a verbal commitment was made between the former clinical director of the agency and Katherine, with no official signed contract, supervision should not have begun until signed documentation existed. Because of liability issues, Katherine would have been wise to make sure that a legal contract was in place before beginning supervision. Katherine, although not an employee of the agency, is still responsible as Audrey's supervisor for her actions. Considering vicarious liability, Katherine can be held liable for neglectful acts performed by Audrey while she is under Katherine's supervision. In addition, Katherine has an indirect relationship with Audrey's clients. Although Katherine will not be working directly with Audrey's clients, she is legally and ethically responsible for monitoring their welfare.

There are several factors to consider when evaluating this case. First of all, when Audrey reported to Katherine that the agency had a new clinical director, Katherine's first order of business should have been to contact Dr. Michaels to set up a meeting between all parties concerned. At the meeting, the contract between Katherine and the agency to provide Audrey's supervision should have been negotiated. According to the Association for Counselor Education and Supervision's *Ethical Guidelines for Counseling Supervisors* (1993), it is crucial that all supervisors have open lines of communication on a regular basis regarding polices and practices. Had this meeting occurred at the beginning, Katherine would have modeled good professional behavior. Second, now that the damage between Katherine and Dr. Michaels has been done, it is even more important that she rectify this situation. Katherine should call a meeting immediately to deal with any confusion between her and Dr. Michaels. It is apparent that Audrey has been triangulated between Dr. Michaels and Katherine. Katherine's professional obligation as the senior member of the counseling profession would be to remove Audrey from the middle. Katherine should be prepared to share with Dr. Michaels her experience in the counseling profession and her justification for being able to provide Audrey's supervision. Katherine should explain to Dr. Michaels the importance of receiving supervision from a supervisor in Audrey's profession in addition to valuing the working alliance in support of the agency's licensure mandate. This will afford Audrey the opportunity to develop a more pronounced professional identity as a counselor. Last, in order to prevent any future communication problems, while negotiating the contract, Katherine should include a schedule of regular face-to-face meetings between herself and Dr. Michaels. It is suggested that these meetings take place at the agency. This would give Katherine opportunities to experience the everyday workings of the agency and to develop a better understanding of the policies and procedures that govern Audrey's behavior.

In this situation, it is crucial that Katherine model appropriate professional behaviors for Audrey. Learning how to work with other mental health professionals is a very important lesson for novice counselors to learn. Katherine should demonstrate an ability to work effectively with other mental health professionals, her supervisees, and clients. In addition, it is Katherine's ethical obligation to deal with the professional responsibilities related to supervision such as securing contracts, providing informed consent, and establishing the parameters of supervision.

References

Association for Counselor Education and Supervision. (1993). *Ethical guidelines for counseling supervisors.* Alexandria, VA: Author.

Bernard, J. M., & Goodyear, R. K. (1998). *Fundamentals of clinical supervision* (2nd ed.). Boston: Allyn & Bacon.

Merriam-Webster's dictionary. (1994). Springfield, MA: Merriam-Webster.

Chapter 19

A Dual Relationship and a Sticky Situation

R. Reneè Evans

Topics

- Dual relationships
- Confidentiality
- Seeking supervision in a clinical agency setting

Background

Elaine is a licensed professional counselor with 8 years of experience and is currently employed within a clinical agency setting that provides employee assistance services to client companies and their employees. The services are prepaid by the client companies and offered as a benefit to employees. Therefore, as employees need to seek out counseling-related services, they may do so by contacting the agency and making an appointment. As a result of the agency having a contract with the company, which in turn directly affects company employees, there are two clients to consider when practicing counseling in this agency: (a) the client company and (b) the client employee. All of the counselors in the agency provide brief counseling to clients, which lasts on average approximately six sessions. If client employees' problems expand beyond their contracted six sessions, the standard procedure is to refer client employees to a professional counselor in the community. All of the counselors in the agency consult and seek supervision often among one another regarding client cases.

Elaine has recently received a new client, Tammy, and had a successful initial assessment with her. Elaine and Tammy also discussed Tammy's goal for seeking out counseling with the agency and what she would like to work through over the course of the six sessions. It was noted, per Tammy's discussion with Elaine, that her husband was not aware that she was seeking counseling. Elaine shared the agency's policy on confidentiality as well as the 24-hour line in the event that Tammy needs to contact the agency before her next visit.

Incident

As Elaine began to enter her notes regarding Tammy's visit, she noticed that Tammy's story sounded familiar. Elaine recognized that Tammy's story sounded similar to that of one of her husband's male family members. Elaine reviewed Tammy's chart again in an effort to see if she recognized the names of the family members in Tammy's household. Elaine had always known her husband's family member by a nickname and was not aware of his first name. Elaine was also aware that the family member had recently married; therefore, Elaine wondered if Tammy was the family member's new wife.

Elaine began to feel very uncomfortable about continuing with Tammy as a client but knew that she needed to identify whether or not Tammy was indeed her husband's family member's wife. Because of confidentiality, Elaine knew she could not call her husband. Therefore, she sought supervision in an effort to identify the best way to handle the situation. After seeking supervision, Elaine contacted Tammy within 1 hour of Tammy's initial session. Elaine shared with Tammy that she had not noticed it during the session, but they might be related to the same people. Elaine sought clarity from Tammy regarding her husband's actual name and nickname. After seeking this clarification, Elaine immediately realized that Tammy was the wife of her husband's family member and that she needed to make immediate arrangements to refer out. Elaine explained that although they had not met formally as family members prior to today, she knew that they were bound to be at family functions together. Elaine further explained to Tammy the obligation to refer her to another counselor because of the closeness of their relationship and because of concerns regarding dual relationships. Elaine assured Tammy that she was bound by law and professional practice to maintain confidentiality about her visit to the agency and that she could refer Tammy to another counselor in the agency or to a professional counselor in the community. Tammy appreciated Elaine's immediate response to the concern and was open to being referred to an outside agency.

However, within an hour of talking with Tammy, Elaine received a phone call from her husband inquiring about "what was going on." An upset Tammy had called him and told him not to share with Tammy's husband the fact that she had received counseling. Elaine began to feel uncomfortable and recognized that although she had expressed to Tammy that she would maintain the confidentiality of her visit, Tammy had just placed Elaine in a difficult situation as a result of Elaine's husband now being aware of the visit. Elaine immediately shared with her husband that she was bound by law and could not discuss her work with him. Later that evening while at home, Elaine's husband also received a call from Tammy's husband with concerns about how this experience (Tammy receiving counseling from Elaine) would affect the family.

Discussion

Elaine's senior colleague, who also worked in the agency as a professional counselor with over 20 years of clinical experience, served as a consulting supervisor regarding the client case. Because the issues of dual relationships and confidentiality were being presented, there were immediate concerns regarding how Elaine might be immediately removed from the client case and the best plan of action to ensure that the agency upheld its contract with Tammy's employer, the client company (to provide quality services to the company's employees as a benefit to employees), and with Tammy as the client. The supervisor also debriefed Elaine about how this was affecting her personally because Elaine was so close to the case.

Questions

1. How might you as the supervisor have assisted Elaine in removing herself from the client case?
2. Do you believe that Elaine has to remain involved in the case until a referral is located for Tammy?
3. What is the agency's obligation to the client company and the client employee?
4. Although clients are able to share their own counseling experiences, what are the issues around dual relationships and confidentiality in this case for Elaine and Tammy?
5. How might this have caused significant concerns for Elaine in her professional life and personal life?
6. What would be the best way for Elaine to respond to her husband regarding his inquiry about Tammy's visit?

Response
Geof Yager

As Elaine's supervisor, I would definitely feel responsible to aid in the immediate transfer of Tammy's case to another counselor in the agency. As a long-time employee of the same clinical agency, I would act to encourage another counselor to accept the case and to contact Tammy for an appointment time as quickly as possible. Although I don't expect that finding another counselor would be a problem, I would take Tammy's case myself if no one was immediately available. Although not directly obligated to see Tammy, I do feel some responsibility for her care given that I was the supervising counselor when Elaine initially accepted Tammy as a client. There may be a delay in completing a referral to an outside agency, which appears to be Tammy's expressed desire, but she will be covered by a counselor referral inside the agency until the additional referral has been set up.

I think Elaine's involvement in the case has been completed. She explained to Tammy that she was obliged to refer her to another counselor and, very importantly, assured her of confidentiality. There is no reason to allow an already uncomfortable situation to worsen with additional contact.

The "provision of quality services to the client company's employees" has, fortunately, not been compromised in this situation. Yes, Elaine did not realize immediately that she had a family connection to Tammy, but the service she provided was appropriate and on target. Her intake interview notes and conceptualizations will be passed on the next counselor. Furthermore, if Tammy so chooses, our agency will continue to provide services through the six sessions that the company contract allows. If Tammy does choose to continue with a counselor outside of the agency, this would also be totally appropriate and within our agency's agreement with the company.

I believe that the question raised in this incident regarding dual relationships and confidentiality addresses the primary areas of difficulty in this scenario. Of course, being an ethical counselor, Elaine will never say anything to anyone in her family (or her husband's family) about the counseling session with Tammy. This silence, even in response to potential questions from her husband or others, ensures the confidential nature of Tammy's visit.

As the question above implies, however, this ethical restriction doesn't apply to Tammy's discussion with her relatives and friends! Tammy was willing to talk immediately to Elaine's husband and, apparently, her own husband. As the *ACA Code of Ethics* (American Counseling Association, 2005) indicates, "Counselor–client nonprofessional relationships [i.e., dual relationships] with clients, former clients, their romantic partners, or their family members should be avoided, except when the interaction is potentially beneficial to the client" (Standard A.5.c). In this scenario, Elaine is explicitly acting to end an accidental dual relationship with Tammy. Because she cannot end the familial relationship with Tammy through her husband's relative, Elaine's only choice is to end the therapeutic relationship (as she did). If Elaine felt her one-session contact was sufficient to create "a counseling relationship," I might encourage her to briefly document the reasons that her one-time visit with a family relative was beneficial to Tammy (see *ACA Code of Ethics*, Standard A.5.d.). Such documentation may be unnecessary, but my personal tendency is to record everything that might be of importance, even if it consists of only a sentence or two. Of course, the file would also contain a short statement from Elaine explaining the family relationship and the fact that this served as a basis for the client referral.

Professionally, Elaine should have a completely clear conscience. (Yes, I recognize that the rational and logical analysis of the situation may or may not be reflected in the emotional response to the same circumstances.) She did not know Tammy prior to the interview, and she only had a vague sense that the concerns Tammy expressed sounded familiar during the initial session. After clarifying that Tammy was a distant family member, Elaine took appropriate action by communicating that their familial relationship would create difficulty in continuing counseling. On the personal level, Elaine may find herself in a few uncomfortable situations at subsequent family gatherings. When put on the spot about the counseling with Tammy, she will need to say (as comfortably as possible), "Oh, come now, Aunt Mabel, you know that I cannot say anything about the work that I do as a counselor. It's all confidential." Such a statement does not even acknowledge that Tammy had even attended a counseling session.

As with her response to Aunt Mabel, Elaine would need to state clearly to her husband that discussion of any client issue would be improper for a counselor. Elaine might say something similar to the following:"If Tammy happens to talk to you about this situation again, I hope that you will reassure her that you know me well enough to know that I would never disclose to anyone the content of a client session. In fact, you might add that you couldn't even get me to confirm that I'd ever seen Tammy for counseling at my agency." Yes, such a statement to her husband does come close to acknowledging that Tammy may have been a client, but it does not actually confirm that the meeting occurred.

Reference

American Counseling Association. (2005). *ACA code of ethics*. Alexandria, VA: Author.

Response

Paul Baird

Based on the written incident, it appears that both Elaine and her supervisor at the agency have acted in a manner that is legally appropriate and in compliance with the *ACA Code of Ethics* (American Counseling Association, 2005). When Elaine began to suspect that she and her client Tammy were in a problematic dual relationship, she immediately sought and received consultation with her supervisor. Following consultation and in a timely manner, Elaine contacted Tammy to confirm the existence of the dual relationship, assured her that confidentiality would be maintained, and explained that a referral could be made to another counselor either within the agency or in the community. It is reported that at this point Tammy "appreciated Elaine's immediate response to the concern and was open to being referred to an outside agency." Later, Elaine's husband asked her about Tammy, and Elaine immediately shared with him that she was bound by law not to discuss her work.

In this scenario, two events occurred that have any number of possible explanations. Despite Elaine's assurances of confidentiality and offer to make a referral, Tammy called Elaine's husband to inform him of what had happened and to urge him not to share the fact that she had sought counseling with her husband. Then, Tammy's husband called Elaine's husband "with concerns about how this experience [Tammy receiving counseling from Elaine] would affect the family."

I am fairly certain that at this point, it is best for Elaine's supervisor to contact Tammy and attempt to facilitate an appropriate referral to another counselor. Tammy should be able to speak more freely to the supervisor. The supervisor is knowledgeable regarding the referral options both inside and outside of the agency. If a referral outside the agency is needed, the supervisor is likely to have the experience and authority to make the financial and contractual arrangements that may be necessary.

If communication between the counseling agency and the employer regarding this matter is appropriate and necessary, the supervisor should be well qualified to perform this responsibility. The clinical agency has an obligation to both the client employee and the client company, but the agency should not compromise the best interests of the client employee in an effort to serve the client company. Given the fact that the contract between the agency and the employer is not available for examination, it is impossible to say with certainty what the written obligations of the parties might be. However, it is hoped that these obligations provide for counseling services that are highly effective, confidential, and flexible.

Should the supervisor attempt to help Tammy and Elaine with their relationship? It might be in both Tammy's and Elaine's best interest for the supervisor to help them look for a way to reduce the discomfort that they might feel at future family gatherings. I am not suggesting anything extensive, and the supervisor should avoid becoming entangled in matters that are clearly not the agency's business. However, I am thinking that a voluntary, brief, face-to-face meeting between Tammy and Elaine in the presence of the supervisor might be helpful. Elaine would restate her commitment to maintaining confidentiality and attempt to establish a level of trust with Tammy that would minimize problems in the future within the family.

If I am the supervisor preparing to make the referral, I might be wondering what happened to Tammy after Elaine's telephone call to her. Although I certainly would not bombard Tammy with questions, in the interest of making the best possible referral I would take note of statements and nonverbal behavior by Tammy that might shed light on the following questions. What were Tammy's thoughts and feelings after her telephone conversation with Elaine? Did Tammy misunderstand confidentiality when it was explained to her? Did she decide that she could not trust Elaine to maintain confidentiality? As a relatively new member of the family, is Tammy afraid of not being accepted? How and in what way did Tammy's husband become aware of the situation? Does the fact that Tammy's husband now knows change Tammy's counseling plans or goals? Does this situation present an opportunity to initiate family counseling?

What about the relationship between Elaine and her husband? She told him that as a counselor she legally (and I would add ethically) could not discuss her work with him. Was Elaine's husband simply acting out of frustration by asking, "What is going on?" or did he not understand counselor confidentiality? Counselors are wise to explain confidentiality to spouses before a specific incident occurs. Of course, explaining in advance does not help if a counselor has shared confidential matters with a spouse in the past. If this has happened, the spouse may assume that confidentiality does not apply to him or her.

Additional points raised by this incident are that counselors must maintain confidentiality, even if it is reported by a third party that the client is talking about confidential material, and that strict confidentiality is important because it is likely to be the only position that can be successfully defended within the context of a family. Finally, Elaine has much to lose personally and professionally if she fails to maintain confidentiality. This incident has the potential to spill out into the community in a way that will damage Tammy, Elaine, and the clinical agency.

Chapter 20

Inclusion, Values, and Alliances: She Has to Quit

Riley Venable

Topics

- Multicultural conflicts
- Therapeutic values
- Working alliances

Background

Central Community Care is a nonprofit social service agency offering a wide variety of services. The following occurred during the regular Friday morning supervision group. This group starts each meeting with each counselor presenting information on new clients seen over the past week. After this discussion, the clinical supervisor assigns the new clients to a team member.

Allen, a 40-year-old White man PhD, is the clinical director of the agency's counseling center. He has over 15 years of experience in a variety of counseling settings and over 4 years of experience as clinical director of the agency.

Tom is a 30-year-old, mixed-race man who holds a master's-level license and has worked at the agency for 3 years. He has recently started a doctoral program in counselor education as a part-time student at a local urban public university.

Karen is a 26-year-old White woman predoctoral intern who attends a local private university. She has started drafting her dissertation, preliminarily titled "A Feminist Response to the DSM." She is currently supporting herself on a graduate fellowship and a trust fund.

Sam is a 47-year-old White man and a new graduate of a local master's in counselor education program. This is his first job after "recareering." Previously he had spent 22 years as a heavy equipment salesman, taking an early retirement for medical reasons.

Lanell is a 32-year-old African American woman master's intern from the local urban public university. A single mother of three, she prides herself on having gone from welfare to a master's degree in 8 years. This is her first semester of field placement.

Incident

Allen: OK, what intakes did you do this week? Tom, why don't you start?

Tom: Susan K. is a 20-year-old White female who came in for career counseling. She is currently attending a community college and plans to transfer to a 4-year school next fall. She needs help determining a major. She is currently working as an exotic dancer at a local gentleman's club. My plan is to . . .

Karen: She must have low self-esteem.

Tom: I didn't pick that up. She seemed pretty goal directed and together to me. She seems to have a good plan to . . .

Karen: She can't feel good about herself, or she wouldn't let herself be objectified and degraded in a job like that.

Sam: Who says it's degrading? Tom, how "qualified" is she for the job?

Allen: Enough, Sam. Tom, what are you thinking about as an initial treatment plan?

Karen: She has to quit that job!

Lanell: No, she doesn't. She's doing what she needs to do. Don't hate the player, hate the game.

Karen [to Lanell]: You are a woman! How could you possibly condone this? I can't believe you don't see how wrong this is!

Allen: Please, everyone, let's get back to the task at hand. Tom, what is your initial treatment plan?

Tom: I was thinking about three sessions, starting with having her complete an interest invent—

Karen: Allen, how can you allow this? Tell him she has to quit that job!

Allen [calmly]: Tom, what is your treatment plan? I didn't get all of it before.

Karen [angrily]: I can't believe this! I won't sit through this! Lanell, how could you? [Karen leaves the room, angrily slamming the door on the way out.]

Sam: What was that about?

Discussion

Supervision groups, like therapy groups, occur with both content and process. Although homogeneous by profession, a supervision group can be heterogeneous across the threads of age, race, gender, social class, ability, and moral values. The multiple intersections of these threads can create challenges for the best group supervisor.

Questions

1. What should Allen do next?
2. What is Allen's professional responsibility to the group? The agency? The clients served?

3. What groundwork should Allen do before next Friday's meeting?
4. How do the issues of race, social class, and gender intersect in this critical incident?
5. How should such differences be addressed within the context of a supervision group?
6. Should Allen direct Tom to rethink Susan K.'s treatment plan to address more than her presenting problem?

Response

Scott Edwards

Initially, I believe it is important to explore my assumptions around the case. I view numerous contextual levels interacting with each other: client, therapy team, agency, and culture. Central to a systemic perspective is the concept of isomorphism, which indicates there can be parallel structures and processes at different but related contextual and relational levels. I assume that attending to isomorphic structures and processes within and between the supervision and therapeutic contexts is important for both therapist development and client growth.

Fundamental to a feminist perspective are concepts of gender, diversity, and power. Reviewing the demographic makeup of the team, there appears to be a modest level of diversity of gender, race, social power, and clinical experiences. Although diversity demographics may be interesting, greatly affecting these supervision and counseling relationships are diversity processes: marginalization, voice, and *power with* versus *power over*. My attention centers around each team member's life and clinical experiences related to gender, culture, and race and their intersection with processes of having or not having a voice as well as power in relationships. Congruent with a feminist perspective, I also attend to relational aspects of openness, respect, curiosity, and accountability to social power, as these may be important in exploring resources and sitting with clients or supervisees as they grow, develop, and change.

Numerous relational processes in the supervision group appear to lack respect, openness, and accountability to power. Demands to each other, sexually degrading comments, and assumptions based on gender are scattered throughout the conversation. Curiosity is absent. Furthermore, female voices of the group were marginalized and silenced each time. Karen's request of Allen to make the client make a career choice speaks to the power in the room; Allen engages in *power over* as decisions are made. Furthermore, Karen's subsequent absence of voice in the room speaks loudly. From a systemic perspective, constraining processes in supervision not only prevent the clinical development of counselors but also constrain parallel processes and the structure of clinical services provided to clients.

Allen may benefit from shifting and restructuring the supervision process. Rather than focusing on treatment planning and counselor assignments, posing questions from a stance of curiosity and accountability to power may be most relevant. For example, "Wow, the silence of Karen's voice is deafening. I must have missed what she was saying [accountability of silencing Karen's voice; builds relational respect]. I am curious about what happened as well, what did you all experience [openness]?" Attending to supervision processes will provide a foundation for attending to client content and decisions around counselor assignment.

After processing their supervision experiences, Allen can shift by posing a question such as "How can what happened in this room be a resource for sitting with this client?" or "Who can see themselves sitting alongside Susan, empowering her to develop informed choices?" Allen has a professional responsibility not only for the clinical care of Susan, but also the clinical development of the supervisees. Allen may be tempted to follow Karen or have someone attempt to engage her; however, he would benefit from allowing Karen the choice of whether and when to rejoin the group. First individually and then with the group, Allen has a professional responsibility to be accountable for marginalizing Karen's voice.

Allen should continue to reflect on ways to shift from *power over* to *power with* his supervisees. In other words, build a collaborative case assignment process using the resources, strengths, and diversity experienced by the team. Preparing questions around themes and resources may allow for information for assigning a counselor as well as development of valuable perspectives within the supervision group, thus facilitating isomorphic processes in the counseling relationship.

Reframing the supervision and case processes from *power over* to *power with* and then presenting this to the supervision group for discussion would certainly begin shifting the constraining supervision processes. For example, a shift would occur by renaming the case "She Has to Quit" to "Empowering Informed Choices" and openly discussing the differences.

Assumptions are made by many individuals around these intersecting topics. Reflecting on diversity processes, there is a recurrent theme of a lack of listening to females and those without power, in both client and supervision contexts. There is also a lack of exploring assumptions based on gender, culture, and power, thus giving more voice to those in power.

By slowing down the supervision processes and attending to diversity processes, Allen might foster opportunities for clinical growth as well as generate valuable perspectives for the client–therapist relationship. For example, after Karen's first comment, "She must have low self-esteem," Allen could have posed a question to unpack her assumptions, such as "What is it that informed you of your comment regarding self-esteem?" By creating space for exploration of personal assumptions, Allen would create isomorphic contexts rich for counselor and client development.

Allen might empower the team to make informed choices as they discuss who might sit alongside Susan, empowering her in making informed choices.

Response

P. Clay Rowell

This incident provides a bevy of issues to address. First, it is important to remember that group supervision requires a multitude of skills that differ from individual supervision. In addition to maintaining the role of supervisor and attending to issues such as client conceptualization and care, treatment planning, and supervisee development, the supervisor must also use her or his group facilitation skills. As many group facilitators would recognize, regardless of setting or purpose, a group is a group is a group. In other words, although this is not a counseling or therapy group, group dynamics and development are vital components of the group's process. Group supervisors must be able to balance the roles of supervisor and group facilitator.

Second, the responses from the group members may indicate the presence of some internalized biases. This incident provided a great moment for supervisee development. It is important for counselors to understand the nature of their reactions to clients in order to minimize the relational effects of their own biases. If counselors do not examine why they react the way they do to various clients, then they may assess their clients, develop treatment plans, and guide the direction of the counseling process on the basis of those biases. Unexamined counselor biases also hinder the ability to develop and demonstrate accurate empathy.

Personal biases are only a part of what constitutes worldview. Unquestionably, one's race and ethnicity, gender, and socioeconomic position (among other demographic variables) directly influence life experiences, which in turn have a major effect on worldview. Life experiences also confirm or contradict one's internalized prejudices that occur during socialization stemming from the macrosocietal messages about groups of people. Karen's experiences undoubtedly have confirmed her internalized prejudices about the occupation of exotic dancer. Her snap judgment about the client is evident because she consistently interrupted Tom during his presentation with comments about the client.

Allen did not handle this situation optimally. Although he maintained a calm disposition, he did not address Karen's escalating reactions effectively. Clearly her biases led to emotions that detracted from the group's process, and Allen allowed it to continue. Moreover, by ignoring Karen, he seemingly fueled her fire to the point that she felt it necessary to leave the group. Allen could have directly addressed Karen's frustrations and the other members' reactions to her and the client's situation. Her level of emotion suggests that Karen may have been willing to share her reasons for her reactions. Then Allen could have used his group facilitation skills to allow all of the group members to examine their own hot buttons that may arise with certain clients or presenting issues. At the very least, however, a validation of Karen's reaction might have allowed the group to continue to discuss the client at hand. If Karen was unwilling to discuss her issue in the group supervision setting, then Allen's responsibility is to speak with her individually to better understand her and help her minimize the effects of her emotional response. Undoubtedly, these or other issues might arise in her future counseling relationships. Such reactions probably would have a negative effect on the client.

Another important issue facing Allen is that his supervisees are at various levels of professional development. Sam's comments illustrate this and display a lack of awareness, and Lanell may be overidentifying with the client. Understanding his supervisees' developmental level is crucial in balancing the multitude of feedback he gives the group. Furthermore, each individual brings his or her own life experiences and worldview to the group. Although exploring the nature of the supervisees' biases is important, it is also essential that Allen not step too far into the counselor role. Although supervisors often vacillate among teacher, collaborator, and counselor roles with their supervisees, knowing the appropriate boundaries of each of these roles is a key supervisory skill. Sometimes supervisors must refer their supervisees for personal counseling when the issues exceed those boundaries.

Although supervisee development is a significant responsibility, Allen's primary duty is to the agency's clients. After Karen left the session, Allen could spend some time processing the event in the here and now with the rest of the group. Karen's escalating emotions and subsequent departure certainly affected the group dynamics and process in some way. He cannot spend too much time with this, however, because a case has been presented, and the assumption is that more cases require attention at this meeting. With a limited amount of time for case presentations, the focus must shift back to helping Tom develop a plan of action for his client.

Chapter 21

Duty to Protect:
Whose Session Is It Anyway?

Heather C. Trepal

Topics

- Technology
- Parallel process
- Vicarious liability and duty to protect

Background

In our counseling center, we have a supervision lab that incorporates technology in several components. Beginning practicum students see community clients in the center, and they are supervised live by program faculty during the sessions. Classmates who don't have clients scheduled are also able to view the live sessions. Supervision techniques include videotaping sessions along with voice-over supervisory comments on the tape, bug-in-the-ear (telephone), and bug-in-the-eye (computer screens on which messages can be seen by the supervisee during the session).

Incident

Beginning practicum students often have the opportunity to complete intakes as a part of their training in the center. One evening, Jamie was scheduled to complete an intake with a community client who was mandated for counseling as a part of his divorce and custody settlement. On the basis of the referral, it seems the client, Jim, had an intense history involving alcoholism, domestic violence, and suicidal ideation. Jamie was a first-semester practicum student, and although she was nervous about completing the intake session with this client, she also diligently prepared by familiarizing herself with the risk assessments and center policies on substance use, domestic violence, and suicide.

Jim showed up for his session on time and nervously met with his intake counselor Jamie, while initially avoiding eye contact. Jamie went over confidentiality and center policies and asked Jim if he had any questions or comments on the information. Jim hesitated and then quietly asked her about the rules for confidentiality regarding suicide. He explained that, in his view, he was mandated for counseling as a way for the judge to continue to keep his children away from him and that any "negative" information given to the judge would affect his seeing his children in the future.

Back in the control room, Jamie's supervisor and fellow classmates watched the session with interest. The supervision protocol called for the supervisor to try the least intrusive form of direct supervision first (bug-in-the-eye) and then move on to bug-in-the-ear and live intervention (i.e., the supervisor entering the room) if resolution of the issue was not reached. Jamie was spending a lot of time focusing on Jim's feelings about the divorce and custody dispute and had yet to ask any questions or make any assessments based on Jim's presenting statements about suicide. The supervisor typed in "complete a suicide assessment," and Jamie quickly saw it flash on the computer screen in front of her. Several minutes went by while Jamie and Jim continued their session discussing Jim's fears of the judge finding out his personal information. Becoming impatient with Jamie, her supervisor decided to call into the session and, once again, reminded Jamie to complete a suicide assessment. Jamie and Jim continued their session, and Jamie decided to pursue a line of questioning related to his substance abuse history. Becoming even more irritated, the supervisor knocked on the door and entered Jamie and Jim's session, taking over and completing a suicide assessment with the client.

Discussion

After the client left, Jamie and her supervisor tried to process what had occurred. The supervisor asked Jamie why she had ignored repeated requests to complete a suicide assessment, and Jamie tried to explain that she intended to do the assessment but that she was trying to work it into the session so as not to further upset the client because he had already stated that he was nervous about revealing information. Jamie asked her supervisor, "Whose session is this anyway?" She replied that it was disconcerting for all involved when the supervisor came in and basically took over the session.

Questions

1. Do you feel the supervisor was justified in the progressive course of action he or she took in live supervision of Jamie's session? Why or why not?
2. Consider Jamie's position and that of the client, Jim. Was there a therapeutic alliance being established and how might the supervision methodology have impeded this?
3. What would you have done in this situation?
4. What strategies might you recommend for supervisors for developing and improving the skills related to emergency assessment and responsiveness among their counseling students and supervisees?

Response

Darcy Haag Granello

In this very challenging supervision case, there are obvious parallel processes occurring between the counselor and client and the counselor and supervisor. There is a client who is angry and trying to find ways to assume control, a student counselor who is angry and fighting to keep control, and a faculty supervisor who is angry and looking for control. I also wonder about the fear that permeates the case: The client is fearful of what will occur if he is truthful about his suicidal risk, the student is fearful about the level of responsibility placed in her lap, and the supervisor is fearful that incorrect management of the case will have devastating results.

Given all of these layers of complexity and emotion, it is perhaps not surprising that none of the discussion among these three individuals is focusing on the intimate and frightening issues of trust and safety. Just as anger, power, control, and fear permeate all the discussions, what is missing from each relationship is a dialogue about trust and safety. The client begins by bringing up trust. Rather than using that to move forward into meaningful dialogue that would naturally allow a suicide risk assessment to occur, the discussion is derailed into areas of power and control. Perhaps it is easier to talk about power from a place of anger than it is to talk about trust from a place of vulnerability. Then, the student and supervisor mirror that discussion by talking about power and control rather than the trust and safety that form the basis of a supervisory relationship.

Of course, the supervisor is justified in taking whatever means are necessary to keep the client safe. The supervisor has a legal and ethical responsibility to the client. The supervisor clearly understands the nature of suicide risk, something that might be rather esoteric to the student, who does not have experience or context. Given the information, it is impossible to know if the student is minimizing the suicide risk, which clearly is problematic, or is overemphasizing the perceived risk and, as a result, feels paralyzed by the pressure. In either case, the student must respond to the prompts by the supervisor. This is nonnegotiable.

Suicide risk assessment is a very complex skill and, in general, one that is difficult for even advanced counselors to manage. Thus, having a first-semester practicum student engage in a suicide risk assessment may be simply developmentally inappropriate. I wonder if the student has been adequately prepared, if there have been role-playing opportunities, if the student has received extensive training in suicide risk assessment, and if she has had an opportunity to witness such an assessment by a more experienced counselor. In retrospect, it is possible that her resistance was simply due to fear about her competence in completing the assessment or fear of not knowing what to do with the information she uncovered.

A therapeutic alliance, in my opinion, could be enhanced with a very clear and comprehensive suicide risk assessment. Framing the assessment in terms of "I want you to be safe" and "I need to understand how you have gotten to this point" are ways to make clients feel understood and validated. Of course, they also lead into a suicide risk assessment.

Therefore, in my mind, it's not a question about methodology; it's a question of a fundamental misunderstanding on the part of the student. The student has an image in her mind that suicide risk assessment is a divisive activity and that by engaging in such an assessment, she will upset the client. This is clearly a training issue. Suicide risk assessment, when done correctly, can actually enhance the therapeutic relationship. The process of conducting the assessment becomes the cornerstone of treatment. We know that the therapeutic alliance is the key to an accurate and useful assessment, but if the assessment is done in the context of care and safety, then it works to develop the alliance. Somehow, the student has the view that a suicide risk assessment is an antagonistic endeavor when it actually can be just the opposite.

I am not sure I want to second-guess the supervisor or the student, given the limited information I have about the situation. In general, I believe (a) the student should have a strong background in comprehensive suicide risk assessment, including a plan for the session, an opportunity to role play, and an opportunity to witness an actual risk assessment before sending her to meet with this client; (b) this young woman in first practicum needs to be assessed to determine her ability to manage the countertransference that might occur in a therapeutic relationship with an older man with a history of violence; (c) the supervisor could conduct the risk assessment and have the student watch, or at least the supervisor could be in the room from the beginning to help as needed, so that the supervisor's interventions would not be seen as intrusive, but rather as that of a cotherapist; (d) the student needs help to understand how suicide risk assessment can enhance the therapeutic relationship; and (e) the student needs to understand that the instructions given through the various technologies are imperatives, not suggestions. Finally, given the situation as it currently stands, I believe it would be important to have a third person to help the supervisor and student process through the supervisory relationship because there is so much emotion involved.

The average amount of training in suicide that counseling students receive is less than 2 hours and appears to be primarily a recitation of risk factors, leaving clinicians unprepared for the complexity of suicide risk assessment. Training activities should improve knowledge (e.g., the basics of suicide risk), skills (e.g., how to conduct a comprehensive suicide risk assessment), awareness (e.g., the magnitude of the problem in the general population and specific risk categories), attitudes (e.g., recognizing one's own reactions to suicide, coming to see suicide assessment as part of one's responsibility), and self-efficacy (e.g., developing the confidence to engage in risk assessments, to feel in control, to know what to do). With this type of training prior to practicum, and ongoing training once students have clients of their own, the type of anger and escalation outlined in this case may be minimized.

Response

Cheri Smith

The supervisor was justified in following the course of action taken in this situation. There was a supervision protocol in place to begin with the least intrusive form of direct supervision and then move on to more intrusive forms of supervision. Both the supervisor and Jamie were aware of the protocol before beginning the session. Jamie began the session by going over confidentiality and the center policies with the client. The supervisor would have begun the supervision process by going over the protocol before Jamie began her training in the center. The possibility of the protocol being implemented began from the moment Jamie walked into the room to counsel the client.

A therapeutic alliance was being established. Most likely the supervision methodology impeded the alliance. The client's perception of whether or not the supervisor and the counselor-in-training were working as a team would be a key ingredient in understanding how much the therapeutic alliance was impeded and what could be done to reestablish it.

The steps for managing this situation should have been in place before the protocol was followed. The supervisor should have begun not only by covering the protocol with the student but also by letting the student know that each step would be used judiciously and that when a step was implemented, the student was expected to respond. If the student did not agree with the suggestion that was proposed, the supervisor should have asked the counselor-in-training to follow the suggestion given and wait until after the session to discuss any disagreement that may arise regarding the proposal. The supervisor should also emphasize in training that precedes actual work with the clients the importance of addressing any statements about suicide as soon as possible.

It is important for counselor educators to provide many opportunities for experiences that involve emergency assessment, especially suicide assessment (Juhnke, 1994). At the same time, it is also important that both the counselor educator and the counselor-in-training have a clear understanding of the parameters of responsibility for each of them. Jamie asked the question "Whose session is this anyway?" From the beginning it would be best to clearly convey to the counseling student that the session belongs to the client, the counselor-in-training, and the supervisor. Thus, a team perspective should be adhered to instead of a me-versus-you approach. Additionally, it would be helpful for the supervisor to continually monitor the counseling self-efficacy of the counselor-in-training. "Understanding the self-efficacy of counselor trainees can provide valuable information regarding how these trainees process training and supervision interventions" (Barnes, 2004, p. 67). A counseling student's delay with regard to implementing an emergency assessment may reflect the student's inability to effectively implement the assessment with the client. Increasing the self-efficacy in this area may be done in a number of ways:

- Using training videos that specifically demonstrate essential components in suicide assessment (Juhnke, 1994)
- Developing role plays so the counseling students have several opportunities to increase their comfort level in this area
- Making sure the steps that need to take place are written down and regularly reviewed with all counseling students as part of their training (Myers & Hutchinson, 1994)

Having beneficial supervisory supports in place will result in the counselor-in-training developing the capabilities and skills to meet the important challenge of emergency assessment and responsiveness.

References

Barnes, K. L. (2004). Applying self-efficacy theory to counselor training and supervision: A comparison of two approaches. *Counselor Education and Supervision, 44,* 56–69.

Juhnke, G. A. (1994). Teaching suicide risk assessment to counselor education students. *Counselor Education and Supervision, 34,* 52–57.

Myers, J. E., & Hutchinson, G. H. (1994). Dual role or conflict of interest? Clinics as mental health providers. In J. E. Myers (Ed.), *Developing and directing counselor education laboratories* (pp. 161–168). Alexandria, VA: American Counseling Association.

Part III

School Counseling

Chapter 22

She Told Me Her Secret: Do I Warn? Who Do I Warn?

Carmen Salazar

Topics

- Ethical decision making
- Therapeutic relationship

Background

Kristina has just begun her first semester as an emergency certified school counselor in a small rural high school. Emergency certified school counselors are hired in situations in which a school counseling position cannot be filled. This often happens when there are no applicants for the job. Kristina has also just begun attending practicum class. Alicia, a 14-year-old Mexican American freshman, came to see her during the first week of classes, saying that she is sad because her 16-year-old sister has run away from home with her boyfriend. The two are living in Mexico near the town where her parents grew up. Alicia lives with her mother, father, younger brother, and maternal grandmother. Since her sister ran away, Alicia's parents have become critical of her, fearing she will turn out just like her sister and run away. Alicia is unhappy because of the increasing pressures at home. Also, she misses her sister, with whom she is very close. She wants to run away to Mexico, find her sister and boyfriend, and live with them. She reported that her brother plans to run away too, as soon as he is old enough.

When Kristina first presented the case in practicum supervision, her concern was twofold: Alicia's level of risk for running away and the possibility that the children are running away to escape abuse in the home. She determined Alicia had no specific plan or means to run away, and the supervision group agreed there was no need to warn the parents. Alicia reported no abuse in the home other than the pressures and criticism she felt. Kristina spoke with the parents by phone and met with them in person, along with Alicia, to get a better sense of family dynamics. The father, who speaks fluent English, did nearly all the talking while the mother remained quiet. Kristina saw nothing to suggest abuse.

Incident

During the sixth session, Alicia told the counselor she is especially unhappy because her parents have forbidden her to see her boyfriend, Cleofas, whom she had been dating for the past few weeks. They object to him because he is too old for her. Alicia's father threatened to call the police if he learns Cleofas and Alicia are still seeing each other. When Kristina asked for details, Alicia disclosed that Cleofas is 23 years old. Her parents believe she is no longer seeing him, but some days she pretends to get ready for school, and as soon as her parents leave for work, she meets Cleofas and spends the day at his house. Alicia also disclosed she had unprotected sex with Cleofas one time but did not plan to do it again because she did not like it very much.

Discussion

When Alicia revealed her relationship with Cleofas, Kristina immediately brought her concerns to practicum class. She realized she was the only adult in Alicia's life who knew this forbidden relationship was continuing and that it had involved sexual contact. She was uneasy about keeping this secret but was unsure how to proceed. She was concerned about the age difference, fearing emotional and physical harm to Alicia through sexual coercion. Although Alicia had insisted she had no plans to engage in sex with Cleofas again, Kristina was very concerned about the risks of continued unprotected sex. Kristina's first impulse was to warn the parents about the relationship because of the potential danger, but she feared the newly established therapeutic relationship would be compromised if she broke confidentiality.

Ours was an all-female practicum class; nearly all the students and the professor were mothers. The group discussed the strong negative reactions some of us were having about Alicia's sexual activity, recognizing for each of us some personalization issues were at play. One of the students urged caution in reporting the sexual activity. She noted if it were reported, Cleofas would be stigmatized for life as a sex offender. The supervision group took this into account but continued to examine the situation. We discussed whether the level of risk to the client was sufficiently high that Kristina had a duty to warn. If so, who should she warn? If not, how should she proceed? The group also voiced concern that Alicia might be more likely to run away from home because she now had an adult boyfriend with the means to enact a plan.

As practicum supervisor, I advised Kristina we needed to do two things before making decisions about duty to warn. First, she needed to consult with her field site supervisor to learn more about the school's stance on situations such as this. Second, I would consult with a colleague in the department, and I would contact Child Protective Services and describe the case as a hypothetical situation to gain clarification on how, or if, this agency might intervene.

Questions

1. What is Kristina's ethical responsibility now that she knows about her client's sexual relationship with a 23-year-old boyfriend?
2. Does Kristina have a legal responsibility given that sexual contact between Alicia and her boyfriend meets the definition of statutory rape?
3. What is her ethical responsibility regarding Alicia's plan to run away from home?
4. If the level of risk is high enough in one or both situations for Kristina to break confidentiality, whom should she warn?
5. If she does warn, how can she proceed in a manner that protects her client yet minimizes damage to the therapeutic relationship and to Alicia's relationship with her parents?
6. If the level of risk is not high enough in one or both situations, what interventions might Kristina use to address her concerns for the client?
7. Might there be stresses experienced in Alicia's family, other than abuse, that could have contributed to the older sister running away and the younger one's desire to follow her lead?

Response

Laurie L. Williamson

Kristina's ethical responsibility is quite clear now that she knows her 14-year-old client is having sexual relations with a 23-year-old man. Alicia has known Cleofas for only a few weeks and is already sexually involved. Every state has its own statute for age of sexual consent, but most states set the age at 16. This is a clear case of statutory rape. Statutory rape is defined as when the defendant engages in vaginal intercourse or a sexual act with another person who is 13, 14, or 15 years old and the defendant is at least 6 years older than the person. Cleofas is 23 and, at his age, may be guilty of a Class B1 felony.

Kristina has a legal responsibility to report the case to the authorities as described in the definition for statutory rape. As a matter of fact, in most states, professional school counselors are criminally liable if they fail to report a suspected case of child abuse. In addition, most states provide professional school counselors with full immunity when acting in good faith.

Kristina's ethical responsibility regarding Alicia's plan to run away from home is part and parcel of the overarching issues. Alicia seems to be experiencing an identity crisis in that she is transitioning into adolescence, and she has to navigate some cultural family dynamics at the same time. She has also, inadvertently, become prey for a sexual predator.

The family's involvement is important here, first because of the fundamental right of parents to be advised if their child is in imminent danger and second because of the strong extended family ties in Latin culture that are indicated by the three-generation household. The family has already lost one child.

The Ethical Standards for School Counselors of the American School Counselor Association (ASCA, 2004a) state that "Information is kept confidential unless disclosure is required to prevent clear and imminent danger to the student or others" (Standard A.2.b.)." Cleofas is a threat not only to Alicia but also to any number of unsuspecting members of the public. Those in violation of rape laws must be held accountable so that such behavior does not continue unchecked.

Instead of viewing the breach of confidentiality as endangering the newly established therapeutic relationship with Alicia, it can also be seen as an opportunity to support and reinforce this family and society's efforts to protect its members. I would encourage an open and honest dialogue about the hopes and hazards of raising a teenager today.

A report should be filed with local law enforcement or child protection agencies. I personally would want to meet with Alicia and her parents to notify them that I have filed the report and explain why. I would offer the school's support in monitoring Alicia and working with the parents to ensure her safety. At this level of legal proceeding, it would be appropriate to refer this family to victims assistance or family counseling through mental health or private practitioners. Kristina might recommend that the parents be involved in a parent support group and Alicia in a teen support group. Kristina could continue to monitor the situation at school and continue to work on behalf of Alicia's educational and social growth and development.

Prior to the beginning of their counseling relationship, Kristina would have explained confidentiality to Alicia as required by the ASCA (2004a) Ethical Standards on informed consent. In this circumstance, Kristina should tell Alicia that she is very concerned about her relationship with Cleofas. She could explain the parameters of statutory rape and the consequences of unprotected sex. She might suggest that the stress Alicia has been experiencing lately may be clouding her judgment and express concern that Cleofas is taking advantage of her.

Kristina should encourage Alicia to talk with her parents because she knows that they care about her and are there to provide her with support and guidance. If Alicia is unwilling, she may want to offer to meet with Alicia and the family together and help to mediate the situation. Again, if Alicia is unwilling, Kristina must inform her that ethically and legally she is required to report the sexual relationship between Alicia and Cleofas. Kristina needs to inform the principal of the situation and make a report to the authorities, preferably in Alicia's presence. She should wait with Alicia until the authorities and her parents arrive and then assist with the investigation as needed.

I would want to explore what else is important in Alicia's life. What are her interests, talents, and skills? Is she involved in extracurricular activities? Is she active in school, church, or community? I would also be curious to know if Alicia and her sister have been keeping in touch. What are the realities for the sister? Is she back in school? What kind of future is open to her in Mexico? What does Alicia want to accomplish with her life? What is her understanding of why the family immigrated here?

In addition, it would be helpful to talk with Alicia's parents about their disciplinary approach to see if some improvements could be made for adolescent needs. I am assuming that the parents are cooperative with the school as they have previously attended joint sessions with the counselor and Alicia. This also tells me that the parents must have given their permission for Alicia to be involved in individual counseling with Kristina. ASCA's (2004c) position statement on parental consent for service states that school counselors must ensure that parents understand the counselor's role, especially in regard to confidentiality, and must respect the inherent rights and responsibilities of parents for their children while working to establish a collaborative relationship with parents. The parents appear to be concerned and doing what they can to be supportive and cooperative. The school should view them as invested allies.

My sense from the incident description is that some of Alicia's difficulties are cross-cultural in nature. ASCA's (2004b) position on cross/multicultural counseling states that professional school counselors "use a variety of strategies to increase awareness of culturally diverse persons and populations, increase sensitivity of students and parents to cultural diversity, [and] enhance the total school and community climate for all students." Practicing as a cross-culturally competent counselor, Kristina would not jump to conclusions about Alicia's family but take cultural influences into consideration. She would know that it is customary in Latin culture for the man to take the lead in dealing with the authorities. Depending on the mother's personality and level of English proficiency, she may or may not be vocal in school meetings. Asking the mother would be helpful and add to a better understanding of the family dynamics. Alicia's parents, and especially the grandmother, may tend to hold traditional values. Alicia and her siblings, first-generation Mexican Americans, may have been raised in a traditional home, but within the borders of a different country, time, and culture. Often times, there is a clash of cultures, and the responsibility to find ways to merge the two falls on the first generation. The school counselor in this scenario has an opportunity to reach out a hand in support.

References

American School Counselor Association. (2004a). *Ethical standards for school counselors.* Alexandria, VA: Author.

American School Counselor Association. (2004b). *Position statement: Cultural diversity.* Available at http://www.schoolcounselor.org/content.asp? contentid=249

American School Counselor Association. (2004c). *Position statement: Parent consent for services.* Available at http://www.schoolcounselor.org/content .asp?contentid=213

Response

Phillip W. Barbee

Kristina's ethical responsibility is to support Alicia's growth and development while ensuring her safety and well-being. The *ACA Code of Ethics* (American

Counseling Association, 2005) emphasizes that a counselor's primary responsibility is to "respect the dignity and to promote the welfare of clients" (Standard A.1.a.). In this case, Kristina is faced with concern for Alicia's safety, while also respecting her right for privacy and confidentiality (see Standards B.1.b. and B.1.c., respectively). Alicia has reported that she has had unprotected sex. The main concern is that Alicia is 14 and her partner is 23 years old. Some cultures may consider this age difference acceptable. The prevailing view in the United States, however, is that this relationship is inappropriate and potentially exploitive, and as such is considered a form of sexual abuse (Nunnelley & Fields, 1998; Smith, 2002).

Although Alicia reported that she only had sex once and does not plan to do it again, future sexual activity cannot be ruled out. She is still seeing Cleofas behind her parents' backs and frequently missing school in the process. Overall, there is an existing, and potential for increasing, harm to Alicia. She is at risk for a sexually transmitted disease or a high-risk pregnancy. Severe emotional trauma is also possible. The Centers for Disease Control and Prevention (2004) reported that adolescent minors have the highest rates for gonorrhea and chlamydia. Most worrisome is that AIDS typically does not manifest symptoms until years after exposure.

Kristina's legal responsibility is clearly defined by federal and state laws. Sexual abuse of a minor is defined as an adult engaging in a sexual act with a person who is under the age of 16 and there is an age difference greater than 4 years, according to Title 18, Part I, Chapter 109A, of the U.S. Code (2003). In most states, the age of consent is between 15 and 18 (Sexlaws, 2006). By these definitions, statutory rape is sexual abuse and requires immediate reporting.

Kristina, as an emergency certified school counselor, is mandated by state law to report this case of sexual abuse. The Federal Child Abuse Prevention and Treatment Act (1974) inspired all 50 states to pass laws that mandate health practitioners, educators, and law enforcement personnel to report all known and suspected cases of child abuse and neglect to appropriate state authorities (U.S. Department of Health & Human Services, 2003).

Kristina's ethical responsibility is to ensure that Alicia's safety is not compromised by her running away from home. Kristina's meeting with the family did not note anything to suggest abuse. However, Alicia has reported that she plans to run away from home to be with her older sister, who has already run away and is living with her boyfriend in Mexico. Her younger brother will do the same as soon as he is old enough. We are not told how old the younger brother is, nor what age is "old enough" for him to run away or and how soon this event may occur. Kristina must determine whether this is what Anna Freud referred to as "Sturm und Drang" adolescent behavior (Craig & Baucum, 2002) or an indicator of something more serious in the home environment.

Notifying child protective services of the sexual abuse incident is warranted. With respect to the threat of running away, more information is still needed in order to determine whether authorities should be notified on this issue alone. The latter issue may provide amplifying information for the sexual abuse report. Child protective services will investigate all aspects of family dynamics and dysfunctions.

As a mandated reporter, Kristina must notify Child Protective Services in a timely manner. Many states specify how much time is allowed between discovery or suspicion of abuse and reporting of the incident. For example, practitioners in Texas must make a report within 48 hours (Texas Statutes, 2005). The fact that she may not have notified Child Protective Services in a timely matter may present a legal dilemma for Kristina and her practicum supervisor. Kristina immediately brought this issue to the attention of her practicum class; however, we are not told when the discovery was made and when the class met. The practicum supervisor advised Kristina to first consult with her field site supervisor. The supervisor would then consult with a colleague, followed by contacting Child Protective Services with a "hypothetical situation" to gain clarification before finally deciding whether to make a report. These actions would further delay reporting within the specified time parameters.

First and foremost, Kristina must inform Alicia of the requirement for notifying Child Protective Services. One hopes this possibility was presented during the informed consent procedure at the beginning of and periodically throughout the therapeutic relationship. The *ACA Code of Ethics* (ACA, 2005) specifies that clients should be given enough information to make a decision as to whether they will participate in counseling or not (Standard A.2.a.) and if and when confidentiality will be breached, such as in cases of danger to the client (Standard B.2.a.). The parents must also be informed because they are legally responsible for Alicia. Alicia should be encouraged to tell her parents. If this fails, Kristina will then have to make a tough decision about when and how to notify the parents.

Given the scenario related in the critical incident, the level of risk is high enough to notify Child Protective Services about the sexual abuse. With respect to the possibility of Alicia running away, Kristina still needs to gather more information to assess the credibility and possibility of this occurring and then decide which interventions to use.

The running-away problem may have stemmed from something other than abuse in the house. In addition to typical stressors associated with adolescent development, other problems may be rooted in cultural nuances or language. Alicia's parents are immigrants from Mexico, which may have contributed to the family stress level and resultant turmoil. The noted family dynamics may have provided some significant clues. The father was exhibiting male dominant behavior by doing all of the talking during the family visit, which in itself is not atypical behavior for Mexican immigrants. The family dynamics need to be accepted. He is fluent in English; however, we are not told if the mother is also fluent. If the mother is not fluent, another family visit could be rescheduled and conducted by a counselor who is well versed in their native tongue and skilled in multicultural competencies. Other family problems may also be the underlying cause of Alicia's at-risk behavior and her siblings' discord with the family. A family therapist should also be considered as another option.

References

American Counseling Association. (2005). *ACA code of ethics*. Alexandria, VA: Author.

Centers for Disease Control & Prevention. (2004). *Trends in reportable sexually transmitted diseases in the United States.* Retrieved July 15, 2007, from http://www.cdc.gov/std/stats/trends2004.htm

Craig, G. J., & Baucum, D. (2002). *Human development* (9th ed.). Upper Saddle River, NJ: Prentice Hall.

Nunnelley, J. C., & Fields, T. H. (1998). Child abuse: Coping with ethical challenges. *The Educational Forum, 63,* 44–50.

Sexlaws. (2006). *Age of consent.* Retrieved July 15, 2007, from http://www.sexlaws.org/ageofconsent.html

Smith, J. (2002). Evaluation, diagnosis, and outcomes of child sexual abuse. *The Child Advocate.* Retrieved July 15, 2007, from http://www.childadvocate.net/child_sexual_abuse.htm

Texas Statutes. (2005). *Family Code, Subtitle E. Protection of the child, Chapter 261. Investigation of report of child abuse or neglect. Subchapter A. General Provisions.* Retrieved August 3, 2008, from http://www.legis.state.tx.us

U.S. Code. (2003). *Title 18, Part I, Chapter 109A: Sexual abuse of a minor or ward.* Retrieved August 3, 2008, from http://www.law.cornell.edu

U.S. Department of Health & Human Services. (2003). *Modifications to the CAPTA state grant program.* Retrieved August 8, 2008, from http://www.acf.hhs.gov/programs/cb/laws_policies/policy/im/2003/im0304.htm

Chapter 23

I've Been Providing University Supervision a Long Time

Christine Suniti Bhat

Topics

- Supervisor's ability
- Effective supervision

Background

This incident is based in a large, urban, racially and ethnically diverse part of the country. As a school counselor educator, I work in tandem with site supervisors based in public schools. My role is to provide university supervision to counselors in training. This is done both in individual sessions with students and in group seminars with other students completing fieldwork and internship requirements.

Incident

During a group seminar, Alice, a Cambodian American student, voiced what she called a "fundamental incompatibility" with her site supervisor. She had completed approximately half of the required fieldwork hours for the semester with this supervisor and announced she could no longer work with him. Mr. Esteban Torres, her supervisor, was a Latino man in his early 30s. He was one of six school counselors based at a high school of around 3,500 students (approximately 40% Latino students, 30% Asian American students, and 10% African American students, with the remaining students being White, biracial, multiracial, or from other racial or ethnic groups). I asked Alice to help us (the rest of her group and myself) understand her reasons for the strong stand she was taking, and this is what she told us: "When I first started working at this school site with Mr. Torres, I felt very hopeful because he seemed open and I liked the fact he was one of the younger supervisors. However, I have since found out he is extremely inflexible in this thinking.

"Two recent incidents have convinced me that I can no longer work with him. First, he insists I only work with Asian American students. He tells me he has the Latinos covered, and Asian American students on his caseload have not received much assistance because they just can't relate to him. I actually think it is the other way around, and he finds it hard to relate to them. I explained to him I thought it was harmful for us to work with clients based solely on their race or ethnicity, to which he replied, "Trust me, I have been at this a lot longer than you have, and I know the best ways to serve my students." I felt he really closed the door on any further discussion and so, although I was not happy with the outcome of that discussion, I started working with Asian American clients only. Of course, it didn't seem to matter to Mr. Torres that these clients were either Vietnamese or Korean. He just seemed to lump them all together.

"I somehow managed to get over my disappointment with the way our last real discussion went and continued with my work. But last week we had our review-of-cases session, and for the second time, I was forced to see how very hard and inflexible Mr. Torres really is. I was discussing with him my case, a 15-year-old Vietnamese student who comes from a fairly affluent family. He was referred for counseling because his mother is unhappy with his lack of focus on academic matters. My client was very resistant to counseling, but eventually, during the third session, he began to express himself more honestly to me. I detected several irrational beliefs and statements that seemed to be guiding his views of his current situation. Therefore I began to work from a rational emotive behavior therapy theoretical perspective with my client, and began to dispute some of his beliefs. My supervisor, Mr. Torres, stopped the tape and asked me why I was 'badgering' the client. He then launched into a long discussion of how solution-focused brief therapy (SFBT) is the best way to work with my client. I tried to interject, but he told me he knew there was sufficient research backing his view. In fact, he told me the counselor education program at which he had trained did not even cover any of the other counseling theories because they are not effective with young people. He told me my best course of action was to go back to the drawing board and learn SFBT. If not, he said, I would never be able to work well as a school counselor."

Discussion

Alice was rather teary by this point. In the group, we processed her reactions to her treatment by her supervisor, and she received validation for her point of view. When asked to sum up her thinking at the end of this session, she said, "He makes me feel as if I am incompetent, and I know I am not. He is so overbearing about what he thinks; he makes me doubt myself. I dread going to supervision with him because I feel like all he does is lecture me and tell me all the things I am doing wrong. My confidence has really been shaken, and I cannot work with him. The worst part is he is so well liked at the school and everyone there (teachers and office staff) tells me how lucky I am to be working with him. But I can't help thinking if he makes me feel so bad, he probably makes some of his clients feel the same way too."

I spent time with Alice individually so we could formulate a plan of action. She told me she had made up her mind, and she would not return to that school site. I tried my best to convince her it would be preferable for us to go in together and talk to Mr. Torres. However, she was distraught and refused to go back. I was concerned that pushing her at this point would further undermine her confidence. So I decided to speak to Mr. Torres instead. I made an appointment to see him and met with him face to face. He told me he was glad Alice had decided to leave of her own volition because he was not sure this school was the best fit for her. When I discussed both incidents from Alice's perspective, he noted they were blown out of proportion. He admitted that he did think Asian American students would be better served by an Asian American counselor, and he admitted he believed strongly in the efficacy of SFBT in schools, but he did not accept he had been inflexible in his approach.

I did not feel that I was able to really have a discussion with him. In the end, I made a note that students from our program would not in the future be placed at that school site for either fieldwork or internship. And I worked with Alice to obtain for her another school at which to complete her remaining hours. Luckily this new school and the new supervisor worked out well for Alice, and she subsequently graduated from the program. Mr. Torres is still a counselor at the same school, and although I have made sure students from our program do not obtain supervision from him, I do know that students from some of the other counselor education programs do go there and work with him under supervision.

Questions

1. At the time, I felt as if I had done the best I could to protect my student and discuss with Mr. Torres what I perceived to be his lack of appropriate supervision. However, he never did seem to get my point of view. What else could I have done?
2. Alice's experiences continued to fuel much discussion in our university supervision seminars. I feel confident this group of students fully understood the pitfalls in Mr. Torres's approach with Alice. But I still feel worried that students from other programs will be indoctrinated to Mr. Torres's worldview. How could I have approached this more effectively?
3. I really believe the lack of training in supervision contributes greatly to a supervisor's lack of skills and abilities in providing effective supervision. But our state does not mandate training in supervision. I advocate for this to happen, but at the same time, I understand the time constraints most school counselors face. How might I have influenced Mr. Torres to seek out professional training in counseling supervision?
4. Alice felt secure enough to raise her concerns during supervision and to take a stand against Mr. Torres. I am concerned situations such as this one may happen at other school sites, and some students in

similar situations may not discuss them with me. I emphasize with my students that supervisors are not always trained in supervision, and they must trust their own judgment and discuss problematic issues with me. What else can I do to ensure my students are receiving quality supervision?

Response

Rose Marie Hoffman

As we teach our students, we never reach a point at which we no longer can benefit from consultation with our professional colleagues. This critical incident seems to exemplify such a case.

The incident involves several ethical principles Alice's university supervisor must consider. The course of action she chose suggests loyalty, as well as her perception of beneficence in this situation, took priority over the others. Although it is understandable that the university supervisor wanted to protect Alice from a subsequent distressing encounter with Mr. Torres while still in a fragile state, her decision to meet with him without Alice present undermined the student's autonomy. Did Alice really benefit from this course of action, or will it promote a continued dependence on others to deal with interpersonal conflicts she will face in her role as a professional school counselor? As an alternative plan, the university supervisor might have limited Alice's options to meeting with Mr. Torres with or without her participation.

Alice's ability to tell Mr. Torres she disagreed with his promotion of ethnic similarity in the counselor–client relationship, her identification to her supervision group of a "fundamental incompatibility" with him, and her steadfast decision that she could no longer can work with him suggest that she can articulate her own opinions, arrive at her own conclusions, and make her own decisions. We do not have evidence of whether Alice stated her concerns about working only with Asian students in the same way she described them to her supervision group. It may be that she, like many counselors in training, needs to develop her skills in effectively communicating and defending her point of view, particularly about beliefs she holds strongly.

The second point of contention between Alice and Mr. Torres was around her choice of theory. If Mr. Torres's manner of communicating was as Alice described, then it clearly was inappropriate. Yet, it is possible he stated in a less dogmatic way his requirement that school counselors in training learn solution-focused counseling. Such a requirement is not necessarily unreasonable, given the time constraints that contemporary school counselors face.

Some skepticism regarding how accurately Alice portrayed her case stems from the fact that we heard of no conflicts between Alice and Mr. Torres until this point, halfway through the semester. Additionally, one would wonder how Mr. Torres can be such a well-liked and respected colleague in his school, as well as a popular site supervisor with other school counseling training programs, if his manner is as abrasive as Alice suggests. Is it possible the university supervisor's loyalty to Alice obfuscated her ability to form an independent, unbiased impression of him? Might the university supervisor's interaction with Mr. Torres been more productive if she had recognized the possibility that Alice might be contributing something to the problem? Did the university supervisor's loyalty to Alice result in her unintentionally putting Mr. Torres on the defensive?

On the other hand, it remains possible Mr. Torres's behavior in this situation was indeed problematic. One way to address these and other issues in supervision is for counselor education programs to provide opportunities for facilitated discussions and other types of workshops for school counselors who supervise students in the field. In an effort to promote participation in such events, locations might vary and should include K–12 settings as well as other nonuniversity venues. Providing such trainings on the counselors' own turf may mitigate possible perceptions that the unspoken message is that the school counselors need university faculty to teach them how to be good supervisors. Recognizing the work of school counselors as site supervisors at the end of the year by providing certificates of appreciation also is recommended.

The university supervisor's point that an absence of formal training in supervision in many school counselor education programs constitutes a serious void in the training of professional school counselors is well taken. When school counselors who act as site supervisors to school counselors in training are not familiar with the various models of supervision, they may lack the ability to conceptualize the dynamics between supervisee and supervisor. They also may experience difficulty in understanding the levels of development of the supervisee. As counselor educators, we need to advocate for curriculum development in this area. Equipping our students with the knowledge and skills to be effective site supervisors before they enter the field will do much to promote the development of their future supervisees, as well as enrich their own experiences as active parties in the supervisory relationship.

Response

Heidi S. Deschamps

Counselor educators are often faced with complex dilemmas as they work to train new counselors. These difficulties are largely a result of the numerous individuals, groups, agencies, and systems involved in the training process. This incident highlights the challenges many counselor educators encounter as they work to collaborate with students, field supervisors, and school systems. Luckily, there are available resources that offer guidance in this situation.

The Association for Counselor Education and Supervision (ACES) has developed ethical guidelines for counseling supervisors (ACES, 1993). These guidelines describe a prioritized sequence of analysis when addressing a source of potential ethical conflict. If the counselor educator in this situation had attended to the following prioritized sequence, additional courses of action may have been illuminated (ACES, 1993, Section 3.20):

1. Relevant legal and ethical standards (e.g., duty to warn, state child abuse laws)

2. Client welfare
3. Supervisee welfare
4. Supervisor welfare
5. Program or agency service and administrative needs

In adherence to this protocol, one must first examine the relevant legal and ethical standards applicable to the situation. The *ACA Code of Ethics* (American Counseling Association, 2005) and the previously mentioned *ACES Ethical Guidelines* are the professional tools necessary to determine the appropriate course of action in this dilemma. Therefore, these resources will be referenced and used to highlight the essential elements of this issue. These documents will also provide guidance as to how the counselor educator might have implemented additional strategies to ensure the welfare of each individual involved.

The second matter to address is the issue surrounding client welfare. According to the *ACES Ethical Guidelines,* "the primary obligation of supervisors is to train counselors so that they respect the integrity and promote the welfare of their clients" (ACES, 1993, Section 1.01). In this situation, there is a concern that the field supervisor is recommending a practice that discriminates against Asian American students. According to Alice, the field supervisor is condoning the fact Asian American students have "not received much assistance because they just can't relate to him." This also presents a violation of the *ACA Code of Ethics* (2005), which clearly directs counselors to "not condone or engage in discrimination" based on ethnicity, race, or other criteria (Standard C.5.). It could easily be argued that this practice may have a negative effect on Asian American students' welfare. If these students are consistently denied services, it may inhibit them from receiving the same level of support provided to other students, which could have a direct effect on their academic, social, emotional, and cognitive welfare.

When one suspects a potential ethical violation, one is ethically bound to attempt informal resolution by discussing the issue directly with the counselor involved (ACA, 2005, Section H.2.b.). Though potentially uncomfortable, this situation provides the counselor educator with an opportunity to train students about how to address ethical violations in their workplace, a situation they will likely encounter in the future.

Although the counselor educator in this incident made an attempt to discuss the issue with the site supervisor, it appears that the concern that Mr. Torres's practices were unethical was not directly stated. Perhaps, if the possibility of unethical behavior was brought to the site supervisor's attention, a collaborative solution could have been sought. Including the student in the conversation would have provided an excellent modeling opportunity, helping her to gain vital conflict resolution skills. In the interest of client welfare, it is crucial that counselor educators attend to such issues directly. Although the counselor educator protected her students from the site supervisor's unethical practices, no action was taken to protect future clients. As long as the site supervisor continues these practices, client welfare is at risk. It is the counselor educator's responsibility to take appropriate action to ensure that the welfare of Asian American students is protected.

The next issue to examine in this scenario is supervisee welfare. This situation presented potential risks for Alice's personal and professional well-being. The hierarchy inherent in the supervisee–supervisor relationship placed Alice in a vulnerable position. Not only was it difficult for Alice to advocate on behalf of her clients, but it was also challenging to advocate for herself. The site supervisor was insisting that Alice abandon her chosen theoretical approach and adopt a solution-focused strategy. This behavior is in direct violation of the *ACES Ethical Guidelines,* which states that supervisors are required to (a) inform supervisees of their "theoretical orientation toward counseling" and "supervision model or approach on which the supervision is based" and (b) support supervisees "to define their own theoretical orientation toward counseling, to establish supervision goals for themselves, and to monitor and evaluate their progress toward meeting these goals" (ACES, 1993, Sections 3.07 and 3.08). Although Alice intuitively sensed the inequity of the situation, she was not armed with resources to address it.

It might have been helpful to educate Alice about the ethical obligations of supervisors and the skills needed to assess quality supervision by providing her a copy of the *ACES Ethical Guidelines.* This type of education might have allowed her to address the situation at an earlier stage, before she reached the point of feeling incompetent and overwhelmed. At minimum, supervisees must be provided with information regarding due process appeal, should a supervisor's actions come into question (ACES, 1993, Section 2.14). These resources might have allowed Alice to trust her professional judgment and inform others about the situation before it became a "fundamental incompatibility." The skill of addressing professional conflicts is an important aspect of counselor development and should be included in the training curriculum. When students are placed in the vulnerable position of being a supervisee, they must be provided with multiple avenues to address supervisor concerns, and must also be given the skills and support to professionally respond to such situations. The counselor educator appropriately protected the student in this situation but might have been able to intervene earlier if training regarding quality supervision were included in the student curriculum.

The fourth area of evaluation in this scenario includes the issue of supervisor welfare. At first, one might have little sympathy for the field supervisor. However, there are several courses of action that could better support his work as a counselor and a supervisor. The *ACES Ethical Guidelines* require counselor educators to "establish clear lines of communication among themselves, the field supervisors, and the student/supervisees" (ACES, 1993, Section 3.14). They must also "communicate regularly with supervisors in agencies used as practicum and/or fieldwork sites regarding current professional practices, expectations of students, and preferred models and modalities of supervision" (ACES, 1993, Section 3.13). In this scenario, the lines of communication were not established until a crisis arose. If regular communication were occurring between the counselor educator and the field supervisor, this issue might have been detected earlier, leaving room for a collaborative resolution and numerous educational opportunities for each individual involved. The counselor educator might have also recognized the supervisor's need for additional training.

The *ACES Ethical Guidelines* clearly require supervisors to have training in supervision before they become supervisors (ACES, 1993, Section 2.01). A university can require field supervisors to receive supervision training. A collaborative means of meeting this need is to provide supervision training to all field supervisors as a free workshop or at a discounted rate. This serves the dual purpose of meeting the field supervisors' obligations for continuing education units and the university's need of having trained supervisors in the field. Offering regular supervision training to one's community is also a means for providing a professional service, a central responsibility of counselor educators. If the site supervisor in this scenario had received quality training in supervision, many of these issues may have been avoided.

The final issue to examine in this scenario is the program or agency service and administrative needs. The initiation of supervision in this situation arises from the needs of the counselor education program. In order to train quality counselors, education programs rely on the supervision of counselors working in the field. The *ACES Ethical Guidelines* indicate "supervisors in university settings should establish and communicate specific policies and procedures regarding field placement of students" (ACES, 1993, Section 3.12). All too often, the expectations of field supervisors are communicated via a written document sent by mail or, at times, not communicated at all. The responsibility of communicating expectations about field placement and training lies squarely on the shoulders of the counselor educators within the university training program. If a counselor education program has a need for quality supervisors, it must provide opportunities for supervision training to take place, make clear guidelines regarding training, develop strong lines of communication, and provide ongoing support to supervisors in the field. To ensure these issues are addressed, it would be wise to provide a yearly or biannual supervisor orientation, make regular site visits, and provide supervisors a clear avenue for addressing supervisee concerns. These programmatic changes might provide a solid foundation for preventing some of the issues addressed in this scenario.

It is important that counselor educators attend to the complex issues involved in counselor training, including ethical standards, client welfare, supervisee welfare, supervisor welfare, and programmatic needs. Students may find themselves in a challenging situation without the necessary skills to address it. It is vital that counselor educators create avenues for ongoing training, communication, and skill development for every individual involved in the educational process.

References

American Counseling Association. (2005). *ACA code of ethics.* Alexandria, VA: Author.

Association for Counselor Education and Supervision. (1993). Ethical guidelines for counseling supervisors. *ACES Spectrum, 53*(4), 5–8.

Chapter 24

How Shall I Evaluate You? Determining Supervisee Inexperience, Impairment, or Incompetence

Barbara C. Trolley

Topics

- Supervisee competence
- Impairment versus incompetence

Background

I am a counselor educator at a private university located in a small-town community. I work primarily in our satellite cohort program, situated in a suburban area approximately 80 miles from the main campus, which is surrounded by three additional academic institutions with similar training programs. Students attending this school are from a highly diversified population, many are confronted with issues of poverty and family problems, and the supply of mental health services does not meet the demand. Sally is a 2nd-year graduate student in our school counseling track. She came into the cohort program with experience working in the mental health field, primarily with adults with chronic mental illness. Sally gave birth to her first child in the past year, which has triggered some unresolved issues for her. She is also having difficulty finding childcare, and she and her husband have experienced financial challenges since she quit her job to enter the program. Sally has been a student in several of my courses, and I am both her academic advisor and her internship supervisor. Sally presents as quite bright, articulate, and perceptive and has a good theoretical knowledge of the counseling field. She presents a strong commitment to addressing the mental health needs of children, often citing that the courses school counselors take in graduate school are the same courses that community counseling students take. She believes school counselors should provide more mental health counseling and less program development as established in the American School Counseling Association's National Model (ASCA, 2003).

Incident

Sally has been working as a school counseling intern in a middle school setting. She had presented audiovisual tapes of two of her counseling sessions in class, which were satisfactory. However, she seemed frustrated during one of the tape presentations because class time ran out and she could not continue showing the tape, engage in discussion, and obtain more feedback. On site, she received a satisfactory practicum evaluation from her site supervisor and began her internship at the same site. I prepared to make the required internship site visit, which involves observing the intern in a counseling session with a student at the school and briefly meeting with the site supervisor and the intern to discuss progress and issues. During my visit, I was struck by two seemingly distinct incidents, both of which raised similar questions surrounding Sally's competence.

The first incident occurred during my observation of Sally's counseling interaction with a student. At the start of the interview, she adeptly reviewed the student's academic progress, motivation, and standing. However, Sally then proceeded to delve fairly quickly and deeply into the student's feelings about recent custody issues, upcoming court dates, and the student's living arrangements. I was wondering during this time how the student felt talking about such intimate issues in the presence of a stranger, how the student would be able to return to class after discussing such emotionally charged topics, what the student's needs for and expectations of the session were, and why they were not addressed. I questioned whose needs were being met by the session: What were Sally's goals, intentions, and motivation in switching the topic to that of the custody hearing? Why was she apparently unable to pick up on the student's apparent emotionality during this discussion? Red flags were also raised when Sally disclosed to me after the counseling session that she was frustrated with the limits imposed by the school as to her counseling role with the student and her desire to be involved in the upcoming custody hearings.

Discussion

Although I have found it is frequently helpful when interns come into a field placement with prior counseling experience, I questioned whether Sally's experience was being appropriately applied in consideration of her specific role as a school counseling intern. I thought back to the academic information shared in the introduction class regarding the role of the school counselor, the ongoing conflict between the ideal and real roles of school counselors, and the various factors that can influence the school counseling role (e.g., number and type of professionals in the school setting that can provide counseling services; school size, location, and level; administrative policies and opinion as to the school counselor role; availability of community counseling services). I also reviewed the field objectives criteria in our field training handbook regarding the school counselor intern's on-site role and wondered if the information was adequate and clear. I tried to remember Sally's involvement in preplacement meetings, whereby field requirements and professional dispositions were discussed.

I remembered that Sally had missed at least one of these meetings because of childcare issues. Had Sally acted appropriately based on her prior work experience in the field, and was she just experiencing issues any novice intern in a new setting would encounter? Had she gotten in over her head? Had she acted in opposition to understood roles? Was she maybe even incompetent?

The second incident that occurred during this visit arose after the meeting with the site supervisor, Sally, and I had ended. During the meeting, the site supervisor focused on varied experiences to which Sally had been exposed during her internship at the school and said very little in response to questions about her progress. I wondered why. When I was leaving, the site supervisor joined me in the stairwell and shared the following information with me. She indicated Sally had requested to be given "more challenging" counseling cases. She stated that although she was quite impressed with Sally's practicum performance, she had concerns more recently during the internship regarding Sally's insistence on doing more mental health counseling with the students. The site supervisor indicated that she had begun to address these issues with Sally, as well as the topic of community referrals.

I knew there was definitely a large need for counseling services because of the existence of a high student–counselor ratio in the school, the reality of long waiting lists for community counseling services, the absence of a school-based family support center, and the existence of few student advocates outside of school. Yet it seemed very possibly that Sally was in violation of most of the competence criteria defined by Kerl, Garcia, McCullough, and Maxwell, as cited by Bernard and Goodyear (2004). Specifically, was Sally not cognizant of, and going beyond the boundaries of, her competencies and expertise? Was she fully aware of and treading cautiously regarding emotionally charged issues or was she delving too deeply, thereby leaving her students drained before their return to the classroom? Finally, in her efforts to provide mental health services to the "most challenging" cases in school, was she surpassing the limits of her ability and clinical training? (There was at least the ethical and potential legal question of how her qualifications were being presented, if not the perhaps more crucial concern of whether students were being negatively affected by her attempted interventions.) Another concern posed by the site supervisor was whether Sally had exaggerated or even misrepresented her clinical skills to families. The site supervisor concluded with her concern about Sally's extensive life demands, which negatively affected her ability to be on site for any concentrated period of time and resulted in her frequent cancellations of sessions. She stated the these issues negatively affected Sally's ability to get the most from the training experience, her functional level within the school, and the students Sally was seeing. I asked the site supervisor to directly address these issues with Sally, let Sally know that she had informed me of these issues, and note these concerns in Sally's mid-semester evaluation. I assured her I too would communicate with Sally and keep her in the loop of communication once Sally was directly confronted and made aware of my knowledge of the issues.

I left the site visit thinking about all that had transpired. Was this a question of impairment, in which Sally's diminished functioning since practicum was related to her new role as a mother, her financial stressors, and her attempt to balance all of the diverse roles in her life? Or was Sally really incompetent (Forrest, Elman, Gizara, & Vacha-Haase, as cited in Bernard & Goodyear, 2004)? Was her strong knowledge base of the field, articulateness, and intelligence a mask for clinical skill deficits? How much bias, associated with my multiple roles with Sally as her instructor, advisor, and campus supervisor, contributed to the problems at hand? Were Sally's problems accepting feedback in supervision and her difficulty in focusing on student needs indicative of her own feelings of inadequacy and compensatory arrogant behaviors rather than the situational factors of being tired and dealing with fairly complex cases?

When I returned to campus, I began to further examine the issue of informed consent around the evaluation of supervisee competence. Sally had clearly been given the program training requirements when she received a field training handbook in her first class. The issue of the standard field evaluation forms located in the handbook were addressed and discussed. Her site supervisor received a copy of both the handbook and a letter in which training requirements were defined. The spillover of Sally's life constraints resulted in at least one group field advisement meeting being missed, during which time prospective interns had an opportunity to raise questions and address the nuances associated with field training issues. Sally did receive follow-up e-mails from me regarding the factual information she had missed.

I began to think about remediation efforts for Sally and about her overall standing in the program. Once I received a letter and the mid-semester evaluation from her site supervisor (indicating what the concerns were and that they had been addressed directly with Sally), I processed these issues with my colleagues at a staff meeting. I developed an outline of the key issues that had surfaced, in terms of academic requirements and professional dispositions such as responsibility, maturity, and integrity. I reviewed this plan in person with Sally, taking a proactive as well as remedial stance, and encouraged her to obtain outside support and counseling. Unfortunately, increasing difficulty in arranging meetings with Sally arose, and when we did meet, our time was brief because of her late arrival. I did have an opportunity to ask her perspective on these issues and asked her to develop ways to address the key points in the remediation plan. I pointed out that it was important to address these issues now so that she could successfully meet and complete the internship retirements. Her response was defensive and aggressive, blaming the school for its shortsightedness in the counselor role and for not giving her the support needed on site. She also indicated she was not given a clear expectation of the program's requirements or assistance from faculty to address the problems on site.

I was left with a consideration of what factors best dictate supervisee competence. Although Sally was bright, ambitious, empathic, and dedicated, with an engaging personality, concerns had arisen with her willingness to discuss cases, openly receive feedback, ask for help, and grow as a professional. The final site evaluation was soon to arrive, and her site supervisor would receive feedback from counseling satisfaction surveys sent to parents of students Sally had seen. These forms may shed further light on the key issues.

Questions

1. Do you think the issues raised are ones of mistakes made by a novice intern, signs of impairment, or representative of incompetence? What type of assessment might be done to differentiate among the three options?
2. What could the site supervisor and I have done differently to address the issues?
3. Were the interventions and assistance provided to Sally consistent with the supervision guidelines set forth by ACES, ASCA, and the Center for Credentialing and Education?
4. In light of the diversity of roles school counselors often play across settings, how can the role of the school counselor, along with specific functional behavioral measures of competence, be defined?
5. What are the most significant aspects of competence (i.e., internal vs. external factors) in the preparation of school counseling interns, and how might they be best measured?

References

American School Counselor Association. (2003). *The ASCA National Model: A framework for school counseling programs.* Alexandria, VA: Author.

Bernard, J. M., & Goodyear, R. K. (2004). *Fundamentals of clinical supervision* (3rd ed.). Needham Heights, MA: Allyn & Bacon.

Response

Patricia J. Neufeld

As in education, a purpose of supervision is to teach, and the role of the supervisee is to learn. Moreover, education and supervision are alike in that there is an evaluative aspect to the intervention. Each ultimately serves as a gatekeeping function, regulating who is legitimized to enter the world of work in a chosen area (Bernard & Goodyear, 2004).

This incident raises a number of salient issues that arise frequently in supervision. The concerns of competence or possible impairment, the potential of internal and external influencing factors during a field placement experience, and the course of action taken to address such issues are common occurrences for counselor educators. The questions raised as well as an examination of the process that ensued during the course of the semester and the supervisee's response to feedback and supervision will be reviewed.

The counselor educator's response to the situation was first to examine if the student had been provided with the information and resources to inform her of the supervisee's role and responsibilities in the internship. The educator thoroughly examined the steps she had taken to identify the possible holes or deficiencies in the supervisee's preparation. Given that, the supervisor was then able to identify what was and was not occurring during the field experience.

Were Sally's issues the result of her lack of experience, impairment, or incompetence? The answer, quite simply, is yes. In some form, all three are factors. The difficulty arises in determining the extent to which each may be operating for Sally. A novice intern might be described as the intern who is uncertain of the parameters, boundaries, and unique cultures of schools. Often, interns are tentative in their approach to situations, carefully examining all the possibilities within the school community. Allocation of time and resources and responding to daily expectations of the school community are often overwhelming for interning students.

It appears several factors are interfacing with Sally's field experience. Most notably, she was not effectively making the shift from mental health provider to school counselor. Mental health counseling is a community-based model with an emphasis on outreach and counseling services. Within the school setting, counseling is integral to the educational mission of schools. Sally's understanding regarding the role, role definition, and responsibilities of a school counseling program within the educational system seems to be lacking. Sally has chosen to pursue the school counseling tract; therefore, the assumption is made that Sally has completed all of the necessary school preparation and course work prior to her field experience. It is possible she has the knowledge base of comprehensive school counseling programs and the role of the school counselor in addressing the personal, social, career, and academic needs of all students. The concern, most clearly, is not one of acquisition of knowledge but rather one of her ability to demonstrate this knowledge and understanding. Two examples are her request for more challenging cases and her desire to be part of custody hearings for the student with whom she was working. These examples reflect the mindset of a mental health intern rather than that of a school counseling intern. This is not to say school counselors refer out challenging cases or do not testify in court. All too often, challenging cases and subpoenas to appear in custody hearings are a part of the school counselor's day. Although it is difficult to determine Sally's internship experiences in delivering the guidance curriculum, individual planning, and system support, their absence in the incident suggests that she was not involved in those important aspects of the school counseling program.

This absence suggests the supervisee was not able to demonstrate her knowledge and skills in those areas and subsequently concentrated most of her energies in individual counseling. What is perhaps most disconcerting about the examples referenced by the university supervisor is that they seem to be firmly rooted in Sally's strong commitment to addressing the mental health needs of children as well as her beliefs that program development should be less emphasized by school counselors and school counseling programs.

The second concern reflects the supervisee's absences, missed meetings, and late arrivals for supervision. It appears from the incident that the supervisor had addressed these concerns, although it also appears the concerns were attributed to child care and other personal concerns. A 100% commitment to the field experience, including following the school calendar, attending in-services, and attending all group supervisor sessions at the university, needs to be one of the requirements for successful completion of the field experience.

Another factor in this incident in determining the differences between mistakes made by a novice intern, signs of impairment, or incompetence can be evaluated or assessed at one level by the supervisee's response to feedback. Most supervisees have a high degree of motivation to learn and use feedback as a means to improve their counseling skills and their ability to function successfully as a school counselor. When Sally was provided with feedback at mid-semester, she became defensive and blamed the site for not providing what she needed in her field experience. It is unclear if the on-site supervisor and university supervisor were jointly responsible for providing a mid-semester evaluation, but the institution is responsible for ensuring candidates have met the requirements for degree completion as well as certification and licensure in their state. The responsibility for timely, clear, and documented feedback is the responsibility of the university supervisor.

A possible future course of action might include a clearly articulated plan of action. When concerns regarding behavior or dispositions arise, feedback can be a necessary and effective measure for initiating change, and an improvement plan that addresses the concerns or dispositions and behaviors that do not meet expectations can become a contract between the student and program faculty. For Sally, areas of specific concern include

- accepts constructive feedback from others,
- takes responsibility for personal learning,
- is punctual and regularly attends classes and group supervision,
- conducts self-assessment through reflection,
- recognizes personal limitations and seeks ways to compensate or overcome them,
- is self-reflective and able to make changes to accommodate student learning, and
- demonstrates ethical behavior.

These seven areas in which she does not meet the expectations for candidates completing the school counseling program could be incorporated into an improvement plan that would not only provide written documentation of the concerns but would also provide examples within each of the concern areas. Most importantly, an improvement plan should articulate the time frame as well as the responsibility for Sally to demonstrate that she meets or exceeds the expectations in all of the areas on the improvement plan in order for her to be recommended for certification or licensure.

A final thought in reflecting on this incident is the question of why Sally wants to be a school counselor. School counselors are often faced with balancing numerous roles of counselor, coordinator, consultant, and teacher. It is imperative that school counselors function as integral members of the school community and strive to meet the developmental needs of every student. Clearly, with the demands of No Child Left Behind, the school counselor's role is pivotal in positively affecting student achievement. The American School Counselor Association model (ASCA, 2005) has provided the profession with a clear, conceptual framework to guide school counselors in meeting the social, personal, academic, and career needs of students through the delivery of a comprehensive school counseling program. Accountability for school counselors will continue to interface with student achievement.

An informal discussion and exploration with Sally as to her career goals and dreams, as well as her interests in pursuing school counseling and working in the school setting, may provide some insight for the university supervisor. Discussion might include the inherent ethical dilemma for the supervisor with Sally's strong commitment to the mental health needs of students as well as her belief that program development should be less emphasized by school counselors. The discussion could reference the preamble to the *Ethical Standards for School Counselors* (ASCA, 2004), which describes school counselors as "advocates, leaders, collaborators, and consultants who create opportunities for equity in access and success in educational opportunities by connecting their program to the mission of school." Repeatedly the ethical standards refer to the school counselor's responsibility in

- meeting the needs of all students,
- working toward the maximum development of every student, and
- providing students with a comprehensive school counseling program that includes an emphasis on working jointly with all students to develop academic and career goals.

Discerning Sally's commitment to the school counseling profession and interest in fostering the development and improvement of the school counseling profession may be of potential benefit in determining Sally's suitability to the profession.

References

American School Counselor Association. (2004). *Ethical standards for school counselors*. Alexandria, VA: Author.

American School Counselor Association. (2005). *The ASCA National Model: A framework for school counseling programs*. Alexandria, VA: Author.

Bernard, J. M., & Goodyear, R. K. (2004). *Fundamentals of clinical supervision* (3rd ed.). Needham Heights, MA: Allyn & Bacon.

Response

Hugh C. Crethar

In reviewing this critical incident, it is apparent Sally did not have a clear understanding of the appropriate role of a competent school counselor as defined by the American School Counselor Association National Model (ASCA, 2005). Sally appeared to believe the main purpose of an effective school counselor was to serve as a mental health counselor in a school setting. As I read the case, I found myself wondering what had been covered in Sally's didactic training. Presuming Sally's training maintained a focus on preparing her to work within the ASCA National Model, it is apparent she was striving to function as a mental health or community counselor.

Although the ASCA National Model states the role of a school counselor varies, it clarifies that the key role for school counselors is advocating for the academic success of every student, serving as a leader in promoting school reform (ASCA, 2005). Competent school counselors do this by promoting the development of all students within the academic, career, personal, and social domains. Sally's interest in performing deeper levels of psychotherapeutic work with the students is not inherently bad, just inappropriate to the role, duties, and typical training of today's school counselors. If Sally feels the students with whom she was working are in need of more psychotherapeutic counseling than is typically provided in the school setting, she is ethically bound to help them acquire such services. With student-to-counselor ratios of 500 to 1 or worse, school counselors are not in the position to provide intensive counseling services and actively advocate for the academic success of all students. This is one of several reasons why most school counseling programs do not offer training that would prepare their graduates to counsel in this manner with competence.

In reviewing the work of Dr. Trolley and Sally's site supervisor, I feel the overall response to the issue was appropriate. Communication was relatively speedy in response to concerns, very clear, and straightforward. I was also impressed with Dr. Trolley's focus on Sally's needs and possible countertransference throughout this process. Dr. Trolley demonstrated appropriate care for the students served by the intern as well as the intern herself. This balance is often tricky in supervisory relationships.

I would like to offer a few suggestions that might aid in avoiding repeats of the challenges that arose in this supervisory relationship. When considering the competence and disposition of school counseling trainees, it is important to consider what coursework is required prior to the start of the internship experience. Although it would be best if all coursework were successfully completed prior to beginning an internship, it seems imperative, at minimum, that students have successfully completed all core school counseling courses, skills and techniques, and practicum.

The internship manual should include a clear outline of student counseling dispositions and behaviors while on internship. The manual should clarify and reemphasize the model of school counseling taught in the program as well as what behaviors and dispositions are expected of the interns. As a safeguard against challenges like the one presented by Dr. Trolley, perhaps the internship manual could be shared with students prior to the beginning of internship, accompanied with a content examination to ensure it has been read and comprehended. Although this would add a little more work up front for all concerned, it might help to avoid the work that comes with students not understanding their roles as counseling interns.

In order to avoid repeat experiences like that with Sally, site supervisors should be invited to regular trainings wherein the model of school counseling taught within the program is emphasized and components of the internship manual are covered. A key focus of these training meetings should be to empower site supervisors to quickly respond to concerns they may have with their interns. These training meetings should emphasize the importance of clear feedback from a unified front of both the site and the university supervisors. I have found it most effective to portray this as a mentoring relationship shared by both supervisors with the trainee.

Finally, in response to the question of how functional behavioral measures of school counseling intern competence might be defined, I refer once again to guidance we receive from the ASCA National Model (2005). The model posits that the delivery system components of effective school counselors are (a) school guidance curriculum, (b) individual student planning, (c) responsive services, and (d) system support. If students are trained to work within this model, they should be expected to demonstrate knowledge and behavioral competence in each of these areas. To be more specific, Sally appears to not have had any experience or training in teaching. Although most states in the United States do not require school counselors to have certification as a teacher prior to school counselor certification, the skills of effective teaching are key to competent school counseling. As the school guidance curriculum is a focal component of any effective school counseling program, I encourage my site supervisors to emphasize this area with interns who do not come from a teaching background. Such a focus would be quite appropriate with Sally and, ultimately, distract her energy away from behaviors more resemblant of mental health counselors.

Reference

American School Counselor Association. (2005). *The ASCA National Model: A framework for school counseling programs.* Alexandria, VA: Author.

Chapter 25

Is This the Proper Use of Technology?

Paul Barnes

Topics

- Appropriate uses of technology
- School counselor training
- Use of technology and confidentiality concerns
- Presentation skills

Background

Elliott has been a full-time counselor educator for 5 years. He is often considered to be a techie by his peers. Despite resisting this label, he does enjoy thinking of ways to infuse technology into what he considers to be a very traditional counselor education program. In his 1st year, Elliott designed and implemented a new digital portfolio for counseling degree candidates. By entering a protected Web site, candidates could add digital content to their individual portfolio. When each portfolio was complete, it provided evidence of an individual's professional competence related to specified standards and requirements. The digital portfolio was created, edited, and viewed entirely over the Internet. Completion of the digital portfolio was required as one aspect of comprehensive examinations for candidates seeking a master's degree in school counseling.

While implementing the new portfolio, it became evident the candidates were enthusiastic about the project and liked the digital format. Additionally, Elliott received recognition from his peers for his new work in this area. Each new semester brought counselor candidates who had innovative ways to enhance their portfolio for the purpose of demonstrating their professional competence. Soon, online portfolios were composed of audio recordings, streaming video of counseling sessions, slideshows of guidance lessons, text, and images of students, teachers, and counselors involved in various guidance activities. Each bit of multimedia was described in relation to specific standards and was included to demonstrate particular counselor competencies.

As an effort to protect confidentiality, each candidate portfolio was password protected. Entering the password was required each time candidates accessed the content of their portfolio. If the candidate wished to share his or her professional portfolio with a prospective employer, the candidate could create an additional temporary password that provided a view-only mode of the portfolio via the Internet.

Incident

Maria recently graduated with a master's degree in school counseling and was actively applying for a job at area high schools. As a former counseling student and advisee of Elliott's, Maria stood out among her peers. Her counseling skills, professional disposition, and personal qualities were impressive. Maria was very proud of her digital portfolio and felt it gave an authentic representation of her diverse skill set. She liked the idea of sharing the portfolio with potential employers as a means of allowing them to view her work in action.

Maria was invited to interview for a school counseling position at a progressive area high school. She had recently completed some of her internship hours at this school and considered it to be her first choice. Despite her typical confidence, Maria was nervous about the school district's interviewing practice that involved a panel of six people: a school administrator, counselor, teacher, student, parent, and one member of the community. When the interview was scheduled, Maria was told to expect a period of questions followed by an invitation for her to share her thoughts that would help the panel make their selection of the new school counselor. Maria considered her digital portfolio to be the edge she needed to stand out among other applicants. Prior to the interview she made arrangements for a laptop and projector to be available at the interview.

The day of the interview arrived and Maria felt ready. She had rehearsed answers to potential questions, was dressed professionally, and had selected a short guidance activity from the portfolio to share during the interview. As the interview unfolded, Maria seemed to be connecting with members of the panel. Her belief that this job was a perfect fit seemed truer as the interview progressed. With the job seemingly in hand, Maria proceeded to the final aspect of the interview. As she projected her portfolio onto the screen and began to share her diverse experiences, the panel was openly impressed. Not only was she a terrific counselor, Maria was demonstrating technical competencies badly needed in the school counseling office. Maria quickly shared some examples of individual counseling sessions and then moved to a video that showed her ability to teach a guidance lesson. She proudly described the objectives for her classroom activity. Maria stated, "I was helping students who have special education needs to form meaningful career goals." "You have no right!" exclaimed a member of the interview panel. The parent representative on the interview team stood up and further declared, "I'll have your license," as she stormed out of the school conference room.

In response to Maria's obvious confusion about what had just happened, the principal thanked and excused the remaining panel members but asked

Maria to remain. The principal explained that Maria's example of a classroom guidance lesson included video of students in the background. Among the students shown was the angry panel member's daughter. After further investigation, the parent confirmed she was livid that her daughter's face was on the Internet and that she and her 17 classmates were identified as having special education needs.

Discussion

For the first time, Maria and Elliott were faced with ethical and legal questions concerning the storage and sharing of portfolio content. Not only did Maria fail to receive the job offer, but she and her institution were now faced with potential litigation. Maria also felt she had suffered damages in not being offered the job after this incident occurred. Furthermore, she claimed she was merely sharing a university-required project with a closed panel of individuals representing the school. No students were identified by name, nor was the portfolio available to the public.

Questions

1. What, if any, ethical principles have been violated in this case? By whom?
2. Does the involvement of the high school internship site or the university's role in candidate supervision change the dynamics of Maria's responsibilities? If so, how?
3. Is it possible for Elliott to implement policies and procedures that would allow for continued use of the online portfolio as an assessment tool without violating ethical standards? What policies and procedures are needed?
4. How might counselors demonstrate their skills in working with real student groups while respecting privacy and confidentiality? How does new technology factor into your answer?

Response

Jill A. Geltner

A number of ethical principles have been violated in this case, the most obvious being the client's right to privacy. This most basic right clearly outlined in the *ACA Code of Ethics* (American Counseling Association, 2005) and the *ASCA Ethical Standards* (American School Counselor Association, 2004) required the professional school counselor to inform clients of limits to confidentiality. These limits include, but are not limited to, presentations to a supervisor, consultation with other professionals, and prevention of foreseeable harm. According to the description, neither the student nor the parent was informed of any of these limits to confidentiality. Furthermore, the *ASCA Ethical Standards* recognizes the counselor's primary relationship with students but acknowledges the parents' inherent rights within these guidelines, requiring counselors to find the appropriate balance. In this case, neither the parents nor students were made aware of their rights as clients. Even as a counselor-in-training, Maria is required to be aware of and understand these rights and ethical guidelines that oblige her to inform students, or parents as appropriate (ACA, 2005).

In conjunction with right to privacy is permission to videotape counseling sessions. Counselors are required to obtain permission from clients prior to recording sessions, observing sessions, or viewing sessions with others, even within a training environment (ACA, 2005). Maria did not obtain permission to videotape, to use the video for her digital portfolio, or to share it at her interview at the school. In addition, counselors are expected to maintain and secure any client records created, including videotapes and information available through any medium, such as a Web site. Although the Web site and portfolios are password protected, they are accessible to students, faculty, and prospective employers. This is outside the boundaries of supervision limits even with proper informed consent. Online portfolios containing images of counseling sessions and students is a breach of the client's right to expected privacy. Encrypted Web sites are to be used to protect client confidentiality as part of informed consent (ACA, 2005). This violation has been committed by Elliott and Maria; both have an obligation to understand and adhere to ACA ethical standards. Furthermore, Elliott, as the supervisor, is required to ensure the supervisee has an understanding of client privacy and confidentiality.

As a counselor-in-training, Maria has the same obligations as a professional counselor (ACA, 2005). Supervision prior to graduation by the internship site and university should have interrupted these events. Unfortunately, it did not. The students in the class were videotaped and the video is available through the Web site. The professional school counselor is expected to "conduct herself/himself in such a manner as to advance individual ethical practice and the profession" (ASCA, 2004, Standard F.1.). In this case, Maria, the site host, and Elliott did not advance ethical practice but violated it. They are all guilty of unethical behavior by having prior knowledge of the circumstances without taking action to rectify the condition (ASCA, 2004). Furthermore, the limitations at the school site may supersede those of the university.

The online portfolio has great promise to enhance the educational experience of school counselors in training. With proper intervention, this program could continue. An encrypted Web site should to be used that requires more than simply a password to enter. The Web site needs enhanced monitoring to ensure that those who graduate or leave the program are no longer able to access the site. Having graduated from the program, Maria would have had limited access, if any, to the portfolio based on this set of guidelines.

Another approach to respecting client privacy is deleting identifying information about the students or schools: Faces and identifying information such as school mottos on classroom walls or teachers' names on the chalkboard can be blurred digitally. This would make it more difficult to examine client reactions in a counseling atmosphere, but it would allow for the counselors in training to be assessed without any violation of individual rights. Perhaps this video would be best used as an assessment tool only and not to demonstrate technological savvy in an interview setting.

As positive uses of technology increase, so does the obligation to properly create, operate, and oversee its daily use. As a counselor educator, Elliott's skills are well received, but little may be understood by the faculty related to risks. Elliott should convene a committee to assist him in making decisions for the online portfolio. Both ACA and ASCA encourage counselors to confer with one another to make important and difficult ethical decisions.

As discussed above, it is possible to illustrate counseling skills without identifying students. Blurring faces, changing voices, or taping only the counselor is a possibility. The skills of the counselor can be demonstrated without the view of the audience. Also, in this case Maria could have attempted to obtain permission from parents for students to be involved in her videotaped counseling session. Being a progressive school, they may have lent support to her efforts, appreciating the need for this type of assessment. Perhaps, with the proper topic, Maria may have had a large number of parents interested in her presentation, and parents and students could have attended together. To truly respect client confidentiality, counselors must inform clients of procedures, policies, goals, and techniques (ACA, 2005; ASCA, 2004) and proceed only with their consent. In the school setting, these clients include students, parents, and other guardians as appropriate. In Maria's case, this could have included informing the panel about the use of the portfolio and who has access. Perhaps with this information, this conflict could have been avoided. But the violations do remain; with new technology comes much responsibility. Elliott can explore what is available to use this portfolio as a tool while still protecting individual rights.

In summary, there are three issues in this vignette. First, videotaping without informed consent from students or parents is the most basic violation. Second, putting the videotape on the Web site was a further violation. This was done without informed consent and broadcast to a larger audience than even a traditional informed consent would permit. The third issue is Maria using the video Web site broadcast for a job interview. These are clearly intertwined but can be examined as independent sequential violations, all being a consequence of improper adherence to basic ethical guidelines.

References

American Counseling Association. (2005). *ACA code of ethics.* Alexandria, VA: Author.

American School Counselor Association. (2004). *Ethical standards for school counselors.* Alexandria, VA: Author.

Response

Lisa Tang

A primary issue in this incident is one of confidentiality. The immediate concern I had when reading that audio and video recordings had been incorporated into Maria's portfolio was whether she obtained permission to use those clips in her portfolio. According to the American School Counselor Association's *Ethical*

Standards for School Counselors (ASCA, 2004), counselors strive to "protect the confidentiality of information received in the counseling relationship...and such information is only to be revealed to others with the informed consent of the student" (Standard A.2.f.). In this incident, Maria has clearly violated the client's confidentiality. If the client is under the legal age to give consent, then Maria needs to obtain parental permission in order to use any counseling session for personal purposes.

Another concern I have involves Maria's clinical supervisor. It was not clear in this incident how Maria obtained the video recording. It is very likely she has kept a copy of the counseling session she had completed from her clinical or field experience course. I wonder what kind of rules and policies were established by her clinical supervisor in safeguarding the confidentiality of the clients throughout Maria's counseling training. According to the Association for Counselor Education and Supervision's *Ethical Guidelines for Counselor Supervisors* (ACES, 1993), the clinical supervisor is responsible for monitoring and supervising counselor trainees to ensure appropriate permission is secured regarding information or materials, including interview notes, test data, electronic documents, and audio and video recordings used in counseling, research, and training and supervision. Furthermore, the supervisor should also ensure that all training materials are appropriately disposed of, destroyed, or erased after the training or course has been terminated. It is very alarming to see Maria has not only used confidential information without appropriate permission but has also kept copies of it for personal use.

I think Elliott has made an effort to protect the confidentiality of his students as well as the information stored in the portfolios. It is evident in his choice of using a password-protected Internet portfolio. It is not clear what type of online portfolio Elliott uses. However, it is recommended that educators use secure servers, encryption, and digital rights management technology (Zambroski, 2006) to protect the safety and privacy of students' personal information. The password-protected access ensures others cannot view students' portfolios without permission.

In addition, as a counselor educator, he has the ethical responsibility to protect the clients' rights to confidentiality. Elliott or the counselor education department needs to establish clear rules and guidelines regarding what types of information can be included in a student's portfolio, especially when completion of a portfolio is a degree requirement. For example, he should provide students with a portfolio submission guideline that may include (a) a confidentiality and originality statement (in such a statement, students are required to state explicitly that some of the examples in the portfolio are the property of the university that has granted permission for these items to be used in a demonstration of his or her work); (b) file format (a list of acceptable and appropriate electronic formats); (c) competency evidence (this should clearly identify types of materials, whether content-based or performance-based, required for meeting the program standards); and (d) personal statements (e.g., counseling philosophy, resume, or reflective statement).

Furthermore, it is also Elliott's professional obligation to screen students' work and to make sure materials included in their portfolios are not only content appropriate but also legally and ethically obtained. Even though Elliot is not a clinical supervisor, he should still make sure the students in his class are aware of and abide by the professional and ethical standards and legal responsibility of the counseling profession. In the incident, it is also not clear if Elliott or the department has any knowledge of or granted permission for Maria to use the portfolio for private purposes. The best approach seems to be not allowing students to use or share the content of the portfolio for any other purpose besides trainees' competency evaluations. To prevent students from abusing the portfolio, Elliott should consider deleting the portfolio after the student has graduated from the program.

Any information and materials obtained as the result of the requirements of a course should only be used for academic purposes. The responsibilities of training and supervising counselor trainees should be clearly identified and shared between the internship site and the university. Before entering the internship, trainees should be informed about their legal and ethical responsibilities as well as any other performance requirements for completing the course and should be required to sign a pledge of ethical standards and confidentiality. The counselor education department should also generate a taping policy and distribute it to internship students. Because Maria seemed to obtain opportunities to work with children through her internship training with the university, she should follow the policies of the university.

Any information and materials she collected during her internship, if they are kept for future training purposes, should be considered the property of the university. She should have no ownership of any of the material unless she has secured clients' or parental special permission for private use. If she was not sure about her rights and responsibility regarding the use and sharing of such sensitive materials, she should have consulted with her supervisor or the department head for further clarification and instruction. Although Maria may think that she has suffered damages and therefore she is also a victim of this incident, I still think she does share equal responsibility for any potential litigation.

I think it is a wonderful idea for counselor trainees to use the online portfolio for job hunting. However, use of authentic examples of student work, transcripts of interviews, photographs, or other documents or narratives in the portfolio raises issues of confidentiality in the public display of this information. Therefore, counselor educators need to provide clear guidance in helping students make better professional and ethical judgments.

In addition to the above-mentioned necessary steps to protect clients' confidentiality, there are several strategies I would suggest counselor trainees adapt in order to safely and ethically use confidential materials in their online portfolio. First, special permission to use confidential information, including audio and video recordings of any counseling sessions, should be secured for the portfolio project. The purpose of the portfolio and the rationale of using the collected information should be clearly explained to the clients. Before uploading materials onto the Internet, trainees should remove any information that would reveal the identity of the client, such as the client's name or address or the school's name. If trainees want to use video clips to demonstrate their skill competency, it would be strongly recommended to focus the camera on the trainee and to avoid exposing the client during the counseling session. If audio clips are desirable, trainees should make sure the segment selected is one in which the counselor played the most active role in the interaction.

Second, if prior arrangement cannot be made for special taping, trainees or counselor educators should seek consultation and explore the possibility of technically blurring or masking the face or any recognizable feature of the client so that the identity of the client remains confidential. Furthermore, the actual recording of the transcripts of the session, with any identifying information edited out, should be used as evidence of skill competency. Trainees should also consider using role-play tapes or mock counseling sessions with their peers as other ways to demonstrate their competency. Because the portfolio is a degree requirement, it is essential that trainees and faculty members are informed about any necessary procedures or accommodations needed to complete the portfolio project, so trainees can be prepared and make prior arrangement for special tapings.

Finally, even with the client's permission, the best way to safeguard the confidential information is to not present it publicly. Students should consider using only nonconfidential materials in their online portfolio. They can list confidential materials as references and only present them when requested. Internet technology has been one of the greatest inventions of the modern society. However, although educators and students enjoy the convenience of this modern technology and its endless possibilities in the classroom, we should not overlook the potential harm it could bring when we misuse or abuse it.

References

American School Counselor Association. (2004). *Ethical standards for school counselors*. Alexandria, VA: Author. Retrieved January 22, 2007, from http://www.schoolcounselor.org/content.asp?contentid=173

Association for Counselor Education and Supervision. (1993). *Ethical guidelines for counseling supervisors*. Retrieved January 22, 2007, from http://www .acesonline.net/ethical_guidelines.asp

Zambroski, R. (2006). Think before you send. *Communication World, 23*(3), 38–40.

Chapter 26

Providing Culturally Responsive Supervision

Lawrence E. Tyson

Topics

- Ethical decision making
- Supervisee–supervisor relationship
- Aligning counseling practices with professional ethics

Background

I am a counselor educator in school counseling at an urban institution. There are 10 school systems in the large metropolitan area surrounding my institution. However, one can drive 30 minutes outside of the city and encounter some of the state's most rural communities. This incident involves a practicum student who currently works as a school counselor in one of these rural communities.

Sam is a former coach who went into school counseling when a position became available at the middle school where he worked. His principal offered Sam the school counseling job before he had finished his degree. As his university supervisor, I met with Sam twice a week to review his counseling tapes and as part of group supervision.

Incident

Sam works as a school counselor in a middle school. Sam's practicum supervision group meets once per week at the university. During group supervision, Sam began talking about his school's policy regarding corporal punishment. (It should be noted that I have deep-seated biases against corporal punishment, at home or in school.) As soon as Sam began talking about his school's stance on corporal punishment and the specific incident, I immediately felt both a physical and an emotional reaction.

Sam said that his middle school's disciplinary policy allowed for the paddling of students and that sometimes paddling was a necessary and useful deterrent for some children. As he shared this comment, I was amazed when three out of the other four counseling students nodded and verbalized agreement. All (except one) commented that they had used corporal punishment at home with their children or that if they had children in the future they would use corporal punishment, depending on the situation.

As I listened I was very aware of my own feelings. I questioned them about participating in acts of corporal punishment at their school sites, asking them if they had administered paddlings, participated as witnesses, or were involved in other ways. Before they answered, I went to my office and downloaded the American School Counselor Association's (ASCA, 2000) position statement regarding corporal punishment. As with many supervision sessions, I wanted to use this time as a teachable moment. I handed the position statement to each student. As we read the statement, Sam said the following: "You know, we don't paddle after 1:00 in the afternoon." The room became very quiet as I wondered what was behind this comment. He continued, "We don't paddle after 1:00 in the afternoon because the administration doesn't want red marks to be left on the child when she or he goes home."

I sat in total disbelief at what I was hearing, and Sam must have noticed the look on my face. He then said, "Dr. Tyson, I've lived in this community all my life. I know many of these parents and their families. This is where we live. The parents expect us to discipline their children when they deserve it, and that includes paddling if needed." He continued, "However, we're not stupid. The reason we don't paddle after 1:00 p.m. is that we don't want the child to go home with red marks. No one wants to get sued." As I looked around the room, most of Sam's peers were nodding and echoing agreement by saying, "You're right" and "I understand."

Discussion

I sat in total disbelief. As the school counseling advisor and coordinator, I teach all the school counseling courses, advise students, help with job interviews, and promote school counseling throughout the state. I honestly did not know how to respond. I believe school counselors should be change agents and work for systemic change. To me, it is incongruent for school counselors to promote healthy living while at the same time working in a system that believes it is acceptable to hit people to get them to do what you want. I have a fundamental problem with that philosophy.

As these thoughts swirled around in my head, I realized I had to respond in some manner that modeled my professional beliefs. I asked Sam to continue talking about having grown up in the community himself and how that related to social justice, systemic change, and advocating for all students. We ended the session that night with each explaining how they believed corporal punishment fit into those three areas.

Questions

1. Professionally, I know it was correct for me to introduce ASCA's position statement. Sometimes I've heard, "What's done nationally

wouldn't work here; we're different." How could I have helped them to make the connection between a national and a local perspective?

2. As I went home, I thought I should have been more assertive in pushing them to advocate for changes in terms of their school's corporal punishment policy. Should I have been?

3. I was bothered by Sam's comment, "I've lived in this community all my life." Should that matter?

4. I've had several students say their school administers corporal punishment, but they do not participate, witness, or in any other way become involved. I have never heard of the added rationale of why a child should not be paddled after a certain time of day. I'm very confused about what to do with this information (assuming it is true). Is there any additional action that I should take?

Reference

American School Counselor Association. (2000). *Position statement: Corporal punishment.* Retrieved June 12, 2004, from http://www.schoolcounselor .org/content.asp?contentid=199

Response

Rachelle Pérusse

According to the *ACA Code of Ethics* (American Counseling Association, 2005, Standard A.5.), it is imperative that counselors not make value judgments or allow their biases to affect their work with their clients. The same is true for supervisors and their supervisees. That is, supervisors must not allow their own values to interfere with their supervisory relationship. On first glance at this incident, it would appear that the supervisor is allowing his "deep-seated biases against corporal punishment" to influence his supervisory experience.

However, I believe this case is mitigated by the reality that corporal punishment has been shown to have deleterious effects on children. Corporal punishment has been banned by most industrialized countries, with the exception of 22 states within the United States (National Coalition to Abolish Corporal Punishment in Schools [NCACPS], 2004a). Over 40 professional organizations have called for or written position statements supporting the abolition of corporal punishment in schools, including the American School Counseling Association (ASCA) and the National Association of Elementary School Principals (NCACPS, 2004b). Furthermore, data disaggregated by gender and ethnicity show that students of color and males are more likely to receive corporal punishment (NCACPS, 2004a). Therefore, this issue rightly falls within the realm of advocacy, social justice, and systemic change and fits with the counselor educator's view of the school counselor's role. This view of school counselors is also consistent with the ASCA National Model (ASCA, 2003).

The counselor educator in the case study rightly produces the position statement of ASCA regarding corporal punishment. The ASCA position statement reads, "Professional school counselors promote understanding of and research on alternatives to corporal punishment, seek legislative solutions and advocate for the use of more effective and affirmative discipline methods" (ASCA, 2000). If the counselor educator truly wishes for his students to learn advocacy skills, he must be willing to model these skills to the students. This counselor educator clearly needs to educate these students on the perils of corporal punishment. If students armed with knowledge about the effects of corporal punishment still do nothing to help promote a healthy change for the system, then the counselor educator should take it upon him- or herself to advocate for students and systemic change in local school districts and at the state level. It is not good enough to expect others to fight and advocate for the best interest of students; school counselor educators should have that same responsibility.

The counselor educator states that several students have argued that "what works nationally wouldn't work here; we're different." Such statements lead to inaction. When Sam states, "I've lived in this community all my life," it may signify that Sam is unable to advocate for students for fear of being disliked by those he serves. To this end, the circumstances leading up to this comment might reflect student recruitment or prescreening issues, or possibly an oversight in the preservice training program. Students must understand that their responsibility as professional school counselors will include advocacy, and at times, such advocacy may make them unpopular with some stakeholders. Students need to be willing to let go of being liked by everybody all of the time in order to become effective.

The counselor educator asks whether he should have been more active in pushing students to advocate for change. I think this is the wrong approach. Modeling advocacy and raising students' awareness about corporal punishment would be more effective than trying to force others to act, especially if their failure to act might reflect a lack of education or awareness on their part.

Students who say that they do not participate, witness, or in any other way become involved with corporal punishment are reminiscent of those throughout history who have turned a blind eye toward social injustice. To not advocate against the status quo is to support the status quo. Inaction and ignorance are not fundamentally sound reasons to allow others to suffer.

Besides educating students about their responsibilities as advocates, there are many actions that the counselor educator might take. For example, he might educate others about corporal punishment through conference presentations, guest lecturing, or local workshops; provide workshops to educate parents about alternative discipline methods; and join forces with local and national professional associations to lobby for changes in the state law.

References

American Counseling Association. (2005). *ACA code of ethics.* Alexandria, VA: Author.

American School Counselor Association. (2000). *Position statement: Corporal punishment.* Retrieved June 12, 2004, from http://www.schoolcounselor .org/content.asp?contentid=199

American School Counselor Association. (2003). *The ASCA National Model: A framework for school counseling programs.* Alexandria, VA: Author.

National Coalition to Abolish Corporal Punishment in Schools. (2004a). *United States: Corporal punishment and paddling statistics by state and race.* Retrieved June 12, 2004, from http://www.stophitting.com/disatschool/states Banning.php

National Coalition to Abolish Corporal Punishment in Schools. (2004b). *United States organizations opposed to school corporal punishment.* Retrieved June 12, 2004, from http://www.stophitting.com/disatschool/usorgs.php

Response

Carolyn B. Stone

The American School Counselor Association (ASCA) provides ethical codes to guide us and to provide us with a framework for our actions and behaviors in the course of completing our professional obligations (ASCA, 2004). Ethical codes are situational. The codes must be applied to community and institutional standards, as these can differ significantly based on geographical location. It is sometimes difficult to accept that professional behavior varies based on the prevailing standards of the community in which the school counselor is practicing. Counselors need to be aware of and respect institutional and community standards. For example, it is acceptable behavior for school counselors in certain schools and communities to refer pregnant students to Planned Parenthood, whereas in many communities this would be considered a serious breach of ethics and an infringement on parents' rights to be the guiding voice in their children's lives.

Acknowledging the prevailing standards of a community does not mean we accept unconditionally the standard if we believe a practice, policy, or law of a particular school or community is in any way detrimental to a student. The ethical counselor advocates in a responsible manner when community standards or the standards of the school need to change so that students are protected (ASCA, 2004, Standard F.1.D.).

The counselor educator in this critical incident could help the supervisees understand the significance of an ASCA position statement on corporal punishment. The fact that all 50 states had representatives who gave input and eventually approved the position statement on corporal punishment is crucial information because it shows that this is the prevailing national standard for the profession. The process demonstrates the value that should be placed on these statements by the membership of the school counseling profession. An important discussion could ensue so that these supervisees understand that their ethical codes and position statements are the norms, customs, and beliefs of their profession that have withstood the test of time. It would be helpful if they could realize that to step too far outside the bounds of what their profession advocates (i.e., abandoning corporal punishment) is to risk going against the prevailing beliefs or norms of their profession.

If possible, the counselor educator could adjust the assignments for the supervisees or challenge them to (a) find research articles that support corporal punishment or refute the effectiveness of corporal punishment in school; (b) interview supervisors in Child Protective Services to determine what constitutes abuse, the level of incidence for the community, the number of students who have been removed from homes for abuse, the number of children per capita who have died at the hands of parents as compared with the same figures from other parts of the United States, and other important information to see how a community that believes corporal punishment is appropriate compares to geographical locations who do not endorse corporal punishment; (c) write a thought paper that requires them to wrestle with the issue by supporting the opposite point of view; or (d) engage in a debate with others who do not believe in corporal punishment.

School counselors are respectful of the values of their students and their families and are vigilant to avoid imposing their own values on their students and their parents or guardians. It is in this same spirit that counselor educators are sensitive to and cautious about imposing their values on the students they are preparing to be school counselors. However, it is also the responsibility of counselor educators to prepare trainees to practice as systemic change agents, challenging them and teaching them to examine practices and advocate for change when practices adversely stratify students' opportunities. It is therefore appropriate—indeed, an ethical responsibility of counselor educators—to ask tough questions and encourage trainees to evaluate their stance on controversial topics such as corporal punishment. This counselor educator is correct in believing that he should have been more assertive with these practicum students in pushing them to critically examine their opinions to advocate for change in terms of the school's corporal punishment practice. The counselor educator would have been correct in asserting his authority to challenge these practicum students to critically examine their position on corporal punishment.

School counselors more than any other person in the school setting must have a penchant for social justice and be willing to improve their awareness, knowledge, skills, and effectiveness in working with diverse populations: ethnic and racial status, age, economic status, special needs, English as a second language or English language learners, immigration status, sexual orientation, gender, gender identity or expression, family type, religious or spiritual identity, and appearance (ASCA, 2004). The statement "I've lived in this community all my life" is derogatory and generally reserved to describe those whom the speaker believes to be inferior, wrong, dim-witted, or offensive. This counselor educator was justified in being disturbed by the statement, as counselor educators are duty bound to send people into the profession who operate with strong personal and social consciousness skills. To graduate a candidate with dogmatic, prejudicial views is to risk placing someone in the profession who will be unwilling or unable to advocate for all students and instead be content to select and sort those students "worthy" of his or her attention.

School counselors are mandated child abuse reporters, and it is cause for concern when school officials set cut-off times for paddling so as not to leave red marks. If this secondhand information is true and if school officials fear a lawsuit, then they must believe that their actions are bordering on potential child abuse. If corporal punishment is to be administered, it needs to follow strict procedures and policies as authorized by the school system. This counselor educator needs to have a discussion about the seriousness of mandated child abuse reporting with the practicum students. A phone call to district-level administrators to share the cut-off time information may well save the school district a costly lawsuit in the future and students additional harm. The counselor educator would be prudent to carefully choose whom to call and to negotiate the politics so that the report has a chance of being received without suspicion or hostility. One would hope that there would be a reasonable response that does not damage the relationship between the school district and the university and that district administrators would investigate and deliver professional development to their principals. Depending on how the conversation with the practicum students proceeds, a phone call to Child Protective Services may be in order.

Reference

American School Counselor Association. (2004). *Ethical standards for school counselors.* Alexandria, VA: Author. Retrieved August 2, 2004, from http://www.schoolcounselor.org/content.asp?contentid=173

Chapter 27

Putting Out a Fire:
An Intern Misperceived

Jean Sunde Peterson

Topics

- Supervisee professional development
- Direct supervision
- Roles and responsibilities of supervisors and supervisees

Background

A conscientious school counseling intern with no teaching experience had a successful first semester in an elementary school, although she missed several days because of colds and flu, not uncommon for those whose immune systems have not yet developed appropriate defenses for the school environment. She received high praise from her site supervisor at the end of the semester for her rapport with children, skills, and conscientious follow-through. Her site supervisor is a split counselor, spending 3 days a week at one elementary school and 2 days a week at the elementary school where her intern is placed. The intern does not spend time at the other elementary school. The site supervisor has been counseling for a number of years. The district offers supervision workshops provided by the local university but does not yet require counselors who wish to supervise a practicum or intern to attend.

Incident

During second semester, the intern continues to cover the bases while her supervisor spends 3 days during the week at another school. Additionally, the intern's absences have continued because she has not completely recovered from her earlier respiratory illnesses. The intern has not worried about her absences because she is ahead of schedule for accruing the required hours at her school site.

Contrary to the site supervisor, the principal has not been impressed with this intern. The principal views the intern as not a team player and who is sick a lot, and frankly, he is unsure of how she spends her time. The intern, who is somewhat shy and a perfectionist, increasingly interprets the principal's unsmiling demeanor and not-so-social personality as critical and nonvalidating. The principal has been aware of her absences and has perceived her increasingly sober and pale countenance as apathy and a lack of enthusiasm for her work. As one of her assigned duties, the intern regularly publishes a high-quality counselor newsletter for school personnel and parents, but some of the teachers, unaware of her other activities such as individual and whole-classroom sessions, believe she has been "just sitting at the computer."

Discussion

The site supervisor is often at the second school site, and the intern has consequently developed a level of autonomy and self-sufficiency that has led her not to ask questions or check out concerns. The site supervisor is not available to "protect" the intern, and a negative spiral of perceptions has by now become well entrenched, even though the intern remains unaware of how she has been, and is being, perceived.

A new adjunct professor is the intern's campus supervisor for the spring semester. This instructor has not followed program guidelines regarding site visits and has not yet visited the site. The program coordinator finally hears, through another local school counselor, that the intern is not doing well and the situation was recently discussed at a district school counselors' monthly meeting.

Questions

1. What roles and responsibilities of campus and site supervisors are pertinent to this situation?
2. How might this situation affect the intern, site supervisor, and program?
3. What recommendations might be made to the site supervisor regarding her ability to supervise future interns?
4. What programmatic and curricular adjustments might the program coordinator need to make to ensure such a situation will not occur in the future?
5. What information, provided to them early in the year, might have helped the principal, the intern, the site supervisor, and the campus supervisor to avoid this unfortunate situation?

Response
Laurae K. Wartinger

The misperceptions in this incident resulted from a lack of clarity around the roles and responsibilities of all parties involved. There seemed to be particular confusion around the roles and responsibilities of the campus and site supervisors. The role of the campus supervisor and site supervisor do overlap in this situation because both parties are responsible for ensuring that the intern develops a suitable professional identity as a school counselor. Additionally, both supervisors should be concerned with the counseling skill development of the intern and the well-being of the students being served by the intern; however, there are differences in the role of each supervisor.

The campus supervisor is primarily concerned with the education and training of the counseling intern and is responsible for assisting the intern in translating counseling theory into practice. The role of the campus supervisor also includes being a liaison between the academic and internship sites. Accordingly, the campus supervisor should have frequent contact with the site supervisor to discuss both progress and issues of concern. Ultimately, it is the responsibility of the campus supervisor to ensure that the intern has adequate support, which includes, but is not limited to, sufficient on-site supervision of school counseling duties.

The role of the site supervisor is to ensure delivery of quality services to students in the school community through regular on-site supervision of the intern. The site supervisor's role includes guaranteeing the services delivered are within the intern's scope of competence. The role of the school counselor involves serving students across academic, career, and personal social domains. Delivery of these services is achieved through individual and small-group counseling, large-group guidance, and consultation. Adequate delivery of these services requires communication with teachers and administrators. The site supervisor is in the best position to communicate expectations related to the internship experience to stakeholders in the school, including what duties are and are not appropriate for interns to perform.

This critical incident will likely affect the intern, site supervisor, and the counselor education program in a negative manner. The intern in this situation stands to have a tarnished reputation as a result of the experience and may have difficulty securing a permanent school counseling position in the immediate area. The site supervisor may lose future opportunities to supervise interns and may have lost the confidence of administrators and teachers. And finally, the program may lose the current placement and future placements in the surrounding area if the program is perceived as not providing schools with competent and adequately supported interns.

The following recommendations could be made to the site supervisor regarding her ability to supervise future interns. The program coordinator should meet with the site supervisor and program supervisor to discuss the purpose of the internship and the program's expectations. The site supervisor should agree to be on-site with interns, provide them with regular supervision, and engage in frequent communication with the program supervisor. Additionally, the site supervisor should agree to attend the supervision workshop and become trained in the delivery of supervision services.

It would also be prudent for the program coordinator to make some curricular adjustments to ensure such situations would not occur in the future. Most important, the program coordinator should require training in supervision for both program and site supervisors. The training could be provided for continuing education credit as incentive for site supervisors taking responsibility for interns. Ideally, the training should include an induction to the roles and functions of both the program and the site supervisors, as well as essential information related to supervisee development.

The program coordinator should also create a manual for the internship experience that outlines the roles of and responsibilities of the intern, site supervisor, program supervisor, and program coordinator. The program coordinator should endorse the use of a supervision contract between the intern, site supervisor, and program supervisor.

The supervision contract would include agreements about the minimum number of site visits from the campus supervisor, minimum hours of supervision from both the site and the program supervisors, and goals for the supervisory relationship between the intern and both supervisors. The program coordinator should also enrich evaluation procedures for the internship experience by including questions directed to the site supervisor, campus supervisor, and intern related to the level of communication and support present during the internship experience. Finally, the program coordinator should establish an advisory committee made up of site supervisors, principals, interns, and program supervisors in order to receive feedback on the internship program.

Essential information provided to the stakeholders in this situation early in the year might have helped the principal, the intern, the site supervisor, and the campus supervisor avoid this unfortunate situation. First and foremost, the intern should have been empowered with the information about the appropriate duties associated with her role. Role induction for the intern is essential for a successful internship experience and should have occurred through interaction with the campus supervisor. The campus supervisor should have been aware of the site supervisor's responsibilities in another school as well as the duties that were being performed by the intern. The campus supervisor is responsible for ensuring that interns are engaging in duties that are consistent with the role and function of school counselors under the direct supervision of a site supervisor. The site supervisor should have been informed about what was expected of the intern, including appropriate guidelines for supervision. The site supervisor should also have known to expect visits and frequent communication from the program supervisor, including what steps to take if the visits were not occurring. The principal should have been given information regarding the duties of interns and expectations about the internship experience procedures for accountability for the intern in the school counselor's absence.

It is much easier to prevent a fire than it is to put one out after it has started. The misperceptions of the well-meaning intern were a corollary to the insufficient communication between the persons charged with ensuring that her internship environment was conducive to her professional development. We can avoid situations such as this with our own interns if we are diligent about communicating the roles and responsibilities of interns, supervisors, internship sites, and counselor education programs in a comprehensive and consistent manner.

Response

Katrina Cook

The importance of the internship experience in helping counseling students make significant progress toward developing their emerging professional identity cannot be emphasized enough. In fact, the internship experience could arguably be the most important experience of the counseling student's academic career. It is often during the internship that novice counselors learn firsthand whether they have what it takes to be a counselor. The habits they develop during this time, whether effective or not, may follow them throughout the remainder of their professional service.

In this case, the intern is approaching the completion of her internship experience. Although she appears to have put her time in and is accruing the hours she needs to meet her course requirements, it seems that important opportunities for professional growth have been lost. I find it very frustrating when students consider internship as just one more hoop to jump through rather than embracing it as a rich opportunity for growth. However, in this case, it would appear that the intern's university and site supervisors could each shoulder a portion of the responsibility for the intern's limited growth during this internship.

The American Counseling Association's *ACA Code of Ethics* (2005) differentiates among the responsibilities that the university supervisor, site supervisor, and counseling student hold regarding internship experiences. The university supervisor is responsible for developing and communicating policies regarding the site supervisor's role and the student's role within the fieldwork experience. The university supervisor is also required to verify that the site supervisors are qualified to provide supervision and are aware of their ethical obligations within this role. It is the university supervisor's responsibility to provide regular feedback to the intern about her progress. In this case, the new university supervisor has not followed the university's policies and has not visited the site. Although unclear, it seems doubtful that the university supervisor has had any contact with either the site supervisor or the student. It is possible that during a site visit, the misperceptions that the staff holds of the intern could have been brought to his or her attention while there was still time to address them.

The site supervisor also appears to have fallen short regarding support for this intern. The *ACA Code of Ethics* (2005) requires supervisors to actively pursue continuing education in counseling and supervision. Although this district offers training for its site supervisors, it is not required. It is unclear from this example whether or not the site supervisor attended this training or not. Supervisors are also expected to assess an intern's progress and provide feedback on a regularly scheduled basis. These meetings could have given the supervisor the opportunity to point out to the intern how she is being perceived by the staff. Together they could have explored options and developed a plan of action for the intern. Instead, it would appear that the supervisor just left the intern alone to do the best she could on her own.

Although the heaviest burden for this situation falls to the supervisors, the counseling intern must also accept some responsibility for this circumstance. The *ACA Code of Ethics* (2005) indicates that counselors must recognize when their own physical problems may harm a client. Although it is unlikely that the intern's cold could harm any of the students she works with, her frequent absences do seem to impede her effectiveness on the campus. Although she may not have control over her susceptibility to colds, she could visit her doctor or take other steps to minimize the effect of the cold symptoms on her health and her ability to meet the requirements of her position. Information from her university or site supervisor about the importance of self-care for counselors as well as feedback about how her current physical condition might limit her effectiveness may have helped the intern to consider alternate options for herself.

The American School Counselor Association's *Ethical Standards for Schools Counselors* (ASCA, 2004) expects that a school counselor "establishes and maintains professional relationships with faculty, staff, and administration to facilitate an optimum counseling program" (p. 3). It is clear that this intern has not successfully developed professional relationships with the principal and other members of the staff. However, the lack of feedback and modeling of appropriate communication skills by her university and site supervisors contribute to this failure. In fact, one could argue that the intern's avoidance of the principal mirrors the site supervisor's unavailability and the university supervisor's absence.

It would seem from the author's description that this supervisee has the potential to be a competent and committed counselor. However, the lack of adequate supervision during her internship appears to have limited her professional growth. Both the university program and the school district program share a responsibility to guide counseling interns on their journey toward professionalism. Strict adherence to the ethical guidelines for supervision, clear and frequent communication about the internship process, and careful, intentional monitoring of each intern's progress could facilitate greater growth experiences for future interns. Interns who benefit from a structured and carefully monitored intern experience may be able to enter the profession with a clearer concept of what strengths and weaknesses they bring to their chosen profession. This enhanced self-awareness could in turn enhance their effectiveness as counselors.

References

American Counseling Association. (2005). *ACA code of ethics.* Alexandria, VA: Author.

American School Counselor Association. (2004). *Ethical standards for school counselors.* Alexandria, VA: Author. Retrieved February 18, 2005, from http://www.schoolcounselor.org/content.asp?contentid=173

Chapter 28

What Happens When My Student Is More Educated Than the Supervisor?

Trish Hatch

Topics

- Supervisee–supervisor relationship
- Training and preparation issues

Background

I am a school counselor educator and university supervisor to 12 fieldwork students in various districts in a metropolitan area. The school systems are highly diverse and vary in their socioeconomic status. My fieldwork students are 2nd-year students who have spent their 1st year completing 200 hours of practicum in highly diverse, economically challenged schools in the city. During this fieldwork year, they are required to complete their final 400 hours. The students are well trained to implement the American School Counselor Association National Model (ASCA, 2003) and become advocates, leaders, and systems change agents. Most of them have been to a National Model Academy and have worked an additional 100 hours in their 1st year implementing federal grants in the local schools. They have been provided a great deal of supervision leading to an increased ability to learn and perform school site activities, measure results, see systems change issues, and use their voice to advocate for additional support for students. They are comfortable asking questions and seeking clarification when they do not understand something. They are still, however, learning the necessity of being politically correct and understanding the chain of command.

Keith is a 2nd-year student who has been referred to a particular middle school by an administrator at the central office who is in charge of the placement of school counselor trainees. According to the central office administrator, the school counseling team she is placing Keith with "is doing great things, understands the National Model, and is a good site for a student to come on board." After meeting with the site supervisor, Keith reports his site supervisor appears to be less than knowledgeable about the model, and he feels she was assigned to him without the preparation necessary to be a good supervisor. He shares with me that she told him he is her first fieldwork student and she has no experience in the area. I e-mail her and introduce myself, offer to answer any questions, and give her an overview of National Model expectations Keith has for the year. She indicates she is looking forward to a good experience.

Incident

On a Friday afternoon the on-site fieldwork supervisor calls and informs me that she has "serious concerns" regarding Keith. Evidently, Keith

1. set up a time to observe an Individual Education Program (IEP) meeting without telling her first;
2. went to the IEP meeting and, according to her, "represented" the counseling department without getting permission to do so;
3. approached a teacher and offered to teach a study skills guidance lesson without asking her first;
4. arranged to get additional hours from another school counselor who was covering the school site during the 4-week intersession; and
5. asked the principal if he could have access to the State Youth Survey data (he wanted to look at site needs, which was part of the requirements for a class he was taking).

According to the site supervisor, Keith lost her trust by doing these things. I was very surprised to hear this. I had spoken with Keith earlier and he had shared with me his excitement regarding arranging hours during intersession, teaching study skills to students, meeting the principal, and learning about IEPs. He also mentioned how well he was getting along with the supervisor. I decided to probe with her further regarding the incidents.

Discussion

As I heard her tell me her concerns, I realized there were several issues that needed to be addressed with Keith, as well as with her. I was determined to assist both of them in doing whatever it took to help her become a good site supervisor and at the same time assist Keith in understanding school politics and chain of command. It appeared from what she stated that Keith had stepped on several toes (intentionally or unintentionally). It was also apparent that the site supervisor felt it important that she approve all activities that occurred in the school counseling department. She was highly offended by Keith's actions. It had been her expectation that she would be consulted before Keith performed any activities. She believed he had usurped her authority and gone behind her back in doing these things, and she certainly felt it was out of line for him to speak with the principal about anything without asking her first.

I realized in talking with the site supervisor that there was a large disconnect between her perspective and Keith's, because I had seen Keith the night before in class and he had indicated everything was going very well. As I was speaking with her on the phone, I realized this situation would require an investment of time and I would need to meet with both of them several times to support them as they began to learn how to work with each other more successfully. I decided it would be a wonderful learning opportunity for Keith with regard to school and department politics. I was planning to tell him it was not in his best interest to know too much or to jump out and start doing things so quickly. Additionally, I planned to tell him to know his place, because it is indeed possible that students coming out of our program know more and have more site experience than their on-site supervisor and have been trained better in how to design, develop, and implement school counseling programs using leadership and advocacy skills. He needed to hear that he did not know this school site's politics, procedures, or history. Therefore, I was prepared to recommend to him—particularly with this supervisor—that he go slow and get permission. I planned to commit myself to the education and support of both the site supervisor and Keith for the entire year, as I decided training in this process would strengthen them both and thus ensure an excellent placement site for future students. I quickly changed my mind, however.

I explained to the site supervisor that Keith was young and although competent and confident, he was still learning. I sympathized with her concern that he needed to learn how to be respectful of her authority and how to ask permission to initiate activities. While sharing with her that I would support her in this process, I heard a tone in her voice that caused me to pause. It was a tone of "I am not invested in supervising him." So I checked in. I told her, "It sounds like you are not sure you want to be Keith's supervisor anymore." She paused, and then said, "I am not sure I trust him." I agreed with her that it sounded very much like Keith had overstepped his boundaries. I shared that he may have been overzealous and that acting without clearing things with her was not appropriate. I explained to her that I would talk with him and support her in helping him to learn the proper process for working at the school site. I offered to facilitate a conversation between her and Keith to clear the air as doing this is always better than moving a student. Again, she hesitated and then said she was not sure she wanted to do that. It was very clear from her tone and inflection that she was not invested in my student. So I asked her, "Would you like me to find him another placement?" She answered, "Maybe." That was all I needed to hear. I knew at that point that she was not invested in teaching my student how to fit into this particular school system. For whatever reason, she decided the investment in him was not worth it for her and she was not going to commit to any more effort in that area. Although I was disappointed, I realized that if she was not invested in my student, then convincing her was futile and he had to be removed. I thanked her for her time and told her I would talk with Keith and that he would not be returning. I also thought that she, unfortunately, was going to miss out on learning some wonderful things from my student and me.

Later that day I met with Keith. I told him I had to remove him from the site. I made the choice based on what I felt was in the best interest of him, as my graduate student. The disconnect between his perception of the experience and that of the site supervisor was shocking to me. Keith had rated his experience very high, and she had, in his opinion, unfairly accused him of things he did not do. From Keith's perspective, she had never laid out the ground rules, had not been available for him to ask questions, and appeared to be supportive of his ideas when he had suggested them. When I asked him what his assessment of the site was, he indicated very positive (9 on a scale of 1–10).

Keith learned a valuable and difficult lesson that day. We talked a long time about how betrayed he felt—how he had no idea she felt that way, and how he wanted to confront her and ask her why she had accused him of those things. Keith was angry. In his enthusiasm, I now believe, he probably had gone in and done his own thing. But in his desire to learn, grow, assist, and be a part of the school system, he missed a very important step—to assess the political lay of the land. As a new supervisor and still learning, she likely felt a strong need to look good in her department. Having a student come in and run his own show, as she saw it, challenged her authority. If Keith would have picked up on her sensitivity in this area and checked in more often—even more than he thought was necessary—this situation might have been avoided. He failed to read her discomfort with his actions and that is what I believe cost him the school site experience.

Questions

1. In this case, the school system coordinator places students from our institution into schools. Is this process problematic in terms of placing students in best practices sites? What could I have done to better prepare for this type of confrontation?
2. What is Keith's responsibility in all of this?
3. How can an increased visibility with local systems help keep this problem from occurring?
4. Is our program remiss in not addressing these types of issues in coursework? If so, how do we remedy this?
5. Did Keith violate any ethical codes or laws? Was it correct to reassign Keith, or should something more consequential happen?

Reference

American School Counselor Association. (2003). *The ASCA National Model: A framework for school counseling programs*. Alexandria, VA: Author.

Response

Judy Bowers

Successfully matching students to supervisors is a significant factor in a successful internship. It is very important that the instructor placing the student at a school site work with the district counseling coordinator or systems coordinator to ensure the most appropriate match. Frequently, students offer names of counselors they want to work with based on the location or because of someone they know at the school. College professors often suggest names of counselors they have previously worked with successfully, without looking at the student's and the supervisor's strengths. Often, students will ask to complete their internship at a school where they are teaching without considering the strengths of the supervisor. Convenience is repeatedly the reason given for this situation. I believe this process of placing students can be problematic if the students' needs are not matched with the school counselor supervisor's strength. The expectations for the internship must be clearly defined for the supervisor.

Placing students in school sites that have an American School Counselor Association National Model (ASCA, 2005) program in place provides an internship experience that models the school counseling profession. Interns, who have been trained as school counselors working for educational achievement rather than as mental health professionals, find this practical experience a laboratory to put into practice what they have been taught in university classes. For this reason, placing students in best practices sites is the most positive internship experience for students. Others comment that putting students in school sites that are not implementing the ASCA National Model provides the students with an experience in which they can introduce and possibly implement new ideas. Sometimes this works, and other times it can present a very difficult experience for an intern.

In this particular case, because the school counselor was a first-time supervisor, the university supervisor could have meet with her and the student before the internship started. This meeting would have included the requirements, timelines, and projects required of the student and the expectations for the supervisor. In this meeting, the university supervisor would probably have been able to determine if the student's needs and the supervisor's knowledge and available time would provide the needed experience for the student. Because this was the supervisor's first internship student, she may not have been familiar with the ASCA National Model (ASCA, 2005), which has the program components and the counselor skills that are part of a 21st-century school counseling preparation program and school site program. Counseling students are being trained to be leaders and advocates at their school sites, to use data, to collaborate, and to create systemic change using the ASCA National Model. When interns go into the school as practicum students, ideally they should have experiences in all of these areas with supervision from the site counselor.

Typically, practicum students like Keith have discussed with several college professors the types of experiences an internship will offer them and their expectations of the practicum experience. In these discussions, it is common for college professors to talk about working under the supervision of various types of counselors. The political framework (Bolman & Deal, 1997) is a topic often included in these discussions so students will become familiar with this important area. Although it is hard to prepare for the political frame one might encounter in a school counseling department, it is always wise for interns to be sensitive to the role of the supervising counselor.

In hindsight, Keith probably knows he should have discussed his plans with his supervisor in advance. The lesson learned is that interns are wise to discuss their plans for implementing their requirements with their supervisor before they take any action. When they start the internship, interns know the hours they need to work in each of the required areas. Keith would have been prudent to talk with his counselor supervisor about the activities he could experience in each of the required areas. This would have given the supervisor an opportunity to suggest teachers to work with, topics to teach, meetings to observe, ways of meeting data requirements, and the opportunity to work with two counselors.

It is great to see the enthusiasm that interns have when they start their site experience. This eagerness to put into practice what they have learned in class should never be minimized because of fear of offending the site counselor. In order to help avoid problems like Keith's, (a) the supervising college professor should meet with the supervising site counselor before the internship starts to discuss the parameters of the internship and to determine if the intern and site counselor would be a good match and (b) the supervising college professor and the supervising site counselor should meet with the intern to discuss responsibilities and the activities, meetings, and lessons the intern will experience to meet those university requirements.

Partnerships established between the local university and local school district school counseling departments will move away from incidents like this. Typically, professors will extend opportunities to provide connections to the local school counseling department in various ways. First, some professors provide professional development to the counselors in a district on current topics. Many university professors plan monthly meetings for the counselors in their area and provide the topics. In areas where the ASCA National Model is just being introduced, university professors can take the lead in teaching the model to the school counselors. Some university professors have provided workshops on parent programs such as the Joyce Epstein (Epstein, 2001) model and on ways to increase elementary academic achievement through the implementation of a resiliency model. This professional development partnership will strengthen the relationship between site counselors and university professors.

Second, more opportunities to collaborate on research are now being developed between site counselors and university professors. School counselors have the data from classroom guidance and small-group activities, and university professors have the expertise to analyze the data. Opportunities for the university professors to go into the schools to discuss a research project will also increase their visibility and strengthen their relationship with the site counselors. This is a way for the university professor to get acquainted with the counselors and to casually talk about the possibility of placing an intern at their school. School counselors will also appreciate getting acquainted with the university professor and having the opportunity to share their program. The idea of supervising an intern is new to many counselors, and having an opportunity to talk might help them to decide to be a supervisor.

A third way to collaborate is by being involved on the state school counselor association board and working on projects together. There is a position on the each state school counseling association board for the Post-Secondary Vice President. University professors are contributing their expertise to the state association's board while also developing relationships with practicing school counselors. Some states have added the responsibility of the state research chair to the Post-Secondary Vice President role. In this role, the university professor is working with a number of school districts to develop joint research projects with school districts and universities.

As school counseling programs are moving to incorporate the four skills of leadership, advocacy, collaboration, and systemic change in the training of school counselors, this example is a reminder that college professors may be inclined to address the political frame when discussing leadership skills for school counselors. A suggestion would be to include the four frames of Bolman and Deal (1997), one of which is the political frame. Students need to be very aware of this area as they come into a school counseling department and community. Interns may be entering a school with a strong political climate that is hard for a new person to become accepted into, and they may need to know how to navigate in this type of situation.

Several new books have been written on leadership skills for school counselors. One of them is *School Counselors as Educational Leaders* (DeVoss & Andrews, 2006). In this book, school counselors are taken through the four ASCA National Model skill areas with many opportunities to practice leadership skills through the readings and discussions. In addition, the authors talk about using the True Colors Word Sort as a way of looking at the intern's leadership style and learning to understand the leadership styles of others. This exercise would provide insight to working with supervisors, counselors, and administrators with different personality types and might help avoid a situation similar to Keith's. The authors also include several leadership assessment skills inventories that could be used as the basis for classroom discussions. A university instructor would have the opportunity to discuss topics such as judgment, organizational ability, decisiveness, sensitivity, and verbal communication while looking at the strengths and weaknesses of each student. Through classroom experiences such as these, a university instructor would be able to help future interns and counselors look at their own leadership, advocacy, and collaboration skills and create plans to continue developing these skills.

Keith was an enthusiastic intern who eagerly went to work. Although he did not violate any ethical issues or laws, as a new person in the school, he probably could have talked with his supervisor before he took off on his own. As a first-time site supervisor, his supervisor apparently felt the need to know everything Keith was doing and to approve all his activities. The fact that she felt he had gone behind her back and usurped her authority while Keith indicated that everything was going fine is an indication of poor communication and a disconnect between the two. Another supervisor might have interpreted Keith's actions as a student who was being proactive.

When the site supervisor didn't seem to want to invest the time in Keith, it certainly was a red flag to the university supervisor. The reassignment of Keith was a decision the site supervisor made based on the facts and also on the circumstances that would provide the best internship experience for Keith. At this point it was essential he have the best experience for his internship. Although reassigning Keith may not have been what some university supervisors would have done, in this case, it seems to have been the best option. Again, it is paramount that interns have the best possible site experience to prepare them to work as professional school counselors.

References

American School Counselor Association. (2005). *The ASCA National Model: A framework for school counseling programs.* Alexandria, VA: Author.

Bolman, L., & Deal, T. (1997). *Reframing organizations: Artistry, choice and leadership.* San Francisco: Jossey-Bass.

DeVoss, J., & Andrews, M. (2006). *School counselors as educational leaders.* Boston: Houghton Mifflin.

Epstein, J. (2001). *School, family, and community partnerships.* Boulder, CO: Westview Press.

Response

Allan A. Morotti

The placement and training issues identified in this critical incident are all-too-common challenges counselor educators face today in attempting to craft a positive supervisory experience for both the on-site supervisor and the supervisee. The fact that a central office administrator is responsible for identifying training sites and placing interns at those sites is problematic for the counselor educator. It is necessary to maintain a positive working relationship with the school districts accepting a program's students; however, this additional level of administrative bureaucracy initially hinders the counselor educator in addressing key components of the development of a collaborative supervisory relationship that promotes the professional growth of both individuals. Some of these include the match between the professional experiences and levels of training of each party; the provision of a variety of training experiences for the intern that coincide with the training objectives of the counselor education preparation program; the level of support for having an intern on site demonstrated by the school's administration and faculty; and the availability of space at the placement site in which the intern can see individuals privately (Roberts & Morotti, 2001). Furthermore, the type of placement process described in the scenario does not indicate that gender, ethnicity, or age variables were factored into the assignment process, nor personality variables like temperament.

It is imperative that counselor educators have frequent contact with the personnel in the districts where their students are placed. This can take many forms, from meeting with central office personnel and school counselors at their respective sites to attending districtwide meetings to discuss the goals of the particular counselor education program. Attending district meetings also provides the broadest forum for seeking input from practicing school counselors on what they see as being necessary in a training program. Seeking input from these individuals goes a long way in solidifying the credibility of a counselor education program. Each of these contacts helps to build professional alliances between the counselor training institution and the school district personnel. Far too often, school personnel believe many counseling internship students lack the requisite knowledge of how schools work and are unfamiliar with the types of problems that arise when working with students, their parents, or the students' teachers. This belief is often magnified because more and more students entering school counselor training programs have no prior work experience in schools (Peterson & Deuschle, 2006).

Ideally, on-site supervisors should receive a copy of the program's internship training manual for their review before the supervisory relationship commences but no later than the 1st week of the internship. A meeting should be scheduled in the aforementioned timeframe so the roles and responsibilities of the site supervisor, the counselor in training, and the university program supervisor are clearly delineated. The goal of this meeting is to help forge an understanding of what each individual can expect from the other. It also fulfills the ethical obligations that counselor educators have to make known these responsibilities to supervisors and supervisees alike (American Counseling Association, [2005]; Association for Counselor Education and Supervision, 1993). Specific to this scenario, some steps that could have been undertaken before the student was removed from the site include requesting the central office administrator to place students at sites that have had previous experience with interns or at a site that has at least one professional school counselor who has been a supervisor; meeting with all site supervisors before allowing students to visit their respective placements; and discussing with the student the fact that the supervisor is new supervisor and how this may affect their supervising relationship.

Internship placements often create a dilemma for students because they wish to display initiative but frequently feel limited by the amount of freedom given to them by their site supervisors. Compounding this frustration is the fact that interns are often are assigned duties that are more clerical than counseling in nature (Dollarhide & Miller, 2006). Students consistently express a strong desire to immediately assume counseling duties once they are at a site, but many fail to realize they must first gain the trust of their supervisor by demonstrating their ability to work within the professional guidelines identified by site personnel (Bradley & Ladany, 2001). In this case, it is difficult to believe Keith thought he could represent the counseling department at an Individualized Education Program (IEP) meeting when he was not specifically requested to do so by his supervisor or another school official who possessed the authority to make such a request.

Regardless of Keith's knowledge of the American School Counselor Association (ASCA) National Model and his rich but limited field experiences during his 1st year of study, he was in the role of student, and therefore the explicit approval of his site supervisor was necessary before he initiated actions on his own. Furthermore, in this case the offending behaviors appear to have occurred within the 1st weeks of his placement, which could indicate the student's lack of knowledge about how school systems work, a mistaken belief about what it means to be a counselor-in-training, or possibly a conscious disrespect for authority. The fact that Keith reported to his university supervisor after his initial meeting with the site supervisor his reservations about her ability to provide the type of professional training experience he was seeking strongly suggests that he acted intentionally. If this is so, it is necessary for the counselor preparation program to initiate some form of remediation with this student.

As noted previously, it is critical for counselor education program faculty members to meet regularly with the practicing professional school counselors who act as site supervisors for their graduate students. The quality of any counselor preparation program is tied directly to the strength of the internship experience. It is during this experience that counselor education students learn how to apply what they have learned in their graduate classes to the real world (Roberts & Morotti, 2001). The importance of supervision cannot be overstated, for it "bridges the gap between basic counseling competence developed in counselor education programs and the advanced skills necessary for complex or acute cases encountered in the reality of the work setting" (Sutton & Page, 1994, p. 33).

Therefore, it is incumbent on counselor educators to meet as often as possible with school district personnel to clearly delineate the goals of their training program; to answer their questions; to seek input on how their students are doing; to ask what they as counselor educators can do to assist the school district's counselors in realizing their program goals; and to solicit suggestions on how to better prepare their students for assuming the role of professional school counselor (Miller & Dollarhide, 2006). Being available and open to all school district personnel, not just the school counselors, helps to develop the good will necessary for building a solid collaborative relationship between the university, the school district, and the community (Bradley & Ladany, 2001). Despite the strengths of any counselor education program and its faculty, the quality of a program's reputation is often based on the perceptions individuals walk away with from these interactions. Likewise, students are representatives of the program, and their actions also affect its reputation.

Counselor education programs already demand more course work and professional training experiences than most master's degrees. It is simply not possible to cover in course work all possible scenarios that may arise in the practice of professional counseling. Furthermore, in the university classroom, all the theories and real-life scenarios presented to underscore a specific concept always work. This is certainly not the case when practicing in the real world. However, as counselor educators, we are obligated to develop in our students a working knowledge of the systems or organizations they will become a part of. In any school counselor education program, students are required to complete a number of courses where this knowledge of systems can be discussed (e.g., foundations, school counseling, ethics, the initial practicum experience). In addition, it is important for the counseling faculty to meet regularly to talk about what is being taught in their classes, review the program as a whole, and discuss individual student progress, making known any faculty concerns about a student's fitness to assume the role of professional counselor.

Keith definitely demonstrated poor judgment in assuming his ideas were approved in total by his supervisor and by not checking back in with her to confirm that what he was about to do met with her approval. He misrepresented his professional expertise and position when he attended the IEP meeting and stated he was speaking on behalf of the counseling department. An IEP is a legally binding document between the school district, the student, and the student's family, and it is not appropriate for a student intern to potentially obligate the counseling staff to delivering services they may not be able to provide. One assumes that internship students have a basic working knowledge of the various ethical codes (ACA, 2005; ASCA, 2004) that apply to them. Therefore, in this case, it appears Keith did commit an ethical violation, whether intentional or not, by the statements he made at the IEP meeting. The two sections of the 2005 *ACA Code of Ethics* that most clearly address Keith's actions are Standards F.8.a. (Standards for Students) and C.2.a. (Boundaries of Competence). At the very least, given this scenario, the student should be required to meet with his advisor to discuss this matter. He should be informed that the details of the incident leading to his removal from the previous internship site will not be discussed with his new supervisor. However, it should be made known to Keith's new supervisor that this is the student's second placement. Keith should also be informed that if another ethical violation occurs at his new placement site, additional remediation measures will be initiated. If the student is unwilling to accept these conditions or does not satisfactorily complete the remediation process as put forward by the counseling faculty, then his place in the program is in jeopardy of being terminated.

If this were my student, I would meet with my colleagues to review the student's past interactions with instructors and students in an attempt to determine if his actions at the site were typical or not. I would pay special attention to the quality of his interactions with both authority figures and women. I would also meet with the site supervisor face to face to gain a clearer understanding of what had actually occurred, what steps if any I might have been able to take to have avoided this situation, and what steps I can take in the future to facilitate the successful placement of internship students at this particular school site and specifically with this individual.

Because there was such a wide variance between what Keith reported had happened at the site and what his supervisor said occurred, I would be inclined to think this situation resulted from a serious breakdown in communication between the parties. Unfortunately for Keith, as a counselor-in-training, he is the party with the least power but the most to lose if he is perceived as lacking in the requisite skills and knowledge necessary to assume the role of professional school counselor. If his actions were an aberration and not indicative of a pattern of such behavior, then he will most likely learn from this situation and not commit a similar infraction in the future. On the other hand, if his behavior is found to be lacking in the personal dispositions required in becoming a professional school counselor, then the counselor education program faculty has an ethical obligation not to endorse the student for admission to the profession (ACA, 2005). Regrettably, these types of situations do not frequently arise until students are advanced to their internships, and by that time the students have invested considerable time and money to realize their goal of program completion.

References

American Counseling Association. (2005). *ACA code of ethics.* Alexandria, VA: Author.

American School Counselor Association. (2004). *Ethical standards for school counselors.* Alexandria, VA: Author.

Association for Counselor Education and Supervision. (1993). *Ethical guidelines for counseling supervisors.* Alexandria, VA: Author.

Bradley, L. J., & Ladany, N. (2001). *Counselor supervision: Principles, process, and practice* (3rd ed.). Philadelphia: Brunner-Routledge.

Dollarhide, C. T., & Miller, G. M. (2006). Supervision for preparation and practice of school counselors: Pathways to excellence. *Counselor Education and Supervision, 45,* 242–252.

Miller, G. M., & Dollarhide, C. T. (2006). Supervision in schools: Building pathways to excellence. *Counselor Education and Supervision, 45,* 296–303.

Peterson, J. S., & Deuschle, C. (2006). A model for supervising school counseling students without teaching experience. *Counselor Education and Supervision, 45,* 267–281.

Roberts, W. B., Jr., & Morotti, A. A. (2001). Site supervisors of professional school counseling interns: Suggested guidelines. *Professional School Counseling, 4,* 208–215.

Sutton, J. M., & Page, B. J. (1994). Post-degree supervision of school counselors. *The School Counselor, 42,* 32–39.

Chapter 29

The Culturally Incompetent Supervisor

Cher N. Edwards

Topics

- Multicultural supervision
- Relationship between university and on-site supervisors

Background

Third-year school counseling graduate students are placed at internship sites to serve a full year as interns under the supervision of a full-time certified school counselor (on-site supervisor). Given the demographics of the local school districts, many schools in which the interns are placed are culturally diverse. Not all school counseling programs, however, provide training in multicultural awareness, knowledge, and skills. Even fewer provide guidelines for cultural competency within the supervisory relationship.

Incident

Anna, a school counseling intern, was placed at Mt. Ridge High School. Anna often meets with students individually or provides large group guidance related to career exploration and after-graduation transition plans. Shauna, a senior at Mt. Ridge, was referred by a classroom teacher to meet with Anna to discuss postgraduation plans. The classroom teacher was concerned to learn Shauna did not intend to apply for college upon graduation. The teacher commented to Anna that this was a "waste" and felt Shauna was most likely staying local and not applying to college to spend more time with her "lesbian lover" (as referred to by the teacher).

After reviewing Shauna's school records, it became apparent that Shauna was an outstanding student and would be a strong candidate for scholarships. In addition to her high grade point average, she was also very involved in a number of school organizations and demonstrated exceptional leadership skills. Anna was unsure how to address the teacher's concerns and sought the guidance of her on-site supervisor, Jim, one of four full-time school counselors at Mt. Ridge.

Anna shared with Jim the concerns of the teacher as well as the information she had discovered after reviewing Shauna's academic records. On the basis of the teacher's report of Shauna's relationship with another female student at Mt. Ridge, Jim was concerned that Shauna might have gender identity disorder and suggested that Anna focus her attention on a referral to a community mental health counselor rather than spend too much time on college or career counseling.

Anna requested a meeting with Shauna during study hall to see how the student was feeling about her senior year. During their meeting, Shauna shared that she was Native American, had a strong tribal affiliation, and lived on a reservation. She added that she would like to attend college but feared her grandparents (who are raising her) may not be supportive.

Anna met with Jim to discuss the meeting. Anna asked Jim what he knew about Native American culture and moving off the reservation to attend a university. Jim shared he didn't feel culture was a part of this and encouraged Anna to revisit the possibility of a referral for community counseling to focus on gender identity issues.

Anna contacted me as her university supervisor to discuss the supervision she was receiving on site. She felt the student's apprehension about attending college was related to her culture and wanted to be sensitive; however, she felt pressure from her on-site supervisor to pursue issues related to the student's sexual orientation and possibly a referral for a disorder.

Discussion

As a school counselor educator and a university supervisor for school counseling interns, I found it unsettling to hear of this situation for a number of reasons. Although many of our current students are receiving training in cultural competency, quite a few of the seasoned school counselors supervising interns have not received such training. I was also concerned about the apparent focus on a mental health disorder by the site supervisor. This not only seemed inappropriate but also outside the scope of practice of a school counselor. Last, I was disappointed in the process of the on-site supervision that the intern received and was unsure how to proceed as a university supervisor.

Questions

1. Given my role as a university supervisor, was it appropriate for me to challenge the supervision of the on-site supervisor?
2. Did I have an ethical responsibility to follow up on the inappropriate comments and bad advice of the on-site supervisor?
3. Should the intern have continued her internship experience at this site under the supervision of this on-site supervisor, given what I knew about his lack of cultural competency?

4. How should I have intervened as the university supervisor to ensure that the intern was receiving culturally competent supervision and that the high school students at the internship site were receiving culturally sensitive school counseling interventions from the school counseling intern?

Response

Ginger L. Dickson

A primary responsibility of the university supervisor is to monitor and ensure the quality of students' internship training experiences (Bernard & Goodyear, 2004). The information provided raises concerns as to whether Anna is receiving culturally competent on-site supervision. In fact, Anna appears to be more knowledgeable than her site supervisor regarding the potential influence culture may have on the student's career goals. The site supervisor's apparent lack of cultural competence is a potential violation of the *ACA Code of Ethics* (American Counseling Association, 2005), which states, "Counseling supervisors are aware of and address the role of multiculturalism/diversity in the supervisory relationship" (Standard F.2.b.) and warrants further examination. Moreover, disregarding the cultural issues that appear to be at play in this situation would be potentially damaging and harmful to the student–client, whose welfare the student intern, site supervisor, and university supervisor each have an ethical responsibility to protect (ACA, 2005, Standard F.1.a.).

These concerns should be addressed, but within the parameters of the relationships established between the university supervisor, student, and site supervisor. Typically, a direct supervisory relationship exists between the student intern and the site supervisor, as well as between the student intern and the university supervisor. Although both the university and site supervisors are responsible for supervising the activities of the student intern, a more indirect liaison relationship exists between the university supervisor and the site supervisor. In other words, the university supervisor does not assume a direct supervisory role over the day-to-day operations of the site supervisor (Scott, 1995).

Rather than challenging the site supervisor's approach directly, the university supervisor could use the relationship established with Anna to begin to address the cultural issues that may be present in this situation. First, although they are not mentioned in the scenario, the university supervisor and Anna should explore and discuss whether there are cultural differences between them that may be affecting their relationship. Likewise, Anna should be encouraged to initiate a similar conversation with Jim (the on-site supervisor) if, in fact, she feels comfortable in doing so. This conversation may be used to segue into a critically necessary discussion of the differences in Anna's and Jim's conceptualizations of the student's problem, thus allowing them to creatively explore culturally sensitive interventions.

Ideally, the site supervisor would initiate these conversations with the student intern, but it is not uncommon for students who experience conflicts within the supervisory relationship to initiate discussions in an effort to work toward conflict resolution (Moskowitz & Rupert, 1983). Furthermore, most students who initiate such discussions with their supervisors report improvement as a result. By supporting Anna in navigating a resolution to this supervisory conflict, the university supervisor maintains the boundaries of the established relationships, and Anna learns how to address conflicts that may arise in the workplace competently, as well as how to advocate successfully for culturally diverse clients.

Anna's university supervisor has an ethical responsibility to address the inadequacies of her on-site supervision. Standard 3.10 of the Association for Counseling Education and Supervision's *Ethical Guidelines for Counseling Supervisors* (1993) states, "Supervisors should obtain practicum and fieldwork sites that meet minimum standards for preparing students to become effective counselors." In addition, the university supervisor, by nature of the supervisory relationship, can be held vicariously liable for the actions of the student intern (Bernard & Goodyear, 2004). Although they provide the foundation for clinical training opportunities for students, field placement sites also present shortcomings (Bernard & Goodyear, 2004). University supervisors can work to bridge the gap between the "ideal" and the "real" internship site in order to promote the professional development of student interns. Through continued supervision with Anna, the university supervisor should keep apprised of the progress that is being made toward resolution of this conflict and the counseling interventions that Anna is providing. If, despite continued attempts, no resolution is achieved, a meeting between the student intern, university supervisor, and on-site supervisor may be necessary.

Whether Anna should remain in this placement depends on the outcome of all of the interventions mentioned above, as well as Anna's desires. Ultimately, Anna and the university supervisor will have to determine if the deficiencies noted with the on-site supervisor outweigh beneficial opportunities that the internship site provides. According to the *ACA Code of Ethics* (ACA, 2005), Anna is free to terminate the supervisory relationship with notice (Standard F.4.d.). Likewise, if the university supervisor believes the deficiencies of the internship site cannot be rectified, termination of the placement should be considered.

In addition to the strategies mentioned above, the university supervisor may want to consider the use of other interventions to ensure that the university and the internship site agree on mutually held training objectives. First, the university supervisor should communicate clearly to the internship site the curricular and clinical training objectives established for students (Bernard & Goodyear, 2004). For example, the university should communicate the emphasis that is placed on multicultural issues in the training of counseling interns and the expectation that students will be encouraged to address cultural issues within both the supervisory and counseling relationships during internship.

In order to ensure site supervisors have opportunities for multicultural training, university supervisors may offer site supervisors complimentary in-service trainings and workshops that address multicultural issues in counseling and supervision. Universities may consider requiring site supervisors to attend these or similar trainings in order to participate in clinical supervision with students. Generally speaking, early and ongoing communication between the university and internship site is the most viable approach to ensuring that student interns are receiving quality supervision that allows them to provide quality and effective counseling interventions to their clients.

References

American Counseling Association. (2005). *ACA code of ethics*. Alexandria, VA: Author.

Association for Counselor Education and Supervision. (1993). *Ethical guidelines for counseling supervisors*. Alexandria, VA: Author.

Bernard, J. M., & Goodyear, R. K. (2004). *Fundamentals of clinical supervision* (3rd ed.). Needham Heights, MA: Allyn & Bacon.

Moskowitz, S., & Rupert, P. (1983). Conflict resolution within the supervisory relationship. *Professional Psychology: Research and Practice, 14,* 632–641.

Scott, J. (1995). Monitoring the professional development of practicum students and interns. In J. C. Boylan, P. B. Malley, & J. Scott (Eds.), *Practicum and internship textbook for counseling and psychotherapy* (2nd ed., pp. 173–228). Washington, DC: Accelerated Development.

Response

Michael Brooks

As the university supervisor, it is very appropriate for you to challenge the on-site supervision. In reading and evaluating this critical incident, I saw at least three places or levels at which an intervention on the supervision would have been appropriate. The supervision quality, in my opinion, has possibly been compromised in the areas of the supervision relationship, evaluation, and appropriate ethical practice on the part of the supervisor. The supervision relationship is an unequal relationship (Bernard & Goodyear, 2004). The supervisors' reactions to the supervisees will have consequences for the counselors-in-training, regardless of the amount of empathy expressed by the supervisors. By insisting that Anna investigate a gender identity disorder diagnosis, the supervisor could have damaged Anna's budding confidence in case conceptualization. It also places the on-site supervisor in an insensitive light.

Supervisors (regardless of the setting) are taught to allow persons in the supervision relationship to be unique and to allow the supervision relationship to developed or be modified by the demands of the various contexts within which supervision occurs. In doing this, supervisors are able to arm their supervisees with tools that allow them to be competent. If the on-site supervisor had substantial reason or evidence to diagnose gender identity disorder (and I do not think this was the case), there was no effort to groom or coach the supervisee on how she might develop her own style in becoming more aware of such diagnostic signs. It appears, instead, that the supervisor was somewhat biased and authoritative.

It is the ethical responsibility of the university supervisor to follow up on the inappropriate comments and apparently poor advice of the on-site supervisor. In short, the *ACA Code of Ethics* (American Counseling Association, 2005) indicates that counselors have a responsibility to police our own:

> Counselors strive to resolve ethical dilemmas with direct and open communication among all parties involved and seek consultation with colleagues and supervisors when necessary (H. Introduction).
>
> Counselors expect colleagues to adhere to the *ACA Code of Ethics*. When counselors possess knowledge that raises doubts as to whether another counselor is acting in an ethical manner, they take appropriate action (H.2.a. Ethical Behavior Expected).
>
> When counselors have reason to believe that another counselor is violating or has violated an ethical standard, they attempt first to resolve the issue informally with the other counselor if feasible, provided such action does not violate confidentiality rights that may be involved (H.2.b. Informal Resolution).
>
> If an apparent violation has substantially harmed, or is likely to substantially harm, a person or organization and is not appropriate for informal resolution or is not resolved properly, counselors take further action appropriate to the situation. Such action might include referral to state or national committees on professional ethics, voluntary national certification bodies, state licensing boards, or to the appropriate institutional authorities. This standard does not apply when an intervention would violate confidentiality rights or when counselors have been retained to review the work of another counselor whose professional conduct is in question (H.2.c. Reporting Ethical Violations).

If no further discussions were scheduled between the university supervisor and the on-site supervisor, I would say the intern should not remain at this site. This intern and the counseling program are fortunate that the student sought guidance from her university instructor. Had she followed the direction of the on-site supervisor, there could have been a number of legal ramifications. Placing students under this current site supervisor appears to be dangerous and threatening to the counseling program.

My intervention in this incident would include several steps. First and foremost, I would document all reports from the supervisee and from these notes create a chronology of events. It is important to be able to account for all of the critical moments that lead up to the student contacting the university supervisor for additional help regarding the school student. I would want to be clear with the site supervisor as to what aspects of supervision have been violated or compromised. In this case, the aspect of diagnosing with respect to culture and the ethics involved in making a clinical diagnosis would need to be discussed. Next, I would present the on-site supervisor with an overview on making assessments and diagnoses and the importance of cultural consideration. Depending on the discussion that follows from these actions, I would recommend additional training before placing future students with this school counselor. Because of the sensitivity of this matter, I would probably prefer that the training be with a credible provider (e.g., National Board for Certified Counselors).

References

American Counseling Association. (2005). *ACA code of ethics*. Alexandria, VA: Author.

Bernard, J. M., & Goodyear, R. K. (2004). *Fundamentals of clinical supervision* (3rd ed.). Needham Heights, MA: Allyn & Bacon.

Chapter 30

When Is It Appropriate for the Site Supervisor to Be Involved?

Rachelle Pérusse

Topic

- Dual relationships

Background

A large university offers both a school counseling master's program and a counselor education doctoral program. Because the university mostly prepares future counselor educators, all doctoral students are expected to shadow at least two different professors and two different courses with the expectation that they will teach those courses during a subsequent semester.

Clara is a school counselor working in a school district near the university. She is also beginning her doctoral work in counselor education. Clara is the only doctoral student with school counseling experience available for a shadowing experience. The professor believes it would be in the best interest of the master's-level school counseling students to have a person who has experience as a school counselor supervising them in practicum. The professor also believes it would be in Clara's best interest to shadow and eventually teach the practicum course to prepare herself to be a good candidate for a school counselor educator position.

Incident

Five school counseling master's-level practicum students were placed in a student support center at a local high school under the supervision of Clara, the director of the center. The center has been the primary site for practicum students since before Clara entered the doctoral program. The center is unique in its services and in the diversity of the student population it serves. For this reason, it is the primary site to which students are assigned during practicum. At the same time, Clara is beginning her doctoral program and ready to shadow a professor. Because Clara has experience as a school counselor and is interested in becoming a school counselor educator, Clara is asked to shadow the practicum class, so she will be prepared to take over a section of practicum in the subsequent semester. The professor thinks it is a good idea because Clara is already supervising these students on-site. The class would be a natural extension of supervision and an opportunity for the supervisor and supervisees to meet formally $1\frac{1}{2}$ hours per week.

Because the professor has no knowledge of the counseling skills these practicum students possess, she gives them an assignment to create a video-tape that demonstrates their counseling skills. Students are asked to make sure they select topics they feel comfortable sharing with everyone in the class, because they will be asked to present their videotapes during class supervision time, where they will be critiqued by all members of the class.

During Week 3, students begin sharing their videotapes in class. They are critiqued by all the students as well as the professor and Clara. The professor believes Clara's feedback is invaluable because she offers them suggestions that are directly related to working with the high school students at the practicum site. After 2 weeks of class videotape presentations, the professor receives an e-mail from one of the master's students in the class who states she has spoken with other students in the class and they think it is wrong for Clara to be in the course watching their videotapes. This student goes on to say she felt "very uncomfortable having Clara there watching and critiquing my videotape. Surely there are other courses this doctoral student could shadow, or other doctoral students that can help you teach the course." In the next class, the professor asked other students if they felt similarly uncomfortable. Four of the five students nodded their heads. One student said she felt embarrassed because Clara had seen what she called her "horrible counseling skills in that particular videotape." She also stated that because Clara had seen her video, she now felt self-conscious at the practicum site because she wondered what Clara thought of her. Another student mentioned Clara had made reference to a topic that had been discussed during class in a meeting conducted at the school counseling site. Even though only members of the class were present at this meeting, the students said, "We thought whatever happened in class was confidential and stayed in class." Students said they also needed a place to "vent" about the practicum site and did not feel comfortable doing so with their site supervisor present.

Discussion

The professor was torn. On the one hand, practicum is a time when students in the program are expected to be challenged and grow as professionals. On the other hand, the practicum class needs to be a safe place for students to explore their thoughts, feelings, and actions. The professor met with Clara and together they decided it would be best if she discontinued her shadowing experience.

Questions

1. In general, is it a good idea to use doctoral students to supervise master's-level practicum students, or is there already an inherent

dual relationship, because all students are technically in the same program?

2. Is there any way that such a scenario could work out? That is, is it possible to successfully integrate a site supervisor into the practicum course?

3. What about the students who felt squeamish about having their site supervisor watch their videotapes? Were they just being overly sensitive? Why would they feel embarrassed to have their site supervisor watch their tapes?

4. Was it wrong for Carla to bring up a topic that had been discussed during class time while at a meeting with members of the class at the practicum site?

5. Is this a direct breach of the dual relationship ethical code?

Response

Gary Goodnough

There is certainly the potential for dual relationships to exist whenever programs use doctoral students as supervisors and instructors. Nevertheless, it would be extreme to suggest that doctoral students should never be able to work with master's degree students in the same program. There are too many benefits to the counselor education program and the doctoral students themselves. Although master's students do benefit from doctoral students working with them, they are probably the group to benefit least from doctoral student participation. This incident is an example of the program and the doctoral student benefiting, but without an open eye to the concerns of the most vulnerable of the three players—the master's students.

There might be a way to successfully integrate a site supervisor into the practicum course. Such an arrangement would acknowledge the fact that Clara had two roles. Careful planning between the professor and Clara would be necessary to protect practicum students' relationship with Clara as their supervisor. Some elements that are typically involved in shadowing might need to be sacrificed in order to protect the supervisee–site supervisor relationship. Doing a focus group with previous practicum students and site supervisors might be a way to gain insight into those areas that could potentially compromise the supervisory relationship.

"Embarrassed" and "squeamish" are perhaps not the most precise words to describe the students' feelings when their site supervisor watched their tapes. In many ways it seems that what they were reacting to was the violation inherent in having one's supervisor be privy to information about their skills beyond that which is typical for a practicum supervisor. Research suggests that beginning students carry significant levels of anxiety about their performance. Students need to be able to process this anxiety in a safe place. University supervision is one place where this anxiety can be addressed. Having Carla there seems to have interfered with this ability and thus rendered the situation less safe for students.

It seems clear that bringing up a topic that had been discussed during class violated students' sense of safety that accrued from confidential group supervision. This insensitivity on Carla's part seems to stem from a lack of understanding of the boundaries of her dual relationship as a site supervisor and her role in shadowing the professor.

The *ACA Code of Ethics* (American Counseling Association, 2005) departs from previous codes of ethics in that it recognizes that nonprofessional relationships can sometimes be beneficial. Thus the dilemma presented is not prima facie evidence of an ethical code violation. According to Standard F.3.a. (Relationship Boundaries With Supervisees), supervisors "work to minimize potential conflicts and explain to supervisees the expectations and responsibilities associated with each role. They do not engage in any form of nonprofessional interaction that may compromise the supervisory relationship." Thus, it is Carla's responsibility to navigate the situation so as to not set up contingencies that negatively affect the supervisory relationship she has in her position as an on-site supervisor. This responsibility extends to the supervisor of the supervisor—the professor.

Reference

American Counseling Association. (2005). *ACA code of ethics*. Alexandria, VA: Author.

Response

Jill A. Geltner

Any university program training both future school counselor practitioners and future counselor educators is forced to deal with issues such as this one. For the doctoral student, an important part of training is learning and enhancing supervision skills. For the school counselor in training, basic counseling skills must also be taught and enhanced through this same supervision process. This pairing, although potentially unsuited, may also be an ideal match. Dual relationships can be found in many professional relationships. The existence of a dual relationship alone should not exclude individuals from providing the potential growth and knowledge that might come from these processes and experiences. It can be argued that "it is inevitable that supervisors and their supervisees will have dual relationships" (Bernard & Goodyear, 2004, p. 60).

Taking into consideration the existence of a dual relationship from the individual perspective, the goals of the program must be considered. This dual relationship is a result of two differing goals of the university's two separate programs, the school counseling master's program and the counselor educator doctoral program. If considered from a department standpoint, these students are really in separate programs, although housed in the same department. They are not, then, technically in the same program. Students are often placed together as in this case, but are necessarily separate and trained in differing ways for different overall goals. However potentially difficult situations like these may be, they can be ethically managed within the department while still aiming to serve the goals of both groups. Furthermore, "conflict in the supervisory relationship is both unavoidable and desirable; in fact, it may even be supervision's most important process" (Bernard & Goodyear, cited in Fall & Sutton, 2004, p.69).

It is possible to successfully integrate a site supervisor into a practicum course. However, certain safeguards should be provided to ensure the comfort and growth of all participants. In this example, the master's students clearly need a safe place to process experiences at the practicum site. It is understandable they may not feel comfortable expressing all concerns or questions with Clara present. But it could also be quite beneficial to have an on-site supervisor to consult with outside the practicum setting.

There are several scenarios in which changes could be made to accommodate all involved. First, although Clara is a counselor at the site, it may not be necessary for her to be the site supervisor for these students. Another counselor at this high school could serve as the site host for these students. Removing the direct supervision responsibilities from Clara may create a more comfortable atmosphere when she assists the group during the practicum course. Second, another avenue for students to express concerns, particularly about site issues, may be necessary. As in any counselor training program, it may be helpful for the students to have additional supervision. For example, some counseling training programs provide students with an individual supervisor in addition to group supervision. In this model, the practicum student would then have the opportunity to discuss an issue where and with whom he or she feels comfortable. An individual supervisor may provide a more private and trusting exchange than a group might allow. In addition, the group continues to provide an atmosphere to collect ideas and feedback from a group of individuals concurrently. Combining individual and group supervision, even on a biweekly basis, is another option.

Finally, perhaps it is necessary for Clara's feedback skills to be enhanced. Although the students have said nothing specific about her skills, conceivably she has room for improvement in her interactions with school counselors in training at the practicum site. It might be possible for the professor to allow the supervision of Clara to include helpful feedback from the practicum students. Also, including Clara in some but not all sessions of the practicum course may allow for students to have time both with her insight and experience and also without. When she is not present, students may then feel the safety they need to discuss potential issues they may be having at the site or with site supervisors. Hopefully, over time they may begin to trust Clara, appreciate her insights and experience, and work through their feelings of uneasiness.

The students' reaction to being videotaped is not unusual. New students counseling for the first time on tape are naturally anxious, and the group viewing adds to the anxiety. Because Clara might know the high school student in the taped counseling session, the students may feel additional pressure to do well. Perhaps with the right positive feedback from Clara, the students would feel more comfortable with the process. Because these students are new to supervision, it would be important for them to feel successful initially. Additional positive feedback on things done well may be necessary along with the gentle, constructive feedback. But it is important to understand that recognition of this conflict, the processing of it, and an open discussion of it are invaluable steps to students in supervision (Fall & Sutton, 2004). This supervision is a developmental process for both Clara and the practicum students.

It may be that the practicum students are having difficulty understanding the boundaries of the relationships and settings. It may be Clara was making an attempt at timely teaching by illustrating a point in a real-life setting with real student clients. Without knowledge of the exact issue, it is difficult to understand why the students would be concerned about the discussion. Again, this is an issue that may provide a growth experience for all involved if it was permissible to discuss it as a group at another time, with the professor serving as a mediator. If the issue was a sensitive one, it may be likely Clara could have discussed it at another time when the setting was more comfortable for the practicum group.

This may be an issue Clara addresses in her own self-growth as a supervisor and future counselor educator. Bernard and Goodyear (2004) stressed the importance of a supervisor accepting responsibility and raising the difficult topics. Clara may need to examine her interactions with the trainees and address concerns to improve her own interactions with them at the site, thus improving her competence and supervisory skills.

Neither the American School Counselor Association (ASCA, 2004) nor the American Counseling Association (ACA, 2005) address this situation exactly in the *Ethical Standards for School Counselors* or the *ACA Code of Ethics*, respectively. ASCA's *Ethical Standards for School Counselors* does have a subsection on dual relationships, which states that "if a dual relationship is unavoidable, the counselor is responsible for taking action to eliminate or reduce the potential for harm" (Standard A.4.). In this case, it is avoidable, and the professor did end the dual relationship. But it could be argued that the dual relationship continues to exist even if Clara no longer participates in the practicum course. The awkward interaction has changed the dynamic between the master's students, and Clara and they will continue working together at the high school.

The *ASCA Standards* (ASCA, 2004) also includes a section on contribution to the profession. In this area, the guidelines are for all school counselors to "contribute to the development of the profession through sharing of skills, ideas, and expertise with colleagues" and to "provide support and mentoring to novice professionals" (Standard F.2.). Clara was attempting to do both these positive things for her practicum students.

The *ACA Code of Ethics* (ACA, 2005) does address responsibilities of counselor educators and supervision specifically. In the area of field placements, counselor educators are to ensure the safety and responsible supervision of counselors-in-training. The professor and Clara certainly did follow this guideline. In the area of relationship boundaries with supervisees, the *ACA Code of Ethics* states "if supervisors must assume other professional roles . . . with supervisees, they work to minimize potential conflicts" (Standard F.3.a.). Clara did discontinue her role in the shadowing experience with the professor, and she was in agreement with this change.

In summary, this scenario is unfortunate but may be largely unavoidable in a comprehensive university program that provides both master's-level training and doctorate counselor educator training. Without addressing the issue more clearly with the students, it is difficult to rectify their discomfort with Clara. Furthermore, Clara's quick dismissal from the practicum course relieves the apparent issue for the professor, but does not address the continuing relationship that the students and Clara will have at the practicum site with Clara continuing as the site supervisor. A step the professor could have taken, recommended by ASCA and ACA, is to consult with another professional when dealing with an unclear ethical issue. Perhaps a university colleague could have suggested another solution to the dilemma. Even in areas such as medicine and teacher education, such supervisory relationship issues do exist. As a practicing school counselor, relationships can often be difficult and clarification with a trusted colleague both protects your decision and assists in the resolution.

References

American Counseling Association. (2005). *ACA code of ethics.* Alexandria, VA: Author.

American School Counselor Association. (2004). *Ethical standards for school counselors.* Alexandria, VA: Author.

Bernard, J. M., & Goodyear, R. K. (2004). *Fundamentals of clinical supervision* (3rd ed.). Needham Heights, MA: Allyn & Bacon.

Fall, M., & Sutton, J. M. (2004). *Clinical supervision: A handbook for practitioners.* Boston: Pearson Education.

Chapter 31

To Whom Do I Report, the Site or University Supervisor?

Walter B. Roberts Jr.

Topic

- Conflicting opinions of university and site supervisors

Background

Kari was in her final year of studies at a Council for Accreditation of Counseling and Related Educational Programs–accredited university and in the middle of her year-long internship placement. She was excited about her ability to secure a placement in a rural setting, as she had strong feelings about the need for school counseling services in largely underserved areas of the country. The product of a small town herself, Kari felt the placement was an excellent fit. Robyn, her site supervisor, was a veteran in the field with nearly 30 years of service, first as a teacher and later as a school counselor. Robyn was well respected and had served in years past as a mentor for more than one or two interns. She was within a year or 2 of retirement.

Incident

On Monday, Kari had a session with Lori, a 9th-grade girl who relayed quite a story of woe, largely originating from the chaos of home. Lori's story was familiar to Robyn, and she had had extensive involvement with the family through the years, having worked with all of Lori's older siblings.

On this occasion, there was an edge in Lori's delivery of what she shared with Kari that alarmed the supervisee. After double-checking several details with Lori about her situation, Kari decided that the chaos in the home was at a level requiring a report to the county social services agency. Although Lori had not directly said anything to cement Kari's suspicions for a firm, mandated report of child endangerment, she was more uneasy about some of what was not said than what had been said.

Per an agreement between Lori and Kari, any contact with social services was to be discussed first with Robyn, as a professional consultation. After listening to Kari's concerns about her session with Lori, Robyn told her the two of them would meet later that afternoon to further discuss the matter. Robyn never did get back to Kari until after school, at which time they customarily reviewed the full day's events. At that meeting, it became clear Robyn was not going to bring up Kari's session with Lori, at which point Kari did. "It's nothing," Robyn replied rather matter-of-factly. "I've known that family as long as I've been here and worked with all their kids. The parents are nuts, there's no doubt about that, and they get a little emotional sometimes with their kids, but they wouldn't do anything to them. Just let it go. We've got those basic skills tests to monitor tomorrow. What time are you coming in? We need to make certain we've got all our ducks in a row."

Kari was dumbfounded at Robyn's seemingly cavalier attitude. Her university supervisor had told her that site supervisors often had a "different view of the lay of the land," and interns were usually more alarmed and sensitive about their interactions with students at the site than their site supervisors might be. However, the university placed a high premium on its interns knowing and implementing mandated reporting of such cases and had a solid record of students knowing the law and procedures.

On the drive home, Kari called her university supervisor and asked for a meeting. She told her story to her program supervisor, who in no uncertain terms indicated there was enough information in what Lori had shared to contact social services, if for no other reason than for a generic consultation on whether agency personnel felt as if a full mandated report was in order.

Discussion

"You know what you have to do," Kari's university supervisor said. "The law says *suspicion* of child endangerment, not *verification*. That's social services' job to confirm. If your best professional judgment tells you to phone it in, then phone it in."

Kari left her advisor's office in a fog. She was caught in the middle of two conflicting sets of advice from two different supervisors, both holding different keys to her future in their hands. She sat in her car with a sickness growing in the pit of her stomach mulling over whom she should listen to.

Questions

1. It is clear that Kari is caught between conflicting sets of advice on what she should do. What should she do?
2. What is the role and responsibility of the university supervisor in working with site supervisors in matters of conflicting opinions of what interns should do?
3. Who should have the deciding power over an intern on site, the university supervisor or the site supervisor?

Response

Linda H. Foster

It appears from a cursory review of this incident that Kari is caught between conflicting supervisory advice. However, on a closer look, the duty to warn takes precedence. In this case, Kari must protect her own client, Lori. Professionals working with children are considered mandated reporters (Boylan, Malley, & Reilly, 2001). Therefore, Kari should be aware of local, state, and federal guidelines concerning the report of child abuse. Subsequently, on the basis of her own knowledge, Kari should follow any required procedures for reporting such child abuse. It is hoped Kari's university supervisor would have advised interns of legalities surrounding such mandatory reporting and educated interns regarding proper protocol for reporting.

This incident likely provides a very accurate scenario of what indeed happens in conflicting opinions of university supervisors and site supervisors. Resolving conflicting opinions over interns' work may need to begin with the university supervisor's selection of sites. It is incumbent on the university supervisor to select sites and field site supervisors in keeping with the goals of the training program to provide an appropriate placement. Along with selecting a site in keeping with the university's program, selection of site placements must also include a thorough review of the field site supervisor's training, level of education and experience, and credentials. A review of the factors at the beginning of site selection may reduce some conflicts. However, clear guidelines must be in place to prevent any discrepancies in terms of who is ultimately responsible for the actions of the intern. Bernard and Goodyear (2004) believed that agreements of understanding increase accountability for the university supervisor, field site supervisor, and the intern. Furthermore, agreements of understanding help to clarify the supervision relationship and promote ethical practice through emphasizing ethical standards. Agreements of understanding can also be used to clearly outline the duties and responsibilities of both the university supervisor and the site supervisor.

In determining who has power over an intern on site, Bernard and Goodyear (2004) cautioned that university supervisors should not relinquish all control to the field site supervisor during either practicum or internship. Again, according to Bernard and Goodyear (2004), when two entities are involved with interns, there may be conflicts stemming from the primary objective of each entity. The university supervisor's objective is to train future counselors, while the site supervisor's objective is to deliver services. Communication between the two entities is recommended as a way to alleviate some of the potential concerns and conflicts that may result from two supervisors working with interns.

In questioning whether the university supervisor placed Kari "at risk" with the site supervisor, it seems this question is not as important as the question of this incident putting the site supervisor at risk for future placements. The site supervisor's years of experience (while valuable) may become detrimental in terms of staying abreast of current issues, trends, and more important, laws that most assuredly affect our profession, if the site supervisor has not continued education and professional development. This situation may prompt the university supervisor to be diligent in selecting the most appropriate site and in selecting an experienced supervisor who is up to date in continuing education. It also may suggest that university supervisors should be working to enhance the professional development of site supervisors.

Moreover, the ethical and legal considerations surrounding this incident are significant. Direct liability and indirect liability for negligence in reporting suspected child abuse would affect the intern, the site supervisor, and the university supervisor. Borders and Brown (2005) stated that the counseling supervisor can be held legally liable for any negligent behavior by the supervisee. This vicarious liability has been termed *respondent superior*. Borders and Brown reinforced this legal principle by stating the supervisor's legal liability increases with higher levels of control over the supervisee. University supervisors have such control, and therefore it is incumbent on the university supervisor, as well as the site supervisor, to adhere to legalities and liability issues affecting both counselors and supervisors.

The initial question of what Kari should do is clear. Reporting of suspected child abuse is mandatory. No question here. Although Kari may have personal misgivings or even fears of reprisal from the site supervisor, there is no question that Kari has a duty to report.

References

Bernard, J. M., & Goodyear, B. K. (2004). *Fundamentals of clinical supervision* (3rd ed.). Needham Heights, MA: Allyn & Bacon.

Borders, L. D., & Brown, L. L. (2005). *The new handbook of counseling supervision*. Mahwah, NJ: Erlbaum.

Boylan, J. C., Malley, P. B., & Reilly, E. P. (2001). *Practicum and internship* (3rd ed.). Bridgeport, NJ: George H. Buchanan.

Response

Nona Wilson

Given the reactions she is getting from her supervisors, it is not hard to imagine Lori would feel vulnerable and anxious and would experience a sense of urgency. Her focus could easily become fixed on threats: What if she did something that harmed the client? What if she disappointed the university supervisor? What if her site supervisor ejected her from the site? This line of thinking would narrow her options—and urge a premature resolution of the situation—much like her supervisors have done. Lori would do well to try, instead, to shift her attention to ways that would help soothe her thinking and open up her possibilities. Two mental tasks can really help with that: cultivating curiosity and generating options.

Lori could begin by being genuinely curious about the perspectives of everyone involved. How is it she and her supervisor have such different responses to the same situation? What might her supervisor know after 30 years that she doesn't? Could there be factors she can see with fresh eyes that her site supervisor doesn't? What was the client trying to communicate? What is her university supervisor attending to that leads her to believe a report must be made? How could the two supervisors help her better understand their positions? How could she advocate for her own point of view? These kinds of questions could help Lori see that rather than being a simple right or wrong scenario, the situation is complex, and multiple ethical options may exist. Understanding this might shift her state of mind from anxious to interested and could lead to better decision making.

Lori might also benefit from generating a list of questions about each of the relationships she is negotiating. Then, using her answers to those questions, she might develop a menu of options for how to respond. With the client, she might ask herself: What is it about what she said that has prompted me to consider reporting? Do I have the information I need? Would it be helpful to talk with the student again? Am I concerned that waiting to clarify could put the student in danger? With the site supervisor, Lori might ask herself: Do I believe I understand something here she does not? Did I adequately convey that conviction to my supervisor? Could she know something I've missed or have information I don't have? How could I let her know I'm not comfortable ignoring this situation in a way that is professional and respectful? Do I feel strongly enough to pursue this against her instruction? Do I know the steps to follow if I were to do that? With her university supervisor, Lori might consider the following: Did I present the site supervisor's perspective fairly and accurately? Was I asking for my university supervisor to endorse my view or to help me critically examine it? What do I need from my university supervisor that I haven't yet gotten in this situation? How can I ask for that in a professional and respectful way?

These kinds of questions could help Lori sort through the nuances of the situation in order to reach a decision she understands and can stand by. Ultimately, in order to develop a sense of integrity about her professional ethics, Lori will need to feel confident not only about the outcomes of her decisions but also about the process by which she reaches them. The only way to do that is to avoid leaping to decisions, learn to consider multiple options, and purposefully think through her choices.

Ideally, the university supervisor works in a close, collaborative relationship with the site supervisor to jointly promote the intern's professional development. Preferably, as part of that teamwork, the university supervisor would discuss the possibility of conflicting opinions during an orientation process with the site supervisor preceding intern placement. The university supervisor would stress the departmental commitments to teaching ethical conduct and decision making, as well as review what is taught to counselors-in-training about reporting requirements. Then the university supervisor could use Lori's situation as a teachable moment and engage Lori through Socratic questioning.

Once Lori has clarified her point of view, the university supervisor could draw on her knowledge of Lori's skills and abilities to determine whether Lori could manage to successfully negotiate with the site supervisor on her own. If Lori has that potential, the university supervisor might serve as coach and help Lori practice how she will approach the supervisor: What is it Lori would want to convey to the supervisor? How could Lori do that and attend to the relationship she has with her supervisor? What are her options if the conversation does not go well? Assisting interns from behind the scenes in this way, without undermining their site supervisor's judgment, is a skill university supervisors must develop and should carefully explain to site supervisors. Doing so promotes interns' development and also minimizes the possibility that site supervisors could feel that university supervisors do not respect their judgment or support their authority. If, on the other hand, Lori didn't have the skills to successfully negotiate with her site supervisor, she might benefit more by observing the university supervisor negotiate with the site supervisor, and then processing it later to anchor the learning. Whichever route they take, the university supervisor's role is to work with the site supervisor to promote the intern's professional development, and that includes learning how to work through differences.

Though the university supervisor is responsible for submitting the final grade for the internship, and quite likely is accustomed to directing the intern's performance in classes, the site supervisor must have final authority over the intern's actions at the site. Site supervisors provide a tremendous service; they invest considerable time and energy into creating opportunities for interns, and in addition they assume substantial responsibility for the intern. The work site supervisors do—most typically with no remuneration—benefits counselors-in-training, the departments in which students are studying, and more broadly the counseling profession. University supervisors can recognize site supervisors' contributions by trusting their professional judgments. It is not unusual for knowledgeable, ethical, experienced professionals to assess situations differently. University supervisors may question or even disagree with site supervisors' judgments; university supervisors may even encourage their students to critically examine the guidance they receive from site supervisors. In the final analysis, however, site supervisors must be empowered to supervise as they see fit. If a university supervisor is unable to respect a site supervisor's judgment in general, then a departmental decision needs to be made about placing interns, but that decision should be made without placing the intern in a bind between competing directives.

Unfortunately, her university supervisor appears to have made two substantial errors in her role with Lori. First, she simply provided her with a conclusion. Doing that disenfranchised Lori as a learner. Lori may not understand how either supervisor reached a conclusion, and if she merely complies with one of them, without really understanding why, then she loses an important opportunity for professional growth. The second error the university supervisor made was in her opening moves in this situation; she trapped Lori in a dichotomy (she said do this; I say do that). Most situations have more than two options, and everyone in this situation would be better off if Lori's choices weren't so precipitously narrowed. Ultimately, the decision will come down to reporting or not reporting, but that choice should be closer to the end of the decision-making process, not the beginning.

The risks that arise from the university supervisor's errors are considerable. Lori may feel like she has to take sides and she will be penalized no matter what she does. That is simply an untenable position for a learner. Moreover, if inexperienced in handling professional politics, Lori could unintentionally compound her predicament by relaying to the site supervisor that the university supervisor thinks she is right and the site supervisor wrong. Were that to happen, the site supervisor might feel disrespected—by both the intern and the university. Even more troubling, the intern might believe the university supervisor has given her permission to act independently of her supervisor's guidance. Lori could conceivably decide to make a report on her own and, in the process, overstep her role as an intern and be vulnerable to the consequences, such as dealing with an upset supervisor, angry family, and potentially incensed school administration. It is not hard to see how this situation could quickly deteriorate. Thus, directly contradicting the site supervisor to the intern is ill advised.

Chapter 32

What Do I Do? I Work Where I'm Completing My Clinical Training

Heather C. Trepal

Topics

- Managing conflict
- Differences between site and university requirements

Background

I am a counselor educator in a large, urban counseling program. One of the courses I teach is practicum, where I have the opportunity to work with both school counseling and community or agency students during the semester. My course requires students to complete their clinical requirements under the supervision of their site supervisor (a certified school counselor or licensed professional counselor) and then complete the university requirement that involves class, group, and individual supervision sessions with me. I require students to audiotape several client sessions and turn them in for feedback. Todd was a first-semester school counseling practicum student who was also a third-grade science teacher. He was completing his practicum in the school where he worked.

Incident

All day long my stomach had been churning. I knew I was going to have to confront a practicum student, but I was not sure how to proceed. I had listened to his client tape, and it did not seem like there was much counseling going on. In fact, it didn't seem as though my student knew this client. Todd arrived on time for his first individual supervision session with me and nervously came into my office. "Todd, before we get started today," I began, "there is something that has been bothering me since I listened to your tape, which I feel I need to discuss with you." "OK, Dr. Trepal, but first let me explain something to you. My site supervisor would not let me ask any of the parents for permission to audiotape their child during counseling. He said he's had other practicum students before and permission was never a requirement. I was really worried. He offered to let me tape one of his relatives, and I didn't want to get in trouble with either of you so I just went ahead and did it." I sat there stunned and confused. Todd's admission answered my questions about the quality of his counseling session tape but raised some important questions about his supervisor and their relationship. I said, "Todd, I'm sorry you did not feel you were able to come to me with this issue earlier." "Dr. Trepal, you have to understand—I still have to work there. I need my job as a teacher and don't want to jeopardize that in any way. I felt really powerless, even though I know it was wrong." I told Todd I would be unable to evaluate his tape, and I needed some time to consult with our faculty regarding this issue.

Discussion

There are many relevant issues involved in this incident. For me, practicum supervision relationships can be quite complex, often involving dual relationships and tenuous boundaries. Given the fact we are working with people, there is always the potential for conflict. Like Todd, some of my students are employed in the setting where they complete their practicum, and this can present a myriad dilemmas. I had a number of issues with this incident; some of them involved my student, and some of them involved the site supervisor. Resolving conflict is usually difficult, but in this incident, I found myself concerned over a number of issues.

Questions

1. What, if any, consequences should the student face? In this case, the student turned in a tape for evaluation and feedback that was not even a real counseling session.
2. How would you resolve this issue with the site supervisor?
3. How do you balance the line between respecting the university's requirements and the student's concerns?
4. Are there any ethical or legal codes that are relevant to this incident? What are your thoughts on the site supervisor's behavior?
5. Could this entire situation have been prevented? What are some ways to deal with outlining counseling, course, and supervision requirements so that all of the parties involved (student, university supervisor, site supervisor) understand and commit to the rules?

Response

Robert Urofsky

The issues in this incident involve potentially unclear or conflicting programmatic and interpersonal guidelines, as well as difficult individual moral choices. It is safe to say that no matter how much structure and how many precautions a counselor education program puts in place, there is no guarantee such a situation will not occur. However, policies addressing and clarifying the program's, student's, site's, and site supervisor's needs minimize problems and are integral to an efficient and effective clinical training component. It is important that there is consensus and relative agreement among program faculty regarding expectations and requirements, so all faculty are communicating similar information. Communication with students about these expectations and requirements should be an ongoing process, not a one-shot deal. This ongoing communication could include presenting information on clinical experiences during initial program orientation sessions; publishing the information in a student handbook and clinical experiences manual that can be provided in a hard copy and online; presenting information during clinical experiences orientation sessions; and publishing the information in clinical course syllabi. It can be useful to have students sign an acknowledgement that they have received and understood specific information (e.g., the field experiences manual prior to registration).

It is the program's responsibility to assist students in knowing what to look for in a potential site; to communicate program expectations to the site; to clearly communicate to students expectations and evaluation criteria and procedures, as well as to review due process procedures with students; to update repeat site supervisors on changes in program requirements; to mediate conflicts between trainee and site supervisor or site; and to monitor quality control (Bernard & Goodyear, 1998). The university supervisor should contact site supervisors prior to the beginning of the experience to establish a supportive connection with the site supervisor, to check in with the site supervisor about the requirements and their ability to meet the expectations, and to respond to any questions or concerns the site supervisor may have. Ideally the university supervisor should follow up this contact with a visit to the site to check on the student's progress as well as once again touch base with the site supervisor about the placement itself. The use of supervision contracts, which, although legally nonbinding, can be extremely useful for ensuring everyone involved in the clinical experience is aware of the goals, requirements, and expectations of the experience from the beginning (Bernard & Goodyear, 1998).

Supervision best practices as described above should help reduce the number of problems arising during the clinical experiences component of a training program; nevertheless, incidents may still occur. Programs need to be as proactive as possible when they identify and remediate problems. This particular incident reveals that relying solely on the student to indicate there is a problem at a site or with a supervisor is problematic. The student may not be the best evaluator of the quality of a site or supervisor, and his or her position as a subordinate visitor at the site may cause him or her to be hesitant to rock the boat. In this incident, both the university supervisor and Todd acknowledged a potential for conflict of interest because of Todd's dual roles at the site. University supervisors, in anticipation and recognition of such potential conflicts, should be very forthright from the beginning in addressing this issue directly with the student and site supervisor. They should also be particularly vigilant in examining the student's documentation records, such as their logs of site activities, for signs of potential problems. Although employment at the site may raise some unique issues, any student may experience ambivalence at his or her site regarding program expectations. It is the university supervisor's responsibility to be supportive and assist students in the identification and resolution of these problems.

Procedural considerations addressed, this incident is particularly troubling because it appears the site supervisor deliberately went out of his way to sidestep the program requirements. Although not excusing the site supervisor's actions, it is important to recognize counselor education programs bear additional responsibilities to site supervisors beyond just communicating program requirements and expectations to them. Many school counseling site supervisors possess little or no formal training in how to engage in effective supervision. As a result, they may simply do what intuitively seems best to them or stay focused only on the administrative or program issues they know best, even though help with counseling skills is what most students at the practicum level want and need (Nelson & Johnson, 1999). Todd's site supervisor may feel he is doing his colleague a favor by not having him make tapes. He may also have his own anxiety about his supervision skills, knowledge, and abilities that may be affecting the choices he is making. All of the above point to the importance of counselor education programs providing supervision orientation and training to their site supervisors. Counselor education programs should consider requiring site supervisor attendance at supervision orientation and training at least every few years, as well as explore alternative formats for this training such as online workshops, video training programs, or state school counselor conferences, which many site supervisors would attend.

Overall, Todd's site supervisor may not fully realize the important role he is playing in Todd's development as a school counselor. Going back to the issue of a possible lack in training in supervision models and methods, Todd's supervisor may not understand Todd's developmental needs as a supervisee, seeing himself as more of a consultant or colleague to Todd rather than an educator, counselor, or evaluator. He may not realize Todd's high need for information and instruction at this stage of development as a counselor, instead perhaps viewing Todd more through the lens of his relationship with Todd as a teacher at the school. The supervisor may be conflating Todd's competence as a teacher with competence as a school counselor. Todd may not be willing to admit to skill deficits and anxiety until there is a solid supervisory relationship built on trust, especially given the existing dual relationship, and so he inadvertently may be assuming a level of competence and confidence that may not be present. Last, Todd's supervisor may not understand the use of tapes in the supervision process, resulting in his focusing more on the potential difficulties in obtaining informed consent from parents than on the value and power of tapes as a training tool. Orientation to supervision as well as personal contact with the university supervisor will assist Todd in his education and other school counselor supervisors in their development as supervisors. It will help improve the supervision students receive and increase supervisor compliance with program requirements.

The university supervisor should meet with the site supervisor to ascertain the reasons behind his actions with Todd and explore the site supervisor's confidence in Todd's abilities. Did the situation develop because of the site super-visor's reluctance to turn students over to Todd? The use of documented live observations by the site supervisor in future supervisory relationships may help him feel more comfortable with a supervisee's work prior to that super-visee working solo and taping. The added advantage for the supervisee is that he or she would receive immediate feedback from the site supervisor. After a thorough discussion with the site supervisor, the university supervisor can then decide the best course of action—from recommending supervision train-ing to, if the site supervisor is unwilling or unable to comply with require-ments, terminating the relationship.

This now brings us to Todd and his specific actions. Todd submitted work under the pretense that it satisfied the requirements set forth by the univer-sity supervisor when in reality it did not. He does come forth with a preemp-tive confession, but only after the university supervisor indicates a problem. He admits knowing his action was wrong and attempts to explain that he felt powerless in the situation because he teaches at the school where he was doing his practicum. Nevertheless, the indiscretion occurred, and at its heart this incident involves an academic integrity issue. All colleges or universities should have an academic integrity policy that should be clearly communicated to students during their orientation to the program and on course syllabi. In accordance with the policy at Todd's university, he must face the conse-quences of his action. Todd must face the consequences for a number of rea-sons. To start, it is not fair to the other students who did properly complete the work for Todd to be let off the hook. Furthermore, all current students, graduates, and faculty, as well as employers of program graduates, have a stake in the integrity of the program. Students, graduates, and faculty want the de-gree they receive to be well respected in the community and for employers to have confidence in the preparation and abilities of program graduates. Allow-ing improper work undermines this integrity as well as attitudes toward the school counseling profession.

Beyond what is stipulated in the institution's academic integrity policy, it is useful to consider Todd's previous actions and interactions in the program. If the program has regularly evaluated students throughout their program, both academically and clinically, then there should be some indications of Todd's character. If Todd has consistently been a fairly positive presence in the pro-gram and acted with integrity up to this point, an appropriate course of action may be for Todd to fail the course but be allowed to retake it, perhaps with a different site supervisor. Remediation may also include requiring a course or workshop in ethics. The university supervisor should sit down with Todd and discuss whether the following semester is the appropriate time for Todd to continue, or whether perhaps he wants to let his personal and professional life settle before continuing in his studies and efforts in the program. If Todd exhib-ited personal or professional problems at other points during the program, on-going evaluation and careful documentation is important. If there had been sig-nificant concerns, then Todd's entry into practicum should have been delayed or allowed to continue with particular stipulations and careful monitoring throughout, including more frequent direct contact with the site supervisor.

In addition, all remediation and possible actions toward program dismissal must involve careful deliberation and documentation and follow all institutional due process procedures.

If Todd had informed the university supervisor of the conflict, the university supervisor might have been able to intervene and work with the site and site supervisor to resolve the problem before this unfortunate incident occurred. One question the university supervisor needs to explore is why Todd did not indicate any problems earlier. It is the university supervisor's responsibility to try to create a supervisory environment of trust and support in which supervisees will be more likely to open up and share important information for the supervision process to be effective. Although not excusing his actions, it is possible that Todd's reluctance to confide the difficulties at his site can be attributed, in part, to weaknesses in the supervisory relationship with the university supervisor. The university supervisor certainly should take the time to examine her supervisory practices to ensure that she is working to establish an environment of openness and trust in his supervisory relationships with students.

The university supervisor poses the question of whether or not there are any ethical or legal codes available to assist in this case. The American School Counselor Association's (2004) *Ethical Standards for School Counselors* provides information pertaining primarily to the actions of the site supervisor and could be potentially useful in communicating obligations to potential site supervisors. Standards F.1.b. and F.2.c. state, respectively, that the professional school counselor "conducts herself/himself in such a manner as to advance individual ethical practice and the profession" and "provides support and mentoring to novice professionals." Section F of the *ACA Code of Ethics* (American Counseling Association, 2005) addresses supervision, training, and teaching, and standards within this section address issues relating to the importance of providing students information about program expectations and policies, evaluation methods, and feedback, as well as the importance of following due process for student remediation or dismissal.

The Association for Counselor Education and Supervision's (1993) *Ethical Guidelines for Counseling Supervisors* is devoted to the work of supervisors in various capacities. Although there are numerous guidelines in this document that pertain to specific aspects of this case, several stand out as particularly pertinent. Guideline 3.10 states, "Supervisors should obtain practicum and fieldwork sites that meet minimum standards for preparing students to become effective counselors. No practicum or fieldwork site should be approved unless it truly replicates a counseling work setting." Guideline 3.13 states, "Supervisors in training programs should communicate regularly with supervisors in agencies used as practicum or fieldwork sites regarding current professional practices, expectations of students, and preferred models and modalities of supervision." Guideline 3.14 indicates that "supervisors at the university should establish clear lines of communication among themselves, the field supervisors, and the students/supervisees." Last, Guideline 3.15 states, "Supervisors should establish and communicate to supervisees and to field supervisors specific procedures regarding consultation, performance review, and evaluation of supervisees."

Todd needed effective and knowledgeable administrative and clinical supervision to help him learn to navigate the relationships and tensions inherent in working in school settings. Counselor education programs benefit themselves and their students when they establish and communicate clear guidelines, provide training for site supervisors, and foster an environment of support and trust.

References

American Counseling Association. (2005). *ACA code of ethics.* Alexandria, VA: Author.

American School Counselor Association. (2004). *Ethical standards for school counselors.* Alexandria, VA: Author.

Association for Counselor Education and Supervision. (1993). *Ethical guidelines for counseling supervisors.* Alexandria, VA: Author.

Bernard, J. M., & Goodyear, R. K. (1998). *Fundamentals of clinical supervision* (2nd ed.). Boston: Allyn & Bacon.

Nelson, M. D., & Johnson, P. (1999). School counselors as supervisors: An integrated approach for supervising school counseling interns [Electronic version]. *Counselor Education and Supervision, 39.* Retrieved June 15, 2005, from http://web.ebscohost.com

Response

Carol A. Dahir

Imbedded in the preparation of every school counselor degree candidate is a thorough immersion in both practicum and internship. It is through these field experiences that the supervisors witness the unbridled passion that our next generation brings to counseling, leadership, advocacy, and ethical behavior—the cornerstones of our profession. It is a given that each graduate student approaches her or his work in the most ethical and responsible manner possible, both on-site and in the classroom. The demonstration and documentation of these experiences goes beyond a grade in class; it is the supervisor's validation that the candidate will become a worthy colleague as a professional school counselor.

It is most unfortunate that Todd chose not to immediately share the challenges he encountered in his placement, which is also his work setting. Todd's fear is entangled in the world of dual relationships and fear of repercussions both from the university and from his site supervisor. The effect of his first decision—not to tell—may affect severely his ability to complete the course and stigmatize his credibility in the program. Is Todd totally to blame? This situation warrants a serious investigation. Let's first explore Todd's choices and actions and then discuss preventive measures that may inhibit or at least diminish future occurrences with site supervisors.

Course Requirements and Case Misrepresentation

By bringing forth a tape under false pretenses, Todd clearly violated the course requirements and the university's academic integrity policy, as well as the American Counseling Association (ACA) and American School Counselor Association (ASCA) ethical codes. Todd did not admit to his actions until such time as he was confronted by the university supervisor who was concerned about the quality of the session (not thinking that the session was contrived). We can sympathize with Todd's struggle to fulfill course requirements and maintain equilibrium and balance in his work setting. Todd well knows that he needs his site supervisor to support future practicum experiences and ultimately his internship. The university supervisor knows all too well not to take this situation lightly and to further consult with colleagues in the department. At a minimum, the charges presented must be addressed on all levels.

Course Requirements

Because the tape submission is glaringly inappropriate, it will be necessary to negotiate another opportunity for Todd to conduct a counseling session. Certainly this warrants a serious conversation with the site supervisor regarding policies and expectations; perhaps the building principal's input will frame the context of what is permissible and what is not. Todd may have to complete his practicum at another site, perhaps working in an afterschool, evening, or Saturday school-based program in which counseling is a critical component. Although this may cause some personal hardship to Todd, it is imperative that he be engaged in the appropriate learning experiences from which he can improve his counseling skills and techniques.

Academic Integrity Policy

The university's academic integrity policy will also influence the outcomes of this situation. Although Todd admits that his action was wrong and provides a rationale, there is still a clear violation of ethical behavior and assignment misrepresentation. Would Todd have admitted to the indiscretion if he had not been confronted by his university supervisor? Circumstances that he claimed rendered him powerless must be set aside; Todd must stand responsible for his actions and be prepared to accept the consequences. Because he is entitled to due process, it will be up to the hearing panel to determine the relationship between his actions and the university sanctions. Academic integrity is at the heart and soul of this infraction. We have an ethical and moral obligation to preserve the integrity of our graduate education programs and respect the contributions of the faculty and students who do their best to meet these expectations.

Todd's previous academic record, faculty observations that describe his character and judgment, and other introduced testimony can certainly influence the hearing process. The outcome of this decision will determine the options available to Todd and could vary from resubmitting the assignment to being discharged from the program.

Ethical Violations

The ASCA's *Ethical Standards for School Counselors* (2004) states that the professional school counselor "conducts herself/himself in such a manner as to advance individual ethical practice and the profession" (Standard F.1.b.). Although Todd is not yet a credentialed school counselor, his preservice education requires that he must at all times abide by the ethical codes that govern the practice of professional school counselors. The *ACA Code of Ethics* (ACA, 2005) states that counselors-in-training have a responsibility to understand and follow the *ACA Code of Ethics* and adhere to applicable laws, regulatory policies, and rules and policies governing professional staff behavior at the agency or placement setting. Students have the same obligation to clients as those required of professional counselors (Standard F.8.). Acting ethically at all times can also be extended to the relationships with university and site personnel and expected levels of practice in supervisory settings. Todd should be remanded to review the ASCA and ACA codes that govern his practice and be required to demonstrate his understanding and application of the codes to this situation and future practice.

Addressing Concerns With the Site Supervisor

The university supervisor must further investigate and qualify Todd's explanation for breaching his course requirements with the site supervisor. This is an experienced supervisor, but it must be made clear to him how these actions (Todd's and his) resulted in violations of the university's academic integrity policy and the ASCA standards for school counselors. The school counseling supervisor "conducts herself/himself in such a manner as to advance individual ethical practice and the profession" (ASCA, 2004, Standard F.1.b.); "contributes to the development of the profession through the sharing of skills, ideas, and expertise with colleagues" (ASCA, 2004, Standard F.2.b.); and "provides support and mentoring to novice professionals" (ASCA, 2004, Standard F.2.c.). Although clearly the responsibility lay with Todd to come forward with the problem, the site supervisor must be made aware of the conflicted situation in which Todd found himself. The site supervisor needs a careful reminder that parental permission for audio (or video) taping is a counselor education department requirement. An offer to meet with the building principal or the district supervisor of counselors would be in order to clarify and align school district and university policies. The site supervisor has jeopardized the candidate's growth and development as a counselor and does not serve as an appropriate role model.

The conversation between the university supervisor and the site supervisor will clarify to what degree the site supervisor purposely circumvented the requirements. This will provide a context in which to take further action, which might include seeking a change in supervision for Todd.

Safeguarding the Integrity of Practicum and Internship

The partnership between the university and the site supervisor is a formal agreement. The organization, administration, and monitoring of practicums and internships cannot diminish the influence of the human element variable, which can be unpredictable at its best. Supervisors, especially at the university level, must structure the policies, procedures, and practices in order to guarantee an equitable situation for the graduate student and for the site supervisor. Todd's situation, that is accessing his work setting for practicum, is not unusual. Teachers who are studying school counselor education often have little or no choice as to their placement. Expectations may differ, especially when the supervisor and supervisee are engaged in a dual relationship. Providing a written document that delineates roles and responsibilities offers guidance when a situation such as Todd's does occur.

University personnel also have an obligation to ensure that site supervisors and graduate students are familiar with all of the ethical standards and codes that govern their practice. The ACES's *Ethical Guidelines for Counseling Supervisors* (1993) reminds us that

> Supervisors should obtain practicum and fieldwork sites that meet minimum standards for preparing students to become effective counselors. No practicum or fieldwork site should be approved unless it truly replicates a counseling work setting. (Guideline 3.10)
>
> Supervisors in training programs should communicate regularly with supervisors in agencies used as practicum and/or fieldwork sites regarding current professional practices, expectations of students, and preferred models and modalities of supervision. (Guideline 3.13)

In addition, Guidelines 3.14 and 3.15 (ACES, 1993) urge collaborative communication among and between university personnel, field supervisors, and the supervisees on all aspects of expectations and practice

The *ACA Code of Ethics* (2005) also addresses the supervisory role:

> Supervisors document and provide supervisees with ongoing performance appraisal and evaluation feedback and schedule periodic formal evaluative sessions throughout the supervisory relationship. (Standard F5.a.)
>
> Counselor educators develop clear policies within their training programs regarding field placement and other clinical experiences. Counselor educators provide clearly stated roles and responsibilities for the student or supervisee, the site supervisor, and the program supervisor. They confirm that site supervisors are qualified to provide supervision and inform site supervisors of their professional and ethical responsibilities in this role. (Standard F6.g.)

The counselor education department is responsible for helping the graduate find an appropriate site; for initiating and maintaining clear communication with the supervisor on-site regarding expectations, evaluation criteria and procedures, and program requirements; and for monitoring, at all times, the quality of the experience (Bernard & Goodyear, 2004). Paramount to successful supervision is the ability of university personnel and site supervisors to come to consensus on the goals for the supervisees. It is important that university supervisors validate each supervisor's willingness to serve and remind the supervisor that the intention is to provide the site with a graduate student who is well prepared and who will contribute to the school in a positive manner. University program representatives should urge the supervisor to carefully review objectives and procedures to make the process a win–win one for all involved.

Supervisors need to understand their three primary roles:

1. Counselor (e.g., participating with the intern in self-exploration, establishing distance, becoming aware of one's values and possible biases, and confronting the range of emotions that inevitably occur in training)
2. Teacher (e.g., imparting new knowledge and helping to refine skills as requested by the intern; discussing the cognitive theoretical orientation of the intern; acting as a role model; assuring that the intern has a range of experiences; and providing feedback on performance)
3. Consultant (e.g., collaborating and case conferencing; providing feedback on counseling approaches and techniques; emphasizing professional commitment, growth, and improvement)

Additionally, the supervisor needs to provide the supervisee with

- A physical area for individual counseling and mailbox for school communications;
- A clear understanding of weekly supervision time, criteria, and method;
- A calendar of school activities (e.g., parent conferences, staffings, site council, counselor meetings with parents, 4-year plans, college planning, parent advisory, staff meetings, school board) and required attendance at these as appropriate;
- Assigned counseling time for the development of strategies and prioritization of strategies for daily activities;
- Regular feedback on classroom guidance, including group and individual counseling while allowing the intern to brainstorm what went wrong, what he or she would change, what was good;
- A packet with all school forms (e.g., referral, reporting, parental information, pertinent board policies) and a copy of the faculty handbook;
- An agreement for the days of week and times for the internship experience, a scheduled time for supervision, preparation needed by the intern for supervision (e.g., lists, video, case presentations, questions or concerns, etc.); and
- A clear understanding of your expectations.

Communication and documentation can significantly reduce misunderstandings and misinterpretations. The development of a practicum and internship handbook can delineate

- Supervisor qualifications,
- Ethical codes and responsibilities,
- Multicultural considerations, and
- Documentation for clinical experiences of school counselor trainees.

Best practices (Henderson & Gysbers, 2006) encourage us to bring our supervisors together for a candid exchange of collaborative practices to protect both the integrity of the counselor education program and the integrity of the on-site experience. Todd's situation may be unique; on the other hand, we must work diligently with every site supervisor to ensure a high level of integrity and ethical practice. It is in the best interests of the future of our profession to collaborate in order to proactively establish the parameters that will result in the next generation of highly qualified professional school counselors.

References

American Counseling Association. (2005). *ACA code of ethics.* Alexandria, VA: Author.

American School Counselor Association. (2004). *Ethical standards for school counselors.* Alexandria, VA: Author.

Association for Counselor Education and Supervision. (1993). *Ethical guidelines for counseling supervisors.* Alexandria, VA: Author.

Bernard, J. M., & Goodyear, R. K. (2004). *Fundamentals of clinical supervision* (3rd ed.). Needham Heights, MA: Allyn & Bacon.

Henderson, P., & Gysbers, N. C. (2006). Providing administrative and counseling supervision for school counselors. In G. R. Walz, J. Bleuer, & R. Yep (Eds.), *VISTAS: Compelling perspectives on counseling 2006* (pp. 161–164). Alexandria, VA: American Counseling Association.

Chapter 33

Speaking Through Art

Jeannine R. Studer and Rhiannon Horne Price

Topics

- Type of therapy
- Relationship between supervisor and supervisee
- Boundaries of professional competence

Background

Students enrolled in the school counseling program at a major research institution receive their clinical experiences in schools that encompass a diverse population of K–12 students, from impoverished inner city to upper middle class environments. During practicum class, students are exposed to a wide variety of creative, expressive techniques as alternative strategies to the traditional Western-based counseling theories. The use of creative arts in practicum allows trainees an opportunity to view their own world differently, to self-reflect, and to explore personal values and beliefs. In addition, trainees are able to adapt these creative approaches to the K–12 counselees whom they are assisting.

Incident

Rhiannon was enrolled in her practicum experiences at a nontraditional K–4 elementary school that operated on a year-round schedule. During the summer months that school was in session, a teacher referred K. S. for individual counseling because of behavioral problems. When Rhiannon spoke with the teacher regarding the referral, she was told that K. S. was constantly interrupting class by engaging in attention-seeking behaviors and had difficulty staying in his seat. During the initial session, Rhiannon attempted to build rapport with K. S., but his reticence and impulsivity made it difficult for her to communicate. As a result, she decided to use art as a tool to harness his energy and as a strategy to counsel him. In order to learn more about his family, Rhiannon asked this diminutive young student to draw a picture of the people who lived in his home. K. S. readily responded to this request by drawing his older brother and promptly scribbled over this representation with red crayon. This brother was often left to care for K. S. while their mother worked, despite the fact that he was not developmentally ready for this task. After drawing his brother, mother, and himself, he drew his mother's boyfriend as a baby whom he strategically placed between himself and his mother. While drawing the boyfriend who also lived in the home and would occasionally care for the boys, K. S. pressed forcibly on the crayon as he angrily cried, "I hate you! I hate you!" It was at this point Rhiannon realized that there were many issues at home that K. S. was acting out at school, and she asked her site supervisor for some advice and direction.

Discussion

The site supervisor suggested she work with K. S. on stress and anger reduction in a structured counseling setting because of the chaos that seemed to be apparent in this child's home. While Rhiannon continued her counseling sessions in a comfortable, trustful setting, K. S. disclosed that the mother's boyfriend sometimes behaved abusively to him. Rhiannon reported this incident and her concerns to her site supervisor, who took the lead in reporting the incident to Child Protective Services.

Rhiannon discussed this situation and her actions during our weekly group supervision class. As Rhiannon described the situation, I reflected on how she must be feeling as a novice counselor in training and on her ability to reconcile her role as a counselor trainee with the relationship she had established with this student. I also wondered whether K. S. would have provided this information if art had not been used as an engaging strategy. Finally, I speculated about the ability of practicum students to use art as an intentional strategy rather than as a distracting gimmick when they don't know what else to do in a counseling session.

Questions

1. Although expressive arts enable individuals to express themselves creatively, art therapists have unique training and education that is often not part of a school counseling curriculum. How should school counselors use expressive arts when they do not have this specialty training?
2. What are some of the legal ramifications for using expressive arts in the school setting?
3. What types of school-aged youths respond better to creative arts in counseling rather than traditional counseling approaches?
4. What are some of the things school counselor trainees need to consider when setting up a counseling room using creative expressive methods (e.g., space, funding, and number of sessions), particularly when the school counselor already has a huge caseload?

5. What is the best strategy for a supervisor for assisting a trainee who is having difficulties in working with an abused child?

Response

Emily Phillips

First let me say that I am thrilled to hear that during practicum class students are exposed to nontalking techniques. I do believe this is atypical. Having taught play techniques for school counselors (note it's not called play therapy), I wholeheartedly believe this is a necessary component of good school counseling programs.

It is challenging to counsel children because of the difference in how they communicate. Their communication is often more subtle, more symbolic, less well related to time. They are less able to verbally label and express feelings, have shorter attention spans, and lack skills for sequential logic for a good part of their childhood. Therefore the use of play, art, and other expressive modalities makes perfect sense in a school setting, especially with younger children who are less able to think and talk abstractly. Play is the natural way they communicate and can be self-healing. It is our job to communicate with them in their way, not ours. We accommodate their cultural style, as we would any cultural minority.

Play is how children talk; it is how they can express themselves, explore relationships, and explain their phenomenology to others. Observing this play helps us learn what has happened in their lives, how they feel, what they need, or what they think about themselves (Landreth, 2002).

This incident does not state how old the child is, but we can surmise that the student is between 5 and 10 because of the K–4 nature of the building. This would be important information to know, as there are great differences in behaviors and expectation in treatment of 5- and 10-year-olds. They may not even remember specific information depending on where their development was at the time of the incident(s). And not all children are damaged or ill because of childhood challenges and stressors.

There are numerous forms of nonverbal treatments, and no school counselor can expect to have had preservice training or certification in all of them. Our *ACA Code of Ethics* states that we are not to practice outside of our scope of training (American Counseling Association, 2005). But in the real world of school counseling, especially to novices, most is or feels like it is outside our specific scope of training. However, that being said, it is still important for in-service counselors to continue to develop professional expertise through ongoing professional development. One college course in a specific topical area or a few activities shared as ideas during practicum does not make for solid training. I spend some time in practicum discussing the use of Scrabble tiles, pipe cleaners, and commercial literature. But it is never enough.

As we in the field of mental health need to remind ourselves, sometimes a cigar is just a cigar. Just because a child draws with black crayon doesn't mean he or she is depressed. I had one child referred to me for depression tell me she did this repeatedly because it showed up best on the paper, nothing more.

Play and expressive arts techniques have varying purposes. Our job is to learn not to analyze every drawing or clay structure but to learn how to be more intentional when we counsel. In this manner, we do not expect feelings-answers if we ask cognitively oriented questions. Play has three general uses. One is to distract a child who may appear anxious about talking with an adult. This is really a technique of talking therapy. Another use is to form a bond with a child through a familiar medium. This helps with trust and creating a safe environment. Finally, it can be used to facilitate growth and development. This is the treatment part of play, where we let them, as Axline (1948) stated, "play out" feelings and problems as they experience them (p. 9).

So it is important not to use play techniques as a way to distract or relax a child and then expect some deep symbolic sharing. What is important is the meaning the child makes out of the drawings, not what the counselor assumes by looking at it. This process of entering the child's phenomenology is what creates the trust to share the secrets. This takes time, especially if the child has trust issues. The drawings made may not have given a total view yet. The door may be just opening a crack. Patience is needed. Several avenues sometimes help, like the use of puppets to provide an opportunity for the child to simulate the conversations and actions witnessed. Play is the medium through which experience is shared but may not be the literal message. Because it is a metaphoric approach, the counselor in this critical incident needed to ask what this or that meant, not assume from her own worldview and experiences. There are many interpretations that can be made, and the only one that really counts is the one the child places on it. Comment on what you see. Ask pertinent and important questions that help clarify feelings.

If this child was really abused, and I assume the author means physically, he will play this out repeatedly as a major theme. The counselor's role is to follow that pain. It is the child who is most important, not the problem. The counselor's office may become the only safe place in a child's life. At home a child might feel that discussion of intense feelings or even subtle display of them might cause increased parental and personal distress. In some families, this would be so unacceptable it could put the child in physical harm. This is especially true of abused children.

We can allow them to act out roles and situations that can form their fundamental orientation to the adult world. We can then work on what emerges. We can help them learn to appreciate themselves and learn coping skills and help provide them with the comfort that comes from sharing the burden. This can help change the unmanageable into the manageable.

School counselors need to consider soliciting support from teachers and principals, and parents, lest they think you are simply wasting time playing games. Explain the outcomes and goals to others. This is one service you provide, and it may not be the only way you provide counseling services. Let them know all you do.

The location of the room, its size, the availability of a sink, and the level of noise allowed are all factors that influence what and how you can incorporate expressive arts. Your own talents can dictate this. I have encouraged many magicians, guitar players, cross-stitchers, and origami folders to use what they are good at as a way to connect with kids. I tell them, however, that they need to be aware of the purposes of play and not confuse method with purpose. Games are the least useful form of expressive arts. Games of skill, reading, and winning can all be counterproductive to the counseling process, although they might provide a sense of distraction. So it is important to assess what you use, how, and when. Some games are used to help children lessen emotional stimulation, especially if they need to return calmly to math or reading. Again, the purpose is key. If the goal is diagnosis, then play is designed for the counselor's purpose; if it is for treatment, then other activities might be selected that increase self-understanding, self-control, and a sense of personal power.

Huge caseloads are not an excuse to jump to conclusions from one or two drawings. Everyone has too many cases and too little time. Each child deserves the utmost attention to what he or she is trying to tell us. Play techniques can actually be more time saving, because we are talking in their language. We have to learn to listen to how this culture speaks and come to understand its subtleties. We cannot fight all the evils in the world for them, but we can help support and guide them in the effort they make toward doing this themselves. We can provide a stabilizing force in their lives as they do the work. Expressive arts can also be soothing and healing. Offering hope to children should be a priority for all school counselors (Phillips & Mullen, 1999). We can help children make sense of their lives, to find positive ways to meet their needs, and to believe in their ability to deal with life's stressors.

References

American Counseling Association. (2005). *ACA code of ethics*. Alexandria, VA: Author.

Axline, V. (1948). *Play therapy: The inner dimensions of childhood.* New York: Ballentine Books.

Landreth, G. L. (2002). *Play therapy: The art of the relationship* (2nd ed.). New York: Brunner-Routledge.

Phillips, E., & Mullen, J. (1999). Client-centered play techniques for elementary school counselors: Building the supportive relationship. *Journal of the Professional Counselor, 14*(1), 25–36.

Response

Christine Suniti Bhat

School counselors, and all counselors for that matter, must practice within the boundaries of their competence, based on their education, training, supervised experience, state and national professional credentials, and appropriate professional experience (American Counseling Association, 2005, Standard C.2.a.). Counseling and art therapy are both established mental health practices with clear criteria differentiating them. This does not preclude a counselor from using tools or techniques from the expressive arts if this is done within the boundaries of competence. Counselors providing counseling services to young clients are unlikely to restrict themselves to talk therapy alone. Establishing rapport is vital with young clients, especially when clients demonstrate resistance, reticence, or impulsivity, as in the case of K. S. The counselor's role in the early phases of the counseling relationship includes finding ways to connect with the client, enter the client's world, and understand the client's background and presenting issues. The use of visual arts can be an effective way to accomplish these early goals. Rhiannon's aim in introducing drawing in this case is focused on obtaining relevant information from a young and not very verbal client. Her strategy to engage K. S. by asking him to draw a picture of his family seems appropriate.

The use of art in counseling sessions with younger clients is helpful because it engages clients and often provides access to the unconscious to express covert conflicts (Gladding, 2005). Drawing helped K. S. verbalize his anger toward his mother's boyfriend. A counselor who uses different types of communication to help a client tell his or her story is not engaging in art therapy. What would be problematic would be for a counselor using art activities to describe himself or herself as an art therapist. Art therapy is an established mental health practice that uses the creative process of art making to improve and enhance the physical, mental, and emotional well-being of clients. Specialized training is required to practice as an art therapist (American Art Therapy Association, n.d.). Rhiannon's supervisor suggested that she work with K. S. to address stress and anger in a structured counseling session. If Rhiannon chose instead to use only expressive arts techniques in all counseling sessions, this would be unethical because of her lack of training in these treatment modalities, and because of her infringement on the role of a credentialed or licensed art therapist.

Focusing on practicing within the boundaries of competence is essential from both a legal and an ethical standpoint. Charges of malpractice may be levied against a school counselor who focuses solely on expressive arts without adequate training and to the detriment of the client's well-being. Working within a school setting also raises specific issues of confidentiality with minors. The American School Counselor Association (ASCA, 2004) reminds us of the ethical responsibility of honoring the confidentiality of clients in schools, while also recognizing that working with minors requires collaboration with parents and guardians. Providing parents and guardians with relevant information is recommended (ASCA, 2004, B.2.c.), as is enlisting their support. Functioning in an open and transparent manner, sharing appropriate information with parents and guardians of minors, and engaging them as allies in the process of counseling are all considered helpful. A school counselor who behaves in a secretive manner regarding the counseling process is more likely to be at risk for legal and ethical challenges than one who is open about ways in which counseling is conducted.

Visual arts are appropriate for use across the lifespan and appeal to numerous clients (Gladding, 2005). Thus, they are likely to be useful in working with students of all ages in schools. Traditional counseling approaches often have limited usefulness for young clients, clients who have not self-referred, or clients who are not personally invested in the outcome of counseling. Students in schools are most often referred for counseling, as in the case of K. S., for problematic behaviors demonstrated in the classroom that hinder their ability to achieve educational goals. Most tasks that students engage in at school are related to verbal and written language. By virtue of being different, expressive arts can make a connection with school-aged clients where words may fail or have limited usefulness. Gladding (2005) also made the point that the use of art in counseling can help transcend cultural boundaries.

School counselors wishing to use expressive arts in their counseling role would have to do so considering available space and funding. They would also have to make decisions about what forms of creative and expressive arts they are likely to use from a practical perspective. For example, working with clay may not be possible, but providing crayons, paints, and colored pencils may be easier to organize. When setting up a counseling room for young clients, counselors are reminded to create a physically and psychologically comfortable environment (Erdman & Lampe, 1996). Providing adequate space, quiet, freedom of movement, encouragement, and time are all considerations for the counselor wishing to use visual arts (Gladding, 2005). Bearing in mind the school counselor's mandate to attend to the academic, career, and personal and social needs of every student (ASCA, 2004, Standard A.1.b.), allowing adequate time for creative expression in schools is likely to pose a challenge.

ASCA's (2003) position statement, *The Professional School Counselor and Child Abuse and Neglect Prevention,* highlights the legal, ethical, and moral responsibility of school counselors to report child abuse. It is essential that school counselor education programs provide school counselors in training with the knowledge and skills required to report child abuse and work effectively with students experiencing abuse. Training should ideally take place before the trainee commences practicum and internship experiences and should include required actions to be taken by the school counselor, reporting procedures, and difficulties likely to be encountered. Resources that permit students to work through realistic case studies such as those in the book by Stone (2005) are particularly helpful.

There is no best strategy to assist trainees who are experiencing difficulties in working with cases of children who have been abused. Developing a strong working alliance in supervision, fostering a sense of open communication, providing emotional and practical support as needed, and addressing skills deficits experienced by trainees all contribute to overall development and confidence in the making of a counselor.

References

American Art Therapy Association, Inc. (n.d.). *About art therapy.* Retrieved February 4, 2007, from http://www.arttherapy.org/about.html

American Counseling Association. (2005). *ACA code of ethics.* Alexandria, VA: Author.

American School Counselor Association. (2003). *Position statement: Child abuse and neglect prevention.* Retrieved February 1, 2007, from http://www.schoolcounselor.org/content.asp?contentid=194

American School Counselor Association. (2004). *Ethical standards for school counselors.* Retrieved February 4, 2007, from http://www.schoolcounselor.org/files/ethical%20standards.pdf

Erdman, P., & Lampe, R. (1996). Adapting basic skills to counsel children. *Journal of Counseling & Development, 74,* 374–377.

Gladding, S. T. (2005). *Counseling as an art: The creative arts in counseling* (3rd ed.). Alexandria, VA: American Counseling Association.

Stone, C. (2005). *School counseling principles: Ethics and law.* Alexandria, VA: American School Counselor Association.